Ex
Libris

C. Andrew Causey

WHEN THEY
READ
WHAT WE
WRITE

WHEN THEY
READ
WHAT WE
WRITE

The Politics of Ethnography

Edited by Caroline B. Brettell

BERGIN & GARVEY
Westport, Connecticut • London

Library of Congress Cataloging-in-Publication Data

When they read what we write : the politics of ethnography / edited by
    Caroline B. Brettell.
       p.   cm.
    Includes bibliographical references and index.
    ISBN 0–89789–325–5 (alk. paper)
    1. Ethnology—Authorship. 2. Ethnology—Fieldwork. 3. Ethnology—
Philosophy.   I. Brettell, Caroline.
    GN307.7.W48   1993
    305.8—dc20   92–43386

British Library Cataloguing in Publication Data is available.

Library of Congress Catalog Card Number: 92–43386
ISBN: 0–89789–325–5

First published in 1993

Bergin & Garvey, 88 Post Road West, Westport, CT 06881
An imprint of Greenwood Publishing Group, Inc.

Printed in the United States of America

The paper used in this book complies with the
Permanent Paper Standard issued by the National
Information Standards Organization (Z39.48–1984).

10 9 8 7 6 5 4 3 2 1

Social analysis must now grapple with the realization that its objects of analysis are also analyzing subjects who critically interrogate ethnographers—their writings, their ethics, and their politics.

—R. Rosaldo (1989:21)

They want to know the results and, unlike laboratory rats, they regard the findings with emotion.

—Haring (1956:61)

It was one thing to publish ethnographies about Trobrianders or Kwakiutls half a century ago; it is another to study people who read what you write and are more than willing to talk back.

—Paredes (1978:2)

CONTENTS

Introduction: Fieldwork, Text, and Audience

Caroline B. Brettell

Cultural anthropology, according to some contemporary practitioners (Rabinow 1986; Tyler 1986), has entered its postmodern phase, a phase characterized by reflexivity, self-criticism, and increasing eclecticism. Postmodernism, it would seem, is a necessary response to the postcolonial world in which anthropology has no choice but to reinvent itself (Hymes 1969). It calls for a reevaluation of what we have been and are doing, of our relationships with informants, and of the written products that our work has generated and will continue to generate.

One manifestation of reflexive postmodern anthropology is a renewed and vigorous interest in the process by which data are gathered—the fieldwork experience (Karp and Kendall 1982; Ruby 1982; Tedlock 1991). This has resulted in the publication of what Van Maanen (1988:7) has described as "confessional tales"—ethnographies that tend to "focus more on the fieldworker than the culture studied." Although works such as Kenneth Read's *The High Valley* (1965) and Jean Briggs's *Never in Anger* (1970) are early examples of such tales, those published since 1970 (for example, Barley 1986; Dumont 1978; Dwyer 1982; Rabinow 1977; Slater 1976; Werner 1984) have perhaps more powerfully drawn attention to the close association between what the ethnographer does in the field and the written ethnography that interprets that field experience. The interpretive perspective in anthropology is characterized by Michael Jackson (1989:182) as a "shift away from the analytic, positivist conception of knowledge to a hermeneutical one which, to adapt Weber's phrase, sees both the anthropologist and the people he or she studies as suspended in webs of significance they themselves have spun."[1]

If the reflexive and interpretive turn is one manifestation of postmodern anthropology,the literary turn is another. Declared to be fictions ''in the sense of something made or fashioned'' (Clifford 1986:6), ethnographies, according to those who advocate this position, are partial or selective truths. They should be approached as texts whose style, rhetoric, and narrative structure can be subjected to the same kind of criticism to which other works of literature are subjected (Crapanzano 1977a; Marcus and Cushman 1982). Writing about culture raises questions about modes of representation, about objectivity and accountability, relativism and ethnocentrism, science and truth. Textualists urge ethnographers to experiment with new forms of writing that are dialectical, dialogic, or polyphonic rather than analytic, authoritative, and univocal (Dwyer 1977; Marcus and Fischer 1986; Clifford and Marcus 1986). Indeed, the omniscient ''I know because I was there'' voice of the post-Malinowskian participant-observer is perceived as a trope that is no longer acceptable in a postcolonial world (Clifford 1983; Pratt 1986).

In this burgeoning literature, questions of readership and audience are considered, although perhaps not as much as they should be given the attention paid to reader-response or reception theory within literary studies in general (Fish 1980; Holub 1984; Tompkins 1980).[2] ''Ethnographies,'' claims Van Maanen (1988:25), ''are written with particular audiences in mind and reflect the presumptions carried by authors regarding the attitudes, expectations, and backgrounds of their intended readers.'' Marcus and Cushman (1982:51ff.) decompose the audience of ethnography into several types: a specialist ethnographic readership, a general anthropological readership, a readership in other social sciences, a student readership, an action-oriented readership, and a popular readership.

Curiously, neither Marcus and Cushman nor Van Maanen (1988) consider ''native'' readers (i.e., those about whom the ethnography is written), and while they refer to general readers, they leave out the press, a readership that often mediates texts for others. Crapanzano (1977a:72) demonstrates an awareness of the native reader in his claim that ''the writer of ethnography writes [for]—and creates—a double audience: the audience of his own people and the audience of those other people whom he refers to in an act of presumptive if not patronizing incorporation as 'my people.' '' And yet, for Crapanzano the audience of ''the other'' is silent, one which simply validates the ethnographer's sense of self. This audience, as he presents it, is not, in short, composed of critical readers.[3]

More recently, Marcus and Fischer (1986) have drawn attention to this native and potentially critical readership, describing it as the most powerful incentive to ''the contemporary experimental impulse in anthropological writing, both as ethnography and cultural critique. Presumably,'' they continue, ''members of other societies, increasingly literate, will read ethnographic accounts that concern them and will react not only to the manifest descriptions of their own societies, but also to the premises about our society that are embedded in the double vision of any ethnographic work'' (Marcus and Fischer 1986: 163). Tyler (1987) and R. Rosaldo (1989) have reiterated this point, attributing the contemporary crisis in ethnographic consciousness in part to a revolution in readership. ''Since the ethnographic other can read, she now presumes to criticize her characterization and to clamour for the right to represent herself. Pity the poor ethnographer'' (Tyler 1987:49).

Tyler claims that the volume *Writing Culture* (Clifford and Marcus 1986) is about reading. But does it go far enough in dealing with the politics of audience reception—of how ethnography is received and interpreted not only by anthropological colleagues and the general public, but also, and most especially, by those who are the subjects, directly or indirectly, of anthropological investigation? Many would answer no. M. Jackson (1989:184), for example, suggests that ''by fetishizing texts [textualism] divides—as the advent of literacy itself did—readers from authors and separates both from the world.''[4]

Although inspired by some of the issues raised by reflexive, interpretive, and literary anthropology, the authors of the chapters in this volume move beyond textualism to consider systematically the relationship between anthropological writers and readers, particularly readers who are informants or who are members of our informants' society and have a vested interest in the anthropological text that has been or will be produced. The idea for this volume began as a session organized for the 1990 meeting of the American Anthropological Association. Its aim was to bring together people who had already had the experience of having the distance between their audience of colleagues and their audience of informants eroded, of having, as R. Rosaldo (1986) has phrased it, ''the natives talk back.''

It became apparent in the discussions following the session that not only were these issues relating to the politics of audience reception, whether real or imagined, rarely treated in print with the kind of brutal honesty and exposure of self that is necessary, but also that the question was complex and multifaceted. In assembling this volume, I have included four papers from the original panel and commissioned seven others that range more broadly in dealing with the relationship between the fieldwork experience and its product—the ethnographic text—on the one hand, and audience/readers on the other. The majority of contributors have worked either in North America or Europe. While this could be viewed as a limitation, it also gives the volume some coherence. Furthermore, it is in these field contexts that the problem has arisen first and most dramatically. The ethnographers are generally writing in a language shared with their respondents, and many of their respondents are readers.

The book is divided into four parts, each of which delineates a different process at stake in the relationship between the ethnographic writer and the audience of readers. In addition, each part emphasizes a somewhat different body of readers of anthropological texts. The first two chapters (Davis, Glazier) address directly the experience of having an ethnographic text contested and challenged by those about whom it is written. These authors write about postpublication responses that were unexpected and often painful. They explore the implications of these responses for future rapport in their respective research communities.

Although Davis made every effort to write a book about the women of Grey Rock Harbour, Newfoundland, that was minimally offensive, she returned to the fieldsite to discover that many of her informants/friends felt betrayed. This sense of betrayal sometimes revolved around the use of a word or phrase that Davis interpreted differently than the woman who had originally spoken it. It also revolved around the easy identifiability of individuals, despite all attempts to disguise them. Davis found that she could both understand and deal with these criticisms. What was harder to cope with were the mistaken rumors about her book that circulated throughout the community to the point where people who had not even read it were voicing opinions about it. Crocombe (1976) describes a similar phenomenon among Samoans with regard to the work of Margaret Mead, and it is an issue also raised by Greenberg in her contribution later in this volume. Ethnographic texts take on a life of their own that is beyond the ethnographer's control. For Davis this complicated the second round of fieldwork in the original research community.

Glazier has returned several times to Trinidad to work with a group of Spiritual Baptists. In his discussion of how his published text *Marchin' the Pilgrims Home* was received by both informants and scholars in Trinidad, Glazier not only raises the issue of how it has affected subsequent fieldwork, but also discusses where it was found wanting by members of his research community. He describes an interesting process whereby the book became a symbol of factionalism within the church and was used to promote the status of some leaders at the expense of others. This was certainly not part of Glazier's intention.

Glazier wrestles with his own feelings about having his work either ignored by local scholars or used but not cited. In her contribution to this volume, Sheehan also deals with the issue of appropriation, but because her informants are Irish intellectuals, the boundaries of ownership for intellectual property are more blurred. Appropriation is also at issue in Glazier's discussion of the misunderstandings and suspicion surrounding the financial aspects of published ethnographies. As the discussion later in this introduction of *Small Town in Mass Society* illustrates, this is a problem that other social scientists have experienced. But few have written about it. It often occurs first within indigenous academic communities. For example, Marilyn Strathern (1987a:20) describes an incident among the student body at the University of Papua, New Guinea, in the 1970s. The students became concerned with the issue of exploitation by foreign scholars, especially anthropologists. They accused these foreign scholars of "using information which belonged properly to Melanesians and deploying it for personal gain."

These indigenous or native scholars are an extremely important readership for our ethnographies. Hanson (1991) claims that the harshest criticisms of his analysis of cultural invention among the Maori came from New Zealand academics. While Glazier discusses this group of readers in his chapter on the reception of his book in Trinidad, the three chapters in Part II of the present volume deal with the problem more directly, focusing on indigenous scholars who are either the subject of research or readers with both the detachment of an informed observer and the involvement of a native participant. Jaffe, Handler, and Sheehan discuss the production of and reactions to texts within highly politicized contexts or ones in which certain power relationships are implicit. In such situations the role of the ethnographer as insider or outsider becomes problematic and has important implications for the authority with which his or her writing is received.

Jaffe conducted her fieldwork on the island of Corsica, focusing her attention on the symbolic importance of language. Corsica is a place that is close enough to home to undermine, she argues, the ethnographer's ability to construct an unproblematic other and hence an unproblematic self. Her chapter centers on three written texts that she produced for various Corsican audiences and a survey that she conducted as part of her research. Each of these forced her to draw or blur the boundaries between insider and outsider. The ambiguity of her status and how it might influence what she wrote drew strong reactions and revealed to her the politics surrounding both knowledge and its representation.

Jaffe's experiences are somewhat akin to those of Maryon McDonald (1987), who has written about being forced to engage in a complex process of code-switching between insider and outsider while conducting her research in Brittany. However, once McDonald's doctoral thesis was published she was quite clearly defined as an outsider. "If I had been accepted as a 'Celt,' I was now 'English' once more, and a 'fascist.' I was 'reactionary' and working for figures and bodies as various as Thatcher and Marchais, the CIA and the KGB" (McDonald 1987:134). Greenberg, an indigenous anthropologist, alludes to a similar process of redefinition—from insider to stranger—in her chapter in Part III of this volume. Both Greenberg and McDonald faced the wrath of a research community that responded powerfully and negatively to newspaper representations of their respective work rather than to the actual text. In McDonald's case, the press was a vehicle for nationalist sentiment. Jaffe's discussion of the change of heart of a weekly magazine that had originally agreed to publish her survey questionnaire is a variant on this theme, although in this case she thinks she was being accorded a symbolic power that did not concur with her personal feelings about her status.

Like McDonald, Jaffe is dealing with issues of nationalism, ethnic identity, and the cultural strength of language. In the field she felt impelled to "take a position" on the question of linguistic diversity. In most of the writing that she published while in the field, she either advocated the "party line" or censored herself by guarding her knowledge of nonpublic events.

Handler's analytical stance with respect to the rage with which his text about Quebec nationalism was received by academics in Quebec universities is somewhat different from that of Jaffe. Like Glazier, he discovers that some of these scholars reject the book by claiming that there is "nothing new in it." Like

Greenberg, he is accused of superiority and condescension. Like McDonald, he is labeled an outsider who cannot possibly understand. In addition, the readers of his text took issue with his argument that what they were doing in their construction of cultural difference was comparable to similar processes in other parts of the world.

Handler suggests that the reactions to his book, a book that fundamentally challenges the way that the Quebecois think about themselves, provide further material for analysis because they tend to recapitulate the nationalist ideology that is the subject of the original text. This leads him to a discussion of "anthropology as cultural critique" and to the position that the insider/outsider dichotomy only tends to reify the culturally bound units we are trying to abandon. Handler urges us not to accept readily the status of ignorant outsider that is often given to us once the "natives" have read what we have written about them. He adopts this position by arguing that our culture is implicated in the culture of the other, and vice versa.

While "native" scholars stood as harsh critics of the texts produced by Jaffe and Handler, Sheehan made these scholars the subject of her research in a cultural arena—Ireland—where there is already a powerful expectation that foreign ethnographers will misrepresent the country and its people. Both she and her informants play dual roles of insider and outsider, thereby complicating both the writing and the reading of ethnography. Like Jaffe, Sheehan wrestles with the question of what is "safe" to write, a decision conditioned for her by her junior academic status, her foreignness, and her concern for the boundaries between the public and private lives of informants who were nationally visible. In the latter case ethical issues came up against ethnographic interests and led to the recognition that anthropological writing is quite different from newspaper writing on the one hand and fiction on the other. Sheehan is not describing what happened when her text was read, but how the anticipation of it being read influenced the decisions she has made in the process of writing an ethnography of an elite social group. This is an issue also discussed by Hopkins in her chapter in Part IV of this volume.

Brettell's chapter in Part III continues the discussion of identity raised in part II, but additionally emphasizes the role of the press as a mediator of her text. In numerous cases the press intervenes and interprets the text for a diverse readership, including readers in the community or population studied by the anthropologist. In Brettell's case, a newspaper account of a lecture she gave about the history of a French-Canadian immigrant community in central Illinois stimulated a strong reprimand from a community leader, an individual who had previously read a published article that dealt with some of the same material and which evoked no response. After dealing with the way that her oral text was misrepresented in the press account, Brettell analyzes the experience for what it adds to ethnographic understanding, particularly of the role of history in human culture. Like Handler, she finds most problematic the generalizations she makes about what her research community understands to be unique.

The furor over Greenberg's book about a development town in Israel was also fueled by an article published in a newspaper, in her case one with a decidedly left-wing political stance. Community people who had read the article but not the book felt impelled to respond, and politicians took advantage of the situation to advance their own careers. Of all the chapters in this volume, Greenberg's does the best job of emphasizing the multiplicity of responses that emerge from a diverse group of readers of one's text or, in this case, a representation of one's text.

Greenberg claims to have approached her subject of study with neutrality and objectivity, but her text was not read that way. This raises the interesting question of varying interpretations of words and phrases by writer and reader. What we as ethnographers assume to be a detached and impartial representation may not be received that way by the people about whom we are writing, especially when we deal with issues that are politically sensitive or that provide the basis for the construction of self. Jean Jackson (1989:138) has recently observed that "our analytical language makes it difficult to describe . . . without using negative, value-laden words, even when we especially wish to sound as neutral, descriptive, and objective as possible." Furthermore, in our postmodernist efforts to use the voice of "the other" by quoting directly, we may in fact open ourselves to more criticism than when we embed what particular respondents tell us in generalities.

Hopkins addresses some of these questions of language and anonymity in Part IV of this volume, which not only raises most forthrightly the ethical issues of ethnographic research and writing, but also focuses on the way in which particular ethnographers have involved their audience of readers, especially those who are the subjects of their research, in the process of writing. Hopkins is particularly concerned with how to write for the diverse audience of readers that she anticipates for her book and how to reconcile the contradictions that she sees as inherent in ethically conscientious research. What can she disclose without threatening anonymity? How can anthropologists promote the rights and welfare of those affected by their work if they cannot write about them directly? Hopkins finds an uneasy solution to these problems in the creation of a composite portrait, a solution which some anthropologists would consider problematic and which, if Glazier's experience is an example, some informants would not like. Glazier's Spiritual Baptist leaders were dismayed to discover that they were not identified by name in his book, and Nancy Scheper-Hughes (1982a:x) tells us that her Irish informants did not like having "bits and pieces of [themselves] strewn about here and there."

Hopkins, like Sheehan, is well aware that there are certain things about which ethnographers cannot write, for to do so would seriously violate confidence and privacy. Once our informants have become readers we can no longer simply pay lip service to this issue. But, as Hopkins points out in her discussion of the teachers, social workers, educational planners, and other officials that she would like to reach through her written text, something that might embarrass her informants if disclosed is essential information to those who are charged with looking after the social and economic well-being of these same informants.

In his contribution to this volume Horwitz writes about some of the same conflicts in the ethics of ethnography and its impact on the written text. He returns to the debate about ethnographic authority, pointing to fundamental differences between the theoretical postmodern position and that which emerges from the more practical considerations that guide what a researcher brings before a Human Subjects Review Committee or a similar body concerned with the ethics of fieldwork and the way it is reported.

Horwitz's solution to the contradictions in the theory and ethics of authority is to be found in a protocol—he calls it a compromise—that guides both his research and the texts that are produced based on his research. Part of this compromise involves showing his informants the written text and inviting corrections. These editing sessions, claims Horwitz, have "ranged from the most congenial to the most acrimonious encounters of my adult life." Unlike Hopkins, Horwitz generally (but not always) uses real names. He also makes his informants aware of the difference between facts about which they can agree and interpretations, which might differ. A discussion of the latter influences what finds its way into print.

While his protocol has generally been successful, Horwitz offers an example of a specific situation where it broke down, and leaves us with the notion that no solution is perfect and that each fieldwork situation will demand flexibility when it comes to what we write and for whom we write. Furthermore, by not pushing a particular informant on certain issues, Horwitz, like Hopkins, has had to wrestle with whether his choice not to disclose, his choice to leave certain things private, unsaid, and unwritten, actually worked against the welfare of this individual and the population he represented.

McBeth pursues collaboration even more thoroughly than Horwitz by discussing her coauthorship of an ethnographic text—the life history of a Shoshone Indian woman named Essie. But her project is about more than collaboration; it is also about negotiation, because it involves balancing the differences between Essie's representation of herself and McBeth's cultural representation of her. Essie wanted to retain control, particularly, McBeth observes, over certain reminiscences about and interpretations of the meaning of her life. Without this kind of control, Essie told her, she would not have agreed to participate. By acceding the process of interpretation as well as that of representation, McBeth produces a text that her informant wants written. This is a different strategy from that followed by Lawless (1992), who showed the women ministers in Missouri who were the source for her book *Handmaidens of the Lord* their life histories and other material that directly emerged from interviews, but did not share with them the interpretive sections. In essence, she privileged her interpretation over theirs, and this became a source of debate once the book was published.

McBeth evaluates both the positive aspects and the inherent problems in writing a life history that is coauthored, not the least of which is the process by which oral communication is made into a written text for a diverse audience of readers. Essie and McBeth were full-fledged partners in this process, thereby avoiding the common trap of informants speaking and ethnographers writing (Van Maanen 1988:137). Both participants edited the text with an acute awareness that it would be a public document. There would be no misunderstandings about what would or would not be included. Essie knew that hers was a subjective interpretation, that she was recalling the past in accordance with her ideas about the present.

In the final chapter of this volume Ginsburg returns to the "traditional" audience for ethnography—our own anthropological colleagues—but with a twist. She discusses a case of mistaken identity: her attempt to adopt the point of view of the other in her representations of the "right-to-life" movement was read as evidence of her having become one of them. Relativism, she was told by some colleagues, "has its limits."

To deal with this reaction, Ginsberg developed a number of strategies for presenting her material that would redirect audience response from the immediate political issues to a broader understanding of the cultural context. She settled on the presentation of life stories, which not only gave a voice to the women who were the subject of her study, but also allowed them to reflect on their own actions. These life stories drew attention to the differences between the interpretations of the anthropologist and those of the actors themselves. One is not necessarily truer than the other; they are simply distinct. If this strategy makes Ginsburg's anthropological colleagues more comfortable, we are left to wonder about the women she interviewed, who may, like the women ministers about whom Lawless (1992) has written, object to the very presence of her interpretation in a text that they have conceived of as representing their voice alone.

Although many of the issues raised in this book are only beginning to find their way into print, a number of comparisons can be made with the experience of other anthropologists working in diverse cultural contexts. Some have been mentioned already, but in order to situate each of the chapters in this volume within a broader framework, the remainder of this introduction draws on some classic cases and instructive examples in order to develop and historicize further what is at stake when the relationship between ethnographer and audience becomes a focus of consideration. The discussion is directed not only to the various readers of ethnography, but also to the processes of contestation, politicization, mediation, and collaboration that organize this book.

WHEN THE NATIVES TALK BACK

Ethnological research carved out a niche for itself in the latter nineteenth century as the study of the far-off and remote "other." Those people among whom the anthropologist worked were often preliterate, and the languages they spoke certainly were not the language in which the ethnographer intended to publish the results of his or her research. There was virtually no chance for the subjects of anthropological investigation to respond, either critically or favorably, to what was written about them. Ethnographic authority survived under the cloak of distance and difference because the "natives" never knew what had been written about them. For Western sociologists, or for those anthropologists who study their own society with the tools and methods of research developed in the study of the far-off "other," the situation has been somewhat different. Perhaps one of the best documented is the furor that erupted over the publication of Arthur Vidich and Joseph Bensman's *Small Town in Mass Society* (1958a).[5]

Small Town in Mass Society was based on participant-observation research carried out in a village in upstate New York. Although community responses to the book were by no means monolithic, a good many inhabitants of Springdale (not the real name) found it offensive because pseudonyms did not effectively disguise particular individuals who were easily recognizable by their social position in the community. In the view of these local critics, privacy and trust had been betrayed and reputations put at risk. People in the community were under the impression that the information they gave would be aggregated into statistical reports of community life. In many cases, it was not.

Residents of Springdale were also perturbed by certain social science terminology. They disliked the phrase "invisible government," used by the authors to describe people who were influential in the decision-making processes of the village without holding office. They felt that insidious implications were being drawn about power-hungry individuals who were acting illegitimately. But the strongest criticism stemmed from a feeling that the book had damaged the town's image of itself, all for the sake of career advancement and personal financial gain.[6] To regain that self-image, and perhaps to exorcise the evil spirit of the participant-observer, community members designed a float for a Fourth of July parade that displayed Vidich in effigy bending over a manure spreader filled with barnyard fertilizer.

Much of this disapprobation was laid out in local newspapers by reporters who had interviewed community residents. An article in the *Oswego Times* (January 31, 1958) claimed, "Mr. Vidich is currently about as popular in [Springdale] as the author of Peyton Place is in her small town and for the same reason— both authors violate what Vidich calls the etiquette of gossip" (quoted in Vidich and Bensman 1964:339ff.). The article went on to describe how offended local businessmen were at the suggestion that the community was at a standstill, and accused the authors of making factually inaccurate statements to bolster that conclusion. A piece in the *Ithaca Journal* (June 13, 1958; quoted in Vidich and Bensman 1964:341) cited some individuals who claimed that the book did more to allay apathy in "Springdale" than anything in a long time, and others who argued that Vidich and Bensman were using big city standards to judge a small community. This latter article ends with the observation that "one thing is certain: walk into [Springdale] and mention 'Small Town' and you won't get away without a reaction. Those reactions range from horse-laughs to polite smiles to the angry bristle of a porcupine."

In a revised edition of the book published in 1968, Vidich and Bensman included a chapter titled "Ethical and Bureaucratic Implications of Community Research" in which they dealt with all the negative responses to their 1958 volume,[7] as well as with the more general issue of the role of the researcher vis-à-vis not only the community studied, but also the organizations sponsoring the research—in this case Cornell University. The project director (Vidich was a staff researcher on the project) formulated a policy that argued that reactions from readers, including some in the community, should receive serious consideration prior to publication of any of the project material. Vidich and Bensman (1958b:3) expressed reservations about this policy at the time and defended their decisions about what to put into print in relation to issues of objectivity and responsibility to science. This stance did not go uncriticized by their professional colleagues, particularly by those who rejected the subordination of questions of moral responsibility to the principle of scientific objectivity. One critic (Bell 1959:49) went so far as to suggest that rather than weakening our scientific integrity, fulfilling our responsibility to the people in the communities we study may in fact improve the scientific validity of the final product.

In an assessment of the debate about *Small Town in Mass Society*, the sociologist Howard Becker (1964:276) has suggested that any good study of a community or organization will necessarily confront "the irreconcilable conflict between the interests of science and the interests of those studied and thereby provoke a hostile reaction."[8] Becker then notes that frequently those who are studied by social scientists do not know what to expect. This obviates any kind of research bargain "where you the researcher think you are educating people as to possible implications because they may not fully understand" (1964:280). In this case, it was apparent that the method of participant-observation itself, whereby an outsider becomes an insider, a stranger becomes a friend, and confidences become data, was not fully understood by the people of Springdale.

One of the first places outside North America where a controversy similar to that surrounding *Small Town* erupted was in Mexico, upon the translation and publication in 1964 of Oscar Lewis's *The Children of Sanchez*. According to Paddock (1965b:63), at the height of the controversy each major metropolitan daily newspaper referred to the book at least a half dozen times in each day's issue. In fact, Lewis and his Mexican publisher were formally accused of obscenity and slander by the Mexican Geographical and Statistical Society, which brought a suit before a Mexican court (Paddock 1965b).

Lewis, in the view of many Mexicans who reviewed or commented on the book, presented an all too gloomy and one-sided view of life among the urban and rural poor of Mexico, a view that shattered a country sensitive about its national image.[9] *The Children of Sanchez*, the critics claimed, was full of absurd generalizations which "present the Mexican people before the world with a moral, economic and cultural level inferior to the tribes of Africa" (*Excelsior*, February 20, 1965; quoted in *Mesoamerican Notes* 6:88). Others expressed irritation about foreign authors doing their social anatomy in Mexico (*Novedades*,

February 18, 1965) or suggested that such research was nothing more than an assault on Mexican institutions for political ends. The form of *The Children of Sanchez* was described as that of "a shameful novel and a political pamphlet" (*El Dia*, March 4, 1965; quoted in *Mesoamerican Notes* 6:117).

Not all the articles published in national newspapers were critical, and some were humorous and satirical. A headline in *Ultimas Noticias* (February 25, 1965) read "A Mexican Is Preparing a Book—Los Hijos de Smith" to be dedicated to Lewis and signed "Unthal Sanchez." A writer for *Excelsior* (February 13, 1965), commenting on the lawsuit, observed that, to be consistent, literary works such as Graham Green's *The Power and the Glory* and Malcolm Lowry's *Under the Volcano* should be equally condemned for their detrimental depiction of Mexico. In the February 17, 1965, issue of *Novedades* the author of an article titled "Savonarola in Mexico" noted that the problem was not the book but the *vecindades* (slum housing), and it was these that should be condemned, as well as the slow efforts of the Mexican government to improve the lives of people like the children of Sanchez.

In defending Lewis's conclusions, the more careful readers pointed to the introduction of *The Children of Sanchez*, in which Lewis claims that his protagonists are members of a particular social class who can be found in countries other than Mexico. But what is most evident is that the voice that goes unheard in this entire exchange is that of the Sanchez family, whose anonymity and privacy, despite Lewis's efforts to protect them, were no doubt destroyed by the debate in the Mexican national press.

A third arena of controversy on the scale surrounding *Small Town* and *The Children of Sanchez* can be found in reactions to ethnographies about Ireland. Published accounts of fieldwork in Ireland did not need to be translated before becoming accessible to those who lived in the communities that had been studied or who shared in the nationality of the ethnographer's informants. As Kane (1982:3) has observed, Ireland is "an almost perfect laboratory for expanding our ideas about the ethics of social science research and publication; its size ensures that it is almost impossible to conceal the identity of the study community, and its sophistication is such that almost anyone can understand, be affected by, and respond to what is written."

Although Irish ethnography by so-called outsiders has been challenged since the days of Conrad Arensberg and Solon Kimball (1940), the two bodies of research that have been most hotly contested are the ethnographies of John Messenger (1969) and Nancy Scheper-Hughes (1979).[10] Indeed, Scheper-Hughes characterizes the reaction of the "most literate and self-reflexive Irish" as "swift, harsh and unsettling" (1982a:v), and Messenger (1989:114) refers to an "inordinate sensitivity of the Irish to what is said of them both by outsiders and by many of their own." "Empirical descriptions," he suggests, " . . . are almost always construed as criticisms—attacks on the nation—rather than as scientific generalizations" (1989:114–115).

In the preface to the paperback edition of *Saints, Scholars and Schizophrenics,*

Scheper-Hughes (1982a) reflects on reactions to her book by asking herself what the people of Ballybran had gained and lost as a result of the publication. She answers her question by reference to a "hitherto unchallenged native interpretation of the meanings of their lives" (p. vii). She presented these people with "an alternative and sometimes shattering vision—that provided by psychological anthropology" (p. vii). As the village schoolmaster put it: "It's not your science I'm questioning, but this: don't we have the right to lead unexamined lives, the right *not* to be analyzed? Don't we have a right to hold on to an image of ourselves as different to be sure, but as innocent and unblemished all the same?"

Scheper-Hughes had exposed what the people of Ballybran would prefer not to have been exposed and, in their words, "created a public shame" (p. viii). As another villager put it to her, "Couldn't you have ignored the warts?" (p. x). In drawing a distinction between "whispering something beside a fire or across a counter and seeing it printed for the world to see" (p. viii), the people of Ballybran were voicing a criticism similar to one directed to Vidich and Bensman by the noted sociologist William Foote Whyte (1958:1) in an editorial in *Human Organization*. "There is a difference," wrote Whyte, "between public knowledge which circulates from mouth to mouth in the village and the same stories which appear in print." Curiously, some Ballybran residents were most concerned by the fact that Scheper-Hughes had written a text that was *so* accessible to them. "Why couldn't you have left it a dusty dissertation on a library shelf that no one would read, or a scholarly book that only the 'experts' would read? Why did you have to write it in a way that *we* could read it and understand exactly what you were saying?" (p. vii). Such a response, however, is clearly not universal. The Spiritual Baptists about whom Glazier writes in this volume were disappointed with the dissertation and eagerly awaited the "real book."

Messenger's experience of "publishing and perishing" (1989) is quite akin to that of Scheper-Hughes, but his reflections on his file cabinet brimming with letters of vilification led him to codify systematically the kinds of reactions that he received to his monograph. These reactions range from accusing him of being ill-informed, ignorant, illiterate, malicious, anti-Catholic, and pro–Anglo-Irish, to warnings about never trusting what an Irishman says, to more general statements about the impossibility of anyone (but especially an outsider) gaining an understanding of the Irish. Some expressed doubt that generalizations could be made about people who were basically individualists or about a whole population based on research with a small segment.[11] A few critics claimed that no one would read the monograph, while others suggested that fiction writers get it better than social scientists. This latter comment is particularly intriguing in light of Clifford's (1986) conception of ethnographic fictions, because it suggests not only that "natives" draw distinctions between works of literature and ethnographies, but also that fiction is often perceived to be more true and real than "made-up" social science. Messenger, as if to echo the remarks of the Mexican writer who compared Oscar Lewis with Malcolm Lowry and Graham Greene, notes that when observations similar to those made by ethnographers are embedded in novels, plays, and short stories they are read as accurate and acceptable. As part of a work of social science, they are challenged.

INSIDERS/OUTSIDERS: WHEN NATIVE SCHOLARS OBJECT

Messenger's research, like that of Scheper-Hughes, was received and read by two quite distinct but interested audiences. On the one hand were those who, like one Inis Beag woman, thought that "everything he [Messenger] says is true" (1989:125). Yet this woman commented to an Irish colleague of Messenger's that the reason he would be lynched if he returned to Inis Beag was that "he had a right not to say it." Like the people of Ballybran and Springdale, the islanders were most offended by the fact that the private had become public— that the ethnographer had foregrounded what the people studied wish to maintain in the background (Herzfeld 1983:163).

On the other hand, there were Irish social scientists, often of a nativist persuasion, who dubbed Messenger's analysis inadequate, invalid, and methodologically weak. He and, by extension, all American anthropologists were accused of studying only "the bizarre, the esoteric, the unusual and the marginal among non-urban societies" (Messenger 1989:128). *Inis Beag* was labeled "pruriently voyeuristic" and its author an arrogant elitist who betrayed confidences. To avoid such betrayal, it was suggested in the pages of both national newspapers and the Royal Anthropological Institute *Newsletter* that in the future ethnographers of Ireland should return to their communities with drafts of what they had written so that data could be corrected and responded to by informants. The Irish anthropologist Eileen Kane (1982) advocated the inclusion of these responses in an appendix to the published ethnography.[12]

While this is not the place to review Messenger's reply to these criticisms,[13] his interaction with native (and sometimes nativist) scholars brings to the forefront another important body of readers. These readers are different from one's professional colleagues at home because they often define themselves as both insiders and outsiders with respect to a specific cultural context. The number of so-called native or indigenous anthropologists is increasing and, aside from the ethnographic work that they produce, they are writing about their particular problems and perspectives on fieldwork in their own society and of their relationship with the larger global anthropological community.

The Kenyan anthropologist Chilungu (1976) was among the first to write in the pages of a prominent professional journal about some of the problems faced by native anthropologists. Initially told by his advisors at an African university that he should not become an anthropologist because it was "for outsiders," Chilungu is critical of the patronizing attitude of Anglo-American anthropologists who treat the societies they study as their personal property. Furthermore, he claims, in their writing these same anthropologists tend to draw comparisons with "our" culture and thus by their very language exclude the non-Western anthropologist as a reader.

The Egyptian anthropologist Fahim (1977) condemns not only a "knowledge for knowledge's sake" approach, but also one that adopts the liberal position that massive change is inherently bad. This is an observation also made by Bennoune (1985:360), an Algerian anthropologist who reflects on his progressive alienation from a field that is fascinated, even obsessed, with the exotic to the point of wanting to freeze evolution and transformation.

Kim (1990), a Korean anthropologist who worked in the southern United States before turning to fieldwork in his own country, complains that the former body of research has been ignored or coolly received because it offers a different perspective (i.e., Anglo-American scholars can be equally nativist). Yet he also suggests that in his own society he can experience the same kind of distance and marginality as that confronting an Anglo-American ethnographer. Kim thus raises the issue of what kind of insiders native anthropologists are.

The question of insider/outsider is also discussed by the African-American anthropologist Delmos Jones (1970), who has carried out fieldwork in Thailand and in a black community in the United States; by the half-Indian/half–German-American folkorist/ethnographer Narayan (1989); by Lila Abu-Lughod (1991), who uses the term "halfie" to refer to people with mixed national or cultural identity who struggle with multiple accountability; and by the Melanesian anthropologist Hau'ofa (1975). Jones suggests that "insider" anthropologists may question certain theories because their own identity is at stake. Yet, he argues, the insider position is not necessarily more privileged. "The outsider may enter the social situation armed with a battery of assumptions which he does not question and which guide him to certain types of conclusions; and the insider may depend too much on his own background, his own sentiments, his desires for what is good for his people. The insider, therefore, may distort the 'truth' as much as the outsider" (1970:256).

Hau'ofa writes of juggling his intellectual persona as an anthropologist with his emotional persona as a Pacific Islander. How does he deal with the claims made by the people of Melanesia and Polynesia that "anthropologists do not really understand us, do not present a complete or fair picture of us, and do not know how we feel" (1975:283)? Like Vidich, Messenger, and others, Hau'ofa too thinks that much of the problem stems from the disjunction between what people expect of anthropological research and the broader theoretical aims of social science. Having taken people into our confidence by telling them that we are going to write a book about them, we then produce works in which our informants "see themselves being distorted and misrepresented. In many cases our field of discourse and our special social scientific language preclude any comprehension of what we are talking about even to those who have started training in anthropology" (1975:284) and are thus presumably reading about themselves.

Using Sahlins's discussion of the Melanesian Big Man as an example, Hau'ofa concludes that "decades of anthropological field research in Melanesia [have] come up only with pictures of people who fight, compete, trade, pay bride-prices, engage in rituals, invent cargo cults, copulate and sorcerise each other. There is hardly anything in our literature to indicate whether these people have any such sentiments as love, kindness, consideration, altruism and so on" (1975:286). Anthropology, he argues, is guilty of the sins of omission and insensitivity, and it is no wonder that angry nationalists come up with an op-posing, if equally one-sided, image of themselves.

One of the more sensitive and reflective treatments of the critical "insider-scholar" is contained in Renato Rosaldo's discussions of Chicano anthropology. Drawing on the writing of Americo Paredes, Rosaldo (1986:10; 1989:49) points to the reactions of Mexican and Chicano scholars to what has been written about them by Anglo anthropologists such as William Madsen, Munro Edmonson, and Arthur Rubel. Madsen's book *Mexican-Americans of South Texas* is, according to Paredes (1978:1), "Exhibit A, to which all Chicanos point with disgust."

Paredes (1978) accuses otherwise politically liberal anthropologists of per-petuating pervasive stereotypes unthinkingly. Chicanos and Mexicans react to ethnographic literature about their culture, according to Paredes, "not so much [with] a sense of outrage, that would betray wounded egos, as [with] a feeling of puzzlement, that *this* is given as a picture of the communities they have grown up in. Many of them are more likely to laugh at it all than feel indignant" (Paredes 1978:2; quoted in R. Rosaldo 1989:50). Rosaldo comments, "The anthropological studies, in other words, appear just off the mark; they seem more parodic than perceptive" (1986:11).[14]

Rosaldo's assessment of this confrontation is that the native is never always right and that the ethnographer, especially a native ethnographer like Paredes, is sometimes wrong. "Instead my claim is that we should take the criticisms of our subjects in much the same way that we take those of our colleagues. Not unlike other ethnographers, so-called natives can be insightful, sociologically correct, axe-grinding, self-interested, or mistaken. They do know their own cultures, and rather than being ruled out of court, their criticism should be listened to and taken into account, to be accepted, rejected, or modified, as we reformulate our analyses" (Rosaldo 1986:50).

WHEN THE PRESS INTERVENES

Elsewhere in his insightful book *Culture and Truth*, Rosaldo (1989:63ff.) recounts an incident with another body of readers, the press. These readers are also writers, and when they write about what they have read they tend to distort and sensationalize for the sake of their own audience of readers. This is precisely what the *Washington Times* and other newspapers across the United States did with an article about Rosaldo and his research among the Ilongot of the Phil-ippines that first appeared in Stanford's weekly magazine. In the magazine article,

Rosaldo mentioned the comments that Ilongot headhunters made to him about the war in Vietnam when they learned of his draft status in the late 1960s. They condemned the soldiering practices of the United States, particularly the tendency to expose comrades to danger, and urged Rosaldo not to "sell his body." As the story was passed from one publication to the next, a headline that read "Headhunting Tribe Provides a Lesson" (*Chicago Tribune*) eventually became "Headhunter Horror: Just 90 Miles from Big City, Bizarre Tribe Still Beheads Innocent People" (*National Enquirer*).

And thus a stereotypical image unintended by the anthropologist was perpetuated largely because an ethnographer cannot control how what he or she puts into print is read, let alone how it is publicly represented. "Cultural studies," Rosaldo comments, "has entered a world where its critical readership, as well as the societies it depicts, no longer can be narrowly circumscribed. Much as Ilongots can comment on modern North American warfare, John Lofton [of the *Washington Times*] and the *National Enquirer* can listen in on my professional talk, and I on theirs. This does not make our lives more comfortable than before, or writing a book for such diverse potential audiences easier than in the classic period, but it does help make apparent how cultural interpretations are both occasioned by and enter arenas of ideological conflict" (1989:67).

Rosaldo's experience with the press as a mediator of his text is by no means unique. Gmelch (1992) writes about an incident described in her life history of the Irish Traveler Nan (Gmelch 1986). In the book Nan relates how Galway youths had stoned her family's tent and injured her baby, who later died. This incident was singled out and became the subject of a headline in the Galway *City Tribune* of October 7, 1986, that read "Fury over Book's claim of Killing of Child in City." The article, according to Gmelch, defended the city's honor, claiming that the incident had never happened. In reflecting on this newspaper account, Gmelch (personal communication 1992) was struck by the fact that it was the *only* incident described in the book that was discussed by the press. This is partly explained by the fact that "the Galway area has a long-standing reputation for hostility and physical assaults against Travellers." Coincidental with the publication of *Nan*, a flare-up between Traveling and settled communities had occurred in the Galway suburb of Rahoon. Gmelch (1992) suggests that any book that challenges people's preconceptions or that strikes too close to home will lead to defensive postures on the part of some readers.

If Gmelch's experience is a good example of how a few paragraphs in a book can be extracted to represent the entire work, Jane Schneider's encounter with elements of the Italian press after the translation and publication of a collection of her essays demonstrates how anthropological writing can be sensationalized and distorted.[15]

The title of the Italian edition of her work, *La Vigilanza delle Vergini*, is taken from Schneider's 1971 article in *Ethnology*, "Of Vigilance and Virgins."[16] In this article, Schneider offered a political and ecological explanation for the prevalence of codes of honor and shame in southern Italy and throughout the

Mediterranean area. Drawing on ethnographic research by other anthropologists for comparative material, she argued that these codes emerged as an adaptation to the intense conflict that external pressures created within and between agri- cultural and pastoral societies in this region. A woman's virginity in some Mediterranean societies, according to Schneider (1971), was central to the sol- idarity of her family of origin, to the preservation of its honor, and hence to its efficacy as a social form. Her shame was crucial to the honor, solidarity, and efficacy of her family of procreation.[17]

The volume of essays came to the attention of the editor of *Moda*, a slick and expensive Italian fashion magazine, who is a Sicilian living in Milan. Keenly interested, he sent a Milanese journalist and photographer to Schneider's field site, a rural interior town that she and her collaborator, Peter Schneider, refer to as "Villamaura" in their published work. The journalist's mission was to investigate local sexual mores, guided by the points raised in the 1971 article. Her effort, a four-page spread enlivened by well-composed photographs of young people in cars and on the piazza, seems condescending; it asserts that such mores remain less progressive in Sicily than in Milan. The argument, reinforced by an archival photograph from the 1920s illustrating a young Italian woman dressed in underwear, fastening her bra while sitting on a bed under an image of the Virgin, draws unwelcome attention to the people of Villamaura, many of whom resented it.

In an insert of several paragraphs entitled "Io Tarzan, tu Jane?" (I Tarzan, you Jane?), the editor of *Moda* also takes on the anthropologist. Portraying Schneider as a "cavalier explorer," he accuses her of generalizing from a rural and backward situation to the entire island, and this after no more than six months of fieldwork. Did she now know that there were cities in Sicily; that a women's movement and a struggle for abortion rights had emerged in these cities? To ignore the urbanity of at least a portion of Sicilian experience was imperialist and racist.

The town of Villamaura publishes a monthly newspaper, for which two local students and an older intellectual wrote responses, as did Schneider. Although all four sent their protests to *Moda* as well, none received a reply, let alone any space in the magazine. Schneider's rejoinder addresses the increasingly vocal questioning on the part of both native laypersons and ethnographers as to whether foreigners, ethnographers or otherwise, can understand the history and culture of other societies or divorce themselves from the kind of cultural exploitation that is unavoidable in such endeavors. She challenges the accusations of racism by reemphasizing the central point of her article "Of Vigilance and Virgins": cultural patterns such as honor and shame "are not ingrained and unchangeable (which would be a racist argument) but relate to the exigencies of organizing rural life in particular environmental and historical settings" (Schneider, personal communication 1991). Finally, she deals with the primitivizing and patronizing tendency of both the *Moda* editor and the journalist vis-à-vis the south of their own country, a tendency she sees revealed in their references to Villamaura as "one of the smallest confines" and a "poor depressed community." Could the Milanese journalist who visited this town for a day and a half claim knowledge superior to that of a fieldworker who lived there for two years (not six months) before producing the 1971 analysis? Perhaps the people of Villamaura deserve an apology from the northern Italian writer who misread and misrepresented her work.

One of the most elaborate discussions of how the media intervene in the reception and reading of ethnographic texts is contained in Wrobel's (1979) study of a Polish-American community in Detroit. Wrobel describes an interview that he gave about his research to a *Detroit Free Press* reporter prior to a scientific conference in Boston. He gave her a copy of the paper that he was about to deliver, in which he discussed the low self-esteem among Polish-American blue-collar workers that was the inevitable result of negative attitudes directed toward them by the larger society. Warned by a Polish sociologist and friend that the words he had chosen would be distorted by the media and lead to a community uproar, Wrobel tried to head off the problem.[18]

But the story was already out of his control. A *Washington Post* article headlined "The Polish Stereotype" told of Polish blue-collar workers who dropped out of high school to go to work because it was the only thing they could do and it paid the bills. It went on to mention wives who do little to help men feel different and marriages that are unhappy though men and women endure them. The quotations drawn form Wrobel's paper had indeed been taken out of context and, in Wrobel's assessment, could easily lead readers to conclude that he was "blaming the victim" (Wrobel 1979:160). Headlines in other papers read "Detroit Poles Feel They're Unworthy, Study Discloses" and "Study Finds Bad Polish Image."

Calls from Polish Americans began to flood Wrobel's office at the Merrill-Palmer Institute, and five parishioners from his study parish showed up at his house to discuss the situation. Having read his work, they were sympathetic and realized that the newspapers "don't tell the whole story" (Wrobel 1979:162). But by this time Wrobel's research was already on the television evening news, broadcast together with interviews with the "Pole on the street." Headlines the next day read "Detroit Poles Attack Study on Self-Image" and "Poles in Detroit Reject Bad Image in Study," and newspapers as far away as Los Angeles to the west and Bangor, Maine, to the east had picked up the story.

Letters to the editor (cited in Wrobel 1979:163–164) suggested that Wrobel's parents had wasted their money in sending their son to college; that no good anthropologist would confine a study to such a small group; that there is nothing wrong with working overtime. Many Poles wrote that they were "Polish and proud of it," and one irate reader, who acknowledged being "extensively involved in Polish affairs," commented that "constructive criticism is always welcome and beneficial but a study with some unprobable [sic] results, doubtful research methods, and suspicion of bias can only mislead the readers and perform unnecessary harm to the parties involved" (cited in Wrobel 1979:163). The last word went to a Pole who expressed resentment at Wrobel's depiction of Poles as stupid and dull. "It wasn't at all representative. I wouldn't attempt to write a thesis unless I first knew what I was writing about. That's where Wrobel wobbled. He sure missed the boat" (cited in Wrobel 1979:164).

Wrobel's final reflections on his encounter with the media are extremely insightful. He points to the distance that separates the anthropologist from the reporter; they meet as strangers, with their respective cultural baggage. "The language of social science is not always understood by journalists, and the time constraints a reporter faces seem incomprehensible and unfair to an anthropologist who is asked to summarize three years of work in three minutes" (1979:171). In his published work Wrobel attempted to minimize social science jargon and eliminate ambiguity. By including the epilogue describing how a part of the work was read and received, he follows Kane's (1982) suggestion as well as the suggestions of some proponents of reflexive anthropology. Indeed, he is perhaps more honest in displaying his naïveté about the impact of his research than many of the more widely known anthropologists writing about reflexivity and experimentation.

STRATEGIES AND RESOLUTIONS

Rosaldo (1986:6–7) has identified three forms of reactions by anthropologists to the challenges of native readers. One he calls the "Chicken Little Reaction"— the experts hear natives talk back and say, "The sky is falling." Either they retreat into hopelessness for the future of anthropology as a discipline, or they react assertively by emphasizing the rightness of their interpretation and the wrongness of the native's response. This reaction is sometimes hard to avoid no matter how reflexive and self-conscious the ethnographer tries to be.

A second he calls the "Two Worlds Reaction," a response emphasizing that anthropologists and natives speak two different languages—that of science on the one hand and of everyday life on the other—and never the twain shall meet. This is Arthur Vidich's reaction in his efforts to deal with the fallout from the publication of *Small Town in Mass Society*, and the response of some of the contributors to this volume.[19] Some of those who offered advice to Davis suggested that she no longer use personal accounts in quotations. Write a more academic book, they said, and your informants will not be interested in reading it, or will not understand it if they do.

Clearly this is a debatable solution, but it should be recognized that even some native readers have suggested that the distance exists and cannot be bridged easily. A few years ago Rosamond Spicer conducted an interview with some of her husband's Yaqui informants about their attitudes toward Ned Spicer's work (Valencia, Valencia, and Spicer 1990). Anselmo, a deer dancer, admitted to consulting some of Spicer's writings, particularly when he wanted to deliver a speech at Pima College. However, his final assessment was that many Yaqui people would not read what Spicer had written because "our idea is that Dr.

Spicer wrote it for the benefit of non-Yaqui so they could understand the Yaqui. And therefore the Yaquis don't know if they have to read it because the Yaquis think they understand the Yaquis. . . . And then because the way the book is written, it's a little bit technical, like lawyer talk'' (1990:103). Yaquis, according to Anselmo, have their own way of explaining things, and no matter how sincere the anthropologist is, he will not explain things in precisely the same way as the Yaqui.

The third reaction to the criticisms of ethnographic writing voiced by native readers is the "One Conversation Reaction." This view, according to Rosaldo (1986:7), emphasizes the new insights that can result from listening to native responses and argues that these insights often outweigh any misunderstandings. This reaction, one that accepts native readers within "the community of scholars that test and contest our ethnographic interpretations," can take different forms.

The form chosen by Wrobel (1979) and Messenger (1989) was to add an appendix to their respective ethnographies that spells out the objections to their work by those about whom they have written. A similar approach has been adopted by Foley (1988) in his study of the role of La Raza Unida in a community in South Texas. Foley took his draft back to the community and incorporated the responses to it in a final section of the book. These responses were by no means uniform, but they add new dimensions to the ethnographer's interpretation and demonstrate how varied the voice of the "native" is according to ethnic, educational, class, and political background. One should always keep in mind that there will never be a single community view or monolithic "insider" reaction to an ethnographic text. Finally, reflecting on what she did and did not show to her respondents prior to publication, Lawless (1992) concludes that she should have included her key respondents' interpretations of her interpretation, as well as her own reinterpretation, in the final text of her book *Handmaidens of the Lord*. "If we insist upon interpreting other people's interpretations, at the very least, we are obligated to allow them space to respond. At the very most, we stand to learn far more than we ever bargained for'' (Lawless 1992:313).

An alternative approach to the more active involvement of ethnographic subjects in their representation focuses on the coproduction of texts, created in what Tedlock (1991:82) has recently referred to as an "interactive Self/Other dialogue." This is precisely the solution pursued by Dwyer (1982) and by Horwitz and McBeth (in this volume). But it is a solution that really works best when a single individual or only a few are the subject of ethnographic research. It is no wonder that such an approach has been most vigorously adopted by anthropologists constructing life histories. According to Blackman (1992), the Haida woman with whom she worked was guided in her telling of her story by issues of intended audience (her local community and the world) and cultural constraints about self-revelation. The manuscript itself was coedited, and numerous family members were free to comment on it.

Blackman, like most of the authors in this book, reflects on the inevitability today that anthropological works will be read, in one way or another, by those in the community studied. Crocombe (1976:68) calls these readers the greatest critics, followed closely by those most closely associated with or identified with those people—native scholars and other elites. Among the reasons for this vociferous criticism he cites the intimate knowledge that these people have about their way of life.

They may be aware of some errors of fact or interpretation that the academic observer has made, but generally and more significantly it is because the academic observer has interpreted things in a different way from what they would have done, or has emphasized different facets of the society, or has held up his mirror to reflect the society from an angle which the society is unaccustomed to. There is also often an understandable feeling that it was improper, impolite, or offensive for certain things which are considered highly personal or sacrosanct to be revealed openly, particularly in written form.

Issues of identity and representation are always at stake, and we need to be aware of this in the preparation of texts that will increasingly be read and contested.

CONCLUSION

In this introduction I have included examples of all the reasons outlined by Rosaldo (1986) for strong negative reactions to what the anthropologist writes, and the chapters of this volume explore them further. In drawing attention to the politics of ethnographic writing, to the impact of audience on both anthropologist and text, this book raises a host of questions of theoretical, ethical, and practical importance for anthropologists who will increasingly be confronted by natives who both read and react. The authors collectively ask us to reevaluate the viability of a distinction between ''insider'' and ''outsider.'' They examine further the issues of ethnographic authority and the politics of representation, and demonstrate how they personally have dealt with the challenges to authority and interpretation that they have faced either during the process of fieldwork or after the publication of the results of their research.

Fieldworkers, according to Karp and Kendall (1982:269), ''are persons who both affirm and deny the validity of native conceptions of existence.'' It is this Janus-like role that is often the source of the controversies that surround an ethnographic text. Furthermore, if, as postmodernists, we have come to accept that we no longer write exclusively for ourselves, even our efforts to ''take the voice of the other'' can result, as Ginsburg so eloquently observes, in reactions for which we are unprepared. By sharing their experiences of what happened when the people they have written about read or responded to what they wrote or intended to write, the contributors to this volume move us one step further toward preparedness, sensitivity, and new ways to involve our ethnographic subjects in their self-representation.

NOTES

The author would like to thank Ellen Badone, Dona Davis, and several anonymous reviewers for their comments and suggestions on earlier versions of this introduction.

1. Jacobson (1991:118) questions whether confessional tales really have any relationship to interpretation. Commenting on Rabinow, he states: "His reflections upon his personal experiences may be interesting, but they do not constitute grounds for his conclusions about Moroccan ways of evaluating the world and their relationships in and to it. His experiences, and his analysis of them, are unrelated to his interpretation, except as rhetorical devices."

2. Reader-response and reception theory shift critical concern from the author and the work to the reader and the text. They focus on questions such as the attitude of the author toward readers, the kinds of readers implied by various kinds of texts, and the role of readers in determining literary meaning. As Fish (1980:3) has put it, "the reader's response is not *to* the meaning; it *is* the meaning."

3. Spencer (1989:148) argues that Geertz's style of writing equally assumes a passive readership.

4. Elsewhere Jackson observes that "behind the current polarization of analytical and interpretive modes of anthropological knowledge lies a struggle for intellectual and moral authority in which scholars promise to save us from false gods only to end up trying to sell us their own idols" (1989:183). This critical stance is equally adopted by Birth (1990), who admonishes Fischer (in his article in *Writing Culture*) for blaming the reader's lack of expertise for the problem of noncomprehension. He goes on to accuse postmodernists of "the very thing they claim to transcend: insensitive writing" and of "displacing the ethical problems of ethnographic representation onto readers" (1990:550). For other critiques see Howes (1990), Jacobson (1991), Polier and Roseberry (1989), Spencer (1989), Roth (1989), and Sangren (1988).

5. Other monographs on communities in the United States, for example William Foote Whyte's *Street Corner Society* and W. Lloyd Warner's *Yankee City*, were also the object of negative reaction.

6. It is likely that many anthropologists have been subjected to accusations of financial gain, though few choose to write about it. In Vidich and Bensman's case, even academic colleagues raised issues of career opportunism. See, for example, the editorial by William F. Whyte in *Human Organization* 17 (2): 1–2.

7. Most of this discussion first appeared in the pages of *Human Organization* in volumes 17, 18, and 19.

8. Commenting on her research in Elmdon, Strathern (1987a:19) makes a similar observation. Ethnographies, she argues, are mixed genres, which are not simply about specific people and specific places and times, but also about theory.

9. The material for this discussion is drawn from the reviews collected and reprinted in volume 6 of *Mesoamerican Notes* (Department of Anthropology, University of the Americas). I am grateful to Robert Van Kemper for bringing this volume to my attention.

10. While he does not deal directly with issues of reception, Glassie (1982) is equally sensitive to the problem of writing simultaneously for his literate rural informants and for the more cosmopolitan readers in Irish and American academies.

11. This latter critique, as well as the broader question of what kinds of generalizations are appropriate and acceptable to the people studied, deserves more attention. Scheper-

Hughes (1982b:13) refers to the process of generalizing from a local study as the "classical anthropological hubris." Marcus and Cushman (1982:32) treat it as a rhetorical device. By creating "common denominator people"—the Nuer, the Irish—ethnographies skirt individual, if not regional, variation. Jacobson (1991:115) suggests that these are not merely issues of rhetoric but also of analytical focus.

12. Messenger (1989:129) reacts to this in a way similar to Vidich. "The advice of the reviewers that I should have discussed my interpretations of controversial issues with my informants and, by implication, should not have written anything with which they disagreed would stultify social scientific research in Ireland. It is my serious contention that at least one islander would have disputed any generalization, controversial or not, set forth in the book." It should be noted that Scheper-Hughes's work was equally taken to task for its "ethnographic inaccuracies, unfounded generalizations, and methodological weaknesses" (Kane 1982:2). Kane also suggests that what most bothered the people of Ballybran was not the question of "for whose good?" but "on whose evidence?" "People here (both scholars and Ballybran residents) are annoyed at . . . the rather numbing sincerity of over-literal interpretations" (1982:3). See Scheper-Hughes (1982b) for a response.

13. See Messenger (1984, 1988, 1989).

14. Many misinterpretations, according to Paredes (1978:4), stem from a lack of fluency in language and particularly from a tendency to attribute literal meanings to figurative expressions. Paredes suggests that enthographers learn from folklorists, who approach the informant as a potential performer and artist. Rhetoric, he argues, is as important to the process of data-gathering as it is to the process of writing an ethnography. Narayan (1989) provides another example of the ethnographer/folklorist who reflects on the relationships between self and other, insider and outsider, and the informant as performer.

15. I am grateful to Jane Schneider for sharing with me the magazine story (*Moda*, April 1989), a copy of her letter of response to it, and her own reflections on the incident.

16. Schneider (personal communication 1991) did not choose the title. It refers to only one article in the book. The other pieces demonstrate subsequent developments in her ideas and research.

17. Schneider's article represents an early attempt to make sense of and synthesize a wide body of literature. Although the concepts of honor and shame as unifying moral values of the Mediterranean region have recently come under criticism (Herzfeld 1980, 1984; Pina-Cabral 1989), her analysis remains thought-provoking and was a significant contribution at the time of its publication.

18. The Polish sociologist underlined a number of sentences in Wrobel's paper that were potentially dangerous. Among them: "Women view a man's attitude towards work as the most important factor to consider in choosing a future husband"; "Polish-American men in this community have one major goal with regard to their role as parents: to raise children whose lives will be significantly different from their own"; "Generally speaking, the men in this community view themselves as unintelligent factory workers unworthy of respect and incapable of accomplishing anything worthwhile except supporting a family through hard work and the ability to sacrifice" (Wrobel 1979:157).

19. It is also evident in Ortner's ethnography of the Sherpas. Throughout the text, Ortner (1978) points to differences between her interpretation and that of her Sherpa informants.

Part I

CONTESTED TEXTS: IMPLICATIONS FOR FIELDWORK AND RAPPORT

1

UNINTENDED CONSEQUENCES: THE MYTH OF "THE RETURN" IN ANTHROPOLOGICAL FIELDWORK

Dona L. Davis

I have Margaret Mead fantasies. I have had Margaret Mead fantasies for some time now.

For me (and probably for numerous other female anthropologists as well), Margaret Mead has been inextricably linked to my mental image of being an anthropologist and going to the field. It was Margaret Mead who convinced me that I wanted to become an anthropologist when I discovered and read *Sex and Temperament in Three Primitive Societies* (1963) in my high school library. During my graduate career I mentally modeled myself as a "Margaret Mead of menopause" as I began my study of women's experience of menopause in the Newfoundland fishing village I call Grey Rock Harbour. Despite the controversies surrounding her career, Margaret Mead continued to dominate my anthropological fantasy life as I prepared to return to Grey Rock Harbour almost twelve years after my first arrival. This time my mind's eye saw Margaret Mead in a boat returning to the shores of Manus. My mental reconstruction of a film clip (Margaret Mead's *New Guinea Journal*) I had seen many years earlier showed friendly natives eagerly awaiting the return of their long lost ethnographer. In a similar vein, I imagined myself returning to Grey Rock Harbour to renew associations with informants who had remained familiar and vital friends in my fieldnotes and whose special relationships with me I had grown to cherish.

My Margaret Mead fantasies guided me through my first fieldwork experience—my anthropological rite of passage. Studying and living in a small, isolated fishing community on Newfoundland's southwest coast, I became immersed in the everyday dramas of the lives of middle-aged women. I also absorbed elements of their identity and romantic self-imagery (Davis 1987, 1986a, 1983b). My Margaret Mead return myths were, however, largely unrealized when I returned for further study in Grey Rock Harbour in 1989. Perhaps it could be said that the Margaret Mead "realities" had set in.

A healthy amount of naïveté got me through my first year of fieldwork. At that time, I felt that my major challenges were to become accepted into the community, to emotionally survive the requisite time period, and to learn all I could about how biological and sociocultural phenomena coalesce to shape local women's experiences of midlife. When I entered Grey Rock Harbour in 1977, I was twenty-nine years old and took on the role of a learner or apprentice to mature womanhood. I wanted to learn how to do fieldwork—to learn how to learn from others. As a single young woman, as a student, I was viewed by Grey Rock Harbour women as socially undeveloped, as a "little girl," as having many important life decisions yet to make. My informants took little interest in how I had come to their village, but sought to mold me to their notions of more natural and responsible female adulthood. This included a firm commitment to a future in the self-sacrificing role of good wife and mother. Being experts at wife- and motherhood, having suffered through good times and bad, my middle-aged informants freely offered advice and guidance to me. They did so by proudly referring to their own life decisions and experiences. I was a "respectful learner" and would beam with pride whenever I received the supreme compliment, "We'll make a Newfie out of you yet." In preparing me to become one of them, they opened up their hearts and souls to me, and I diligently recorded our growing intimacies in my fieldnotes every night.

In 1983 the book *Blood and Nerves: An Ethnographic Focus on Menopause*, the result of this period of fieldwork, was published. I sent complimentary copies of the book to key informants and good friends in Grey Rock Harbour. Through short visits and frequent correspondence, I came to believe that the locals had generally approved of my work and, thus, of me.

In the summer of 1989, I returned to the field, guided by my resurfacing Margaret Mead fantasies, but also intellectually armed with the "new ethnography" (Clifford and Marcus 1986; Marcus and Fischer 1986; Mascia-Lees, Sharpe, and Cohen 1989; R. Rosaldo 1989; Roth 1989). Having had a productive academic career and publications from the first period of fieldwork, I carried with me into the field, for a second time, an intellectualized burden of guilt. I was no longer learning to be an anthropologist; I was a bona fide academic colonialist. Concepts of "other" would also dominate my new sense of identity in the field. I had a well-developed sense of the Newfoundlander as "the other" and a feminist sense of self as "the other" too (Mascia-Lees, Sharpe, and Cohen 1989).

I was ready to face the strategic, situational, accidental, and ethical challenges of fieldwork the second time around. Despite my fantasies of an idyllic homecoming, I was mentally prepared to take the flak I anticipated for my detailed descriptions of very private phenomena, like the characteristics of menstrual effluvia or my discussions of premarital sexual activity. I also anticipated conversations about errors I had made or criticisms of my constructions of such crucial concepts as nerves, blood, women's status, or the nature of the local community. Yet I was secure in my abilities as a good fieldworker and assumed that my first period of residence in the community had earned me the "right" to come back.

What I had failed to anticipate was that I would no longer be seen as their "little girl;"—"a Newfoundlander in the making." My very professionalism and dedication to career were seen by local women as failures in the lessons in life, based on their own lifetime decisions, they had offered to me. I was married but had voluntarily had no children. It was assumed that I must be a bad wife because I had left my husband to spend a year in Newfoundland. To their way of thinking, I had taken a selfish turn in life and was no longer "moldable." My return to the field stimulated a lot of conversation about my moral character, and it also stimulated a great deal of conversation about *Blood and Nerves*. The reaction to both myself and the book was, at best, mixed.

For seven months, in 1989, I lived in Grey Rock Harbour, conducting fieldwork in an environment where controversy over *Blood and Nerves* was a fairly constant factor. The sources and nature of the controversy generated when local people read or discussed what I had written, its consequent effect on my relationship with the community, and its effect on my most recent period of fieldwork are the topics of this chapter. I will discuss what ensued in terms of (1) my failure to anticipate local reactions to the book; (2) the problematic issue of anonymity; (3) how local rumor and confusion affected my reputation; and (4) the stress of daily survival with a dual and volatile identity as friend/champion and villain/pariah.

FAILURE TO ANTICIPATE LOCAL REACTIONS

As I was writing my dissertation, eventually to become *Blood and Nerves*, I remained closely connected to my major informants. Following through on the initial fieldwork, I would return to Grey Rock Harbour between 1978 and 1990, with quotes I had taken from women in normal conversations and as part of their life histories. Where something I said might be seen as offensive or uncomplimentary about a particular woman, I would read the section to her and ask if it was okay to put it in the book. For example, before confederation a woman could receive a widow's benefit, but only if her husband died at sea. One particular woman had a husband who had not fished in years and was dying of tuberculosis. When death became imminent she took her husband out in a boat, and he died at sea. Technically she qualified for the widow's benefit. When I spoke to her, this individual told me to go ahead and put this account into my book. It was a hard decision for her to make. But she was able to keep her children together after her husband's death because of the pittance she had received from the government. She told me she was proud of what she had done. Of all the women I contacted, not one objected to what I said about them as long as I did not use their or the village's real names.

I did not use a signed consent statement, but every woman who agreed to my formal structured and open-ended menopause interview was told that I would write down what she said and might put her comments into a book at a later date. In their formal interviews, many women told me that they had never discussed such (to them) private issues with another human being. I would double-check at this point if it was all right to write this down. Their usual response was that it was up to me, since clearly the entire interview made little sense to them (for a discussion, see Davis 1986b). Informants were very critical of the interview schedule, and our conversations afterwards were an excellent source of information on how their local and my medical and feminist notions of menopause did not exactly overlap. Explaining the use of an interview to someone who has little experience with interviews is difficult. Local women appeared to consent to whatever use I might make of their answers, with the qualification that I was to put what they said in "my own words," to make their statements grammatically correct so that they would not appear "ignorant" or "backward."

When the dissertation was being prepared for publication, I sent the manuscript to two local women, asking them to identify parts they thought might be untrue or offensive to other villagers. Their response was, "We knew it was to be about menopause, and all you said was true, so who can complain." (I now realize that this request to police the manuscript placed an unfair burden on them; I never mentioned them or their approval of the manuscript as criticism of the book began to emerge during the second period of fieldwork.) I worried that my discussions of the nature of premarital sexual activity and the detailed charac-teristics of menstrual effluvia would be reacted to as an unwarranted intrusion into the personal, intimate arenas of their lives. Locals did not fault me for writing a book about menopause. After all, they had been willingly interviewed. Instead, most of their negative reactions were to things I had not anticipated. For example, some complained that I had no business writing that attendance at Sunday church services was usually scanty. Others took offense at examples I had selected from life histories to show what I thought to be positive, admirable characters of local women. For example, to describe how women had a great deal of power as individuals if their domestic domain was intruded upon, I presented a long case history of a woman I had heard described again and again. In short, a decision by village men to divert the village water supply to a herring boat temporarily moored in the harbor interfered with women's after-dinner cleaning. One local woman, fed up with this infringement on her domestic rights, took an axe down to the pump when a small group of men came to reconnect the water to the herring boat. Watched by villagers from their kitchen windows, she axed the hose and threatened the men. Pointing with her axe to the cement base of the pump, she warned them that they would all end up with their asses in cement if they ever again attempted to reconnect the hose at dinner time. To me, she was a feminist heroine. When I read this account to popular women's studies audiences, they sometimes get up and cheer as I deliver the final line. However, when this woman herself read my account of her actions, she was very distressed that I said she had said a bad word, "asses."

THE QUESTION OF ANONYMITY

My intent with *Blood and Nerves* was to write a book that both lay and professional audiences could read. I used extensive quotations from local women, assuming that they would read them and feel that they too had played an active role in the construction of the book. I used fictitious names to disguise the identity of the village and of individuals described in the text. If repeated quotes from the same woman were used in different chapters, I used a new fictitious name for each quote. Some case studies were composites of a number of women, and I attempted to disguise the identity of individual women as far as my standards of truth would allow. Many village women, however, objected that they could still identify those I had referred to in my own narrative sections of the book. (Often they were incorrect.) This I had anticipated—it is a problem inherent in all fieldwork. But it was my extensive use of quotations, or their own words, that most disturbed them.

I had used frequent quotations from local women in my text because the women were so delightfully articulate and because the quotations gave ethnographic depth to my analysis, making my informants, in my view, come alive as individual people in the chapters that dealt with their life histories and their perspectives on the change of life. Besides identifying the women in my own case descriptions, identifying which woman was responsible for which quotation also became a popular pastime. Local women viewed my use of direct quotes as an invasion of their privacy. For example, there is a short description of a woman's fight with bouts of depression. To me it was an extremely heartfelt and moving account of local values and coping strategies; others thought I had no right to portray this woman's private emotions in the book. I might add here that although I was taken to task for not adequately disguising women's identities, the veracity of my or their statements was not challenged, nor was I accused of portraying them as backward.

Local gossips were very interested in discovering who had told me what. (This they were very poor at doing, and a lot of the wrong people got blamed for passing on information to me.) In my interviews, if women reported no difficulties at menopause for themselves, I asked them to describe others they knew who had no problems or who had experienced problems at midlife. During interviews, women were far more comfortable talking about others than about themselves. This was a major source of information for me about women's experience of menopause in the village. This willingness to talk about peers gave me insight as to how women passed judgment on one another and was an important source for cross-checking the truthfulness of informants' statements about themselves. In my opinion (and I would be the one to know), it would be virtually impossible to tell who gave me what information. The information I used was all common knowledge, and each case example I used had multiple informants. It was extremely painful for me to learn that women whose first names I had listed in the dedication of the book were the subjects of severe local censure. I had dedicated the book as a tribute to the special friendships that I had developed with them. In the long run, my tribute only hurt them by falsely branding them as my major informers. In reality they were my confessors, rather than I theirs. This brings us to the third point.

RUMOR AND CONFUSION

What I saw as legitimate complaints about the book did not bother me as much as the rumors and untruths that circulated about it. I realize that in ethnography we take people's own words away from them and reconstruct them for our own purposes (Stacey 1988), just as reviewers and those who quote or refer to our own published works often miss or distort the meaning of our words. As Rosaldo states (1989), our subjects, just like other ethnographers, can be insightful or mistaken. It was the "mistaken" that I found, and still find, most difficult to deal with.

During my first couple of weeks in the village, on my way to a local store, I overheard a village developmentally disabled individual ask his walking companion if she had read my book. She said no, and he then proceeded to inform her that "it was pure shit." Like this man, who could not read, not many people in the village had actually read the book, but everybody talked about it, like this man, behind my back. My return to the field stimulated the circulation of untrue rumors about the book. The years 1988 and 1989 were very.bad for the inshore fishery. There were no fish, and most fisherman and all plant workers were living on unemployment, with little prospect for the return of a successful fishery. My book became a kind of mythological "Rorschach" onto which all their worst contemporary fears about themselves were projected. I was unjustly accused of writing that all the women were crazy and all the men were good for nothing and lazy. Actually, the book had said precisely the opposite.

Worst of all, locals confused my book, *Blood and Nerves*, with Claire Mowat's (wife of Farley) *Outport People*. Also published in 1983, *Outport People* gave a far less flattering account of a nearby village and does refer to the men as lazy. My only defense against this kind of rumor was to supply people with copies of my own book. I discovered the Mowat connection when I brought a woman a copy of my *Blood and Nerves*. She looked it over and said, "Not this one, the one you wrote with the village picture on it." After that the rumor mill accused me of denying that I wrote the "bad book" too. After several months of trepidation, I finally gave a copy of my book to the woman I boarded with. I was afraid that she would read the book and ask me to leave her house. She took the book to bed with her and stayed up the entire evening reading it. The next morning she came into my room and said, "I read the whole thing last night and I'm really pissed off." As my heart sank to the floor, she went on to say that she had heard a lot of terrible things about the book, and not one of them was actually in the book. She told me she could not wait until someone brought my name up again, so that she could tell them they were wrong—that they were being unfair to me.

As this woman noted, the bad things said about me and my book were said largely behind my back. But the effects of the negative reaction to my book are real. Some people refused to have me in their homes. They refused interviews, albeit politely. I could not go to an event that involved heavy drinking because it was thought I would cause a fight to break out. What was frustrating was that I could not combat these rumors. For one thing, no one would openly confront me with them. I felt that any attempt to bring the issue to a head would only contribute to the negative rumors and jeopardize the delicate position of support I did have in the community. My closest village friend advised me to "leave it to others to defend you." The only way I could counter the rumors was to hold my head high, go about life as usual, and pass out free copies of my book (which got to be expensive). Actually, the book was my best defense. The hard part was getting people to read it. As more and more people read the book they were surprised at how tame (boring) it really was.

I was able to share my sense of injustice with only a few people. Their comfort came in the recognition that I was just going through a process that every single one of them has experienced at one time or another. Whatever you do or whoever you are, sooner or later the community will turn against you, and all you can do is hold your head high, ignore what they are saying about you, and go about your business as usual. As I saw similar things happen to others (for example, young girls unjustly accused of abortions, older couples accused of welfare fraud, nasty rumors about the new minister), I was better able to put my own dilemma into perspective. In a way my return and my trial by fire made me a more integral part of the community. I was simply the subject of the very social leveling I had written so much about. I was told by sympathizers, "Now you really know what it is like to live here."

Toward the end of my fieldwork, people began to realize that I knew what they were saying about me. The controversy became more open. A local teacher invited me to speak to high school classes. It was my first opportunity to defend the book in public. In class, a student charged that I had to return to Grey Rock Harbour to "clear my name" because of all the terrible falsehoods I had perpetrated. I asked him to specify what he meant. He made the claim that I had said all the men were lazy. Once faced with the issue, I could begin to straighten out some of the misunderstandings. I admired the young man's courage in speaking out. He had not read the book. Fortunately, his teacher had. The dialogue about my book became more public. Some people began to pity me because I was considered to be an outsider on whom they had imposed punishments which were administered by insider rules. My defenders began to speak up. It actually felt good when a member of my dart team jokingly pointed to a man who came into the club and said, "Watch out Dona, that's ——— and he says if you ever cross his tracks he'll beat the shit out of you." It finally meant I was to be let in on the discourse surrounding my book.

NO PAIN, NO GAIN

That year was full of experiences I hope I never have to repeat. As a professor at the University of South Dakota, every semester I can depend on Native American students raising the issue of resenting (to put it mildly) anthropologists and what they do. Despite the anti-anthropology rhetoric they have grown up with, many Sioux students find the actual study of anthropology very interesting and relevant to their own concerns. Yet selling anthropology as a college discipline is different from legitimizing one's role in the field. I thrive on controversy in the classroom. Controversy in the field is quite a different matter. I always justified my work in Newfoundland as studying my own culture or cultural heritage (English) and felt smug because in 1977–78 my people liked me. Just before I left the field the first time, a woman told me that throughout all the time I had been in Grey Rock Harbour she had not heard a bad word against me. I was proud of that. The second trial in the field was not so idyllic. Moreover, the village itself had fallen on hard times. Grey Rock Harbour was fast on its way to becoming a rural slum (Davis 1990a, 1990b). It is not easy to feel persona non grata for seven months. I did feel very fortunate, however, that I only had to respond to the book and not to every article I had written about them. Anthropology is an intrusive endeavor. The irony of getting informed consent for questionnaires when you are also practicing participant observation has not been lost on me. Many of us are prepared for the criticism that goes with anthropological methods. It goes with the territory. We are prepared for criticism and difficulty in the abstract, but it still is emotionally painful when we have to answer for our actions, intended or not, in the real world. It is hard to be told by someone whose friendship I have grown to cherish, and whose shared life history has helped to build my own career, that while she likes me as a person she does not care for what I do.

I returned to St. John's for a couple of months of additional fieldwork at the beginning of 1990. I was still reeling from my experiences of "when people read what you write." It was a topic I brought up with many different social science colleagues. I was offered diverse sorts of strategies for coming to terms with my dissonance. I was told that it will be a very sad day for anthropology when we let our subjects dictate our ethnographies. I was advised to write my next book in a more academically sophisticated fashion so that my subjects would neither be interested in reading it nor understand it if they did. I was advised to depersonalize my approach to ethnography—to eliminate the use of personal accounts and quotations. I was also counseled by one, whose group was a frequent subject of ethnography, that I had done right. I had stuck it out, opened up the dialogue between those who study and those who are studied, and earned the respect of my subjects and the right to say what I wanted to about them. This is precisely what my own informants had told me. When I asked them what I should put in my next book about them, they told me to tell it as I see it and to put the bad in with the good.

This brings me to the positive side of my recent experience. In a way, living with their censure as an author and as an adult who had decided to make life choices very different from their own gave me both insider and outsider status. I was their ethnographer for better or for worse. By reading my book, some locals came to believe there could be advantages to having me around and having me write about them. I did not have to become one of them; I had a value unique to myself. My current project includes men as well as women. I found that the local men had a lot to say to me and found me to be a source of information on some of the problems they were facing relating to fishing.

People actually sought me out when they had opinions or information they wanted to be communicated in my next book (Davis, in press). I learned that people do not have to like you to give you valuable information. Many informants now see me as a kind of information broker for their concerns to the wider world. Informed consent is a much more meaningful phrase to them now. In truth, I now feel that I have earned the right and the responsibility to be more critical of them. Or perhaps, as Margaret Mead's own stormy career attests, old myths have simply given way, again, to new myths.

NOTE

The original period of research was funded by the National Institutes for Maternal and Child Health in a grant administered by the University of North Carolina at Chapel Hill Population Center. The 1989–1990 research period was funded by a Canadian Embassy Faculty Research Grant, a USD Research Institute Grant, and a Memorial University of Newfoundland Institute of Social and Economic Research Fellowship.

2

RESPONDING TO THE ANTHROPOLOGIST: WHEN THE SPIRITUAL BAPTISTS OF TRINIDAD READ WHAT I WRITE ABOUT THEM

Stephen D. Glazier

Our university sociologists should undertake a serious in-depth study of those believers [the Shouters] who may well represent our only indigenous group. No such study exists and the lack of appreciation may well be solved by greater understanding. We believe that the country as a whole should have an opportunity to know more about the Spiritual Baptists who are still largely a mystery to those of us who know so little about their faith. What are their beliefs, their origins, and their development?

Trinidad Guardian, January 21, 1980

All contemporary ethnography is done is an independent and mutually informed world where the ethnographer and his subjects are both *a priori* familiar and alien to one another.

Marcus and Fischer 1986:112

The traditional view of anthropological texts as "research reports" or "results" is far too restrictive, one-sided, and sterile. It is also a distortion in a world where increasingly those whom anthropologists study can read what is written about them. This traditional, romantic,[1] and hegemonic view has faced much criticism of late, and as Vincent Crapanzano (1977a;1986), George Marcus and Michael M. J. Fischer (1986), and James Clifford (1988) have pointed out, the traditional, nonreflexive view often does violence both to the process of creating an anthropological text and to the actual encounter of anthropologist and informant. It also greatly underplays the significance of the text itself, which, as the chapters in this volume attest, almost always has an existence independent of the author's intentions and the informants' desires.

Anthropological texts may reach unexpected audiences and assume unanticipated significance in unplanned places. Rather than looking at anthropological texts (books, dissertations, films, articles, and so on) as the fruits of research designed to be shared with an audience of scholars (mostly other anthropologists and area specialists), it is becoming more appropriate to view books and articles as integral to the research process itself. This is especially true in the case of long-term field researcher (Foster, Scudder, Colson, and Kemper 1979) or whenever one continues working in an area after the publication of one's initial findings. In my own case, I have worked on the Caribbean island of Trinidad studying a single religious organization, the Spiritual Baptists, for over sixteen years. During that time, having published a number of essays and two books as well as producing a record album dealing with the Baptist faith, I have had to contend with native responses to my publications.

Clifford Geertz (1988) has recently suggested that each anthropologist's life may be seen as a unique personal configuration of works and lives, texts and encounters. Geertz's personal configuration consists of prodigious textual output from a number of relatively short (one- and two-year) field experiences in a variety of settings (Morocco, Bali, Java). However, Geertz, because he has moved from fieldsite to fieldsite, has yet to face so directly the challenges of previous informants. Geertz's configuration of works and life contrasts markedly with my own. Because my research and publications stem from a relatively long-term study of a single cultural organization in a relatively circumscribed area, my published writings have simultaneously opened and closed avenues of research, promoted acceptance and fueled misunderstandings, brought about factionalism and fostered alliances, and deeply affected my life and the lives of my informants in ways that Geertz and his generation of fieldworkers might never have anticipated.

As Geertz so astutely observes, publications simultaneously serve as markers of professional advancement and represent objects of significance in the lives of informants and in the lives of the anthropologists who created them. However, he seems less concerned with the experience of writing ethnographies than with notions of authority or of why we listen to some people and not others on matters of ethnographic importance. Ultimately, he suggests, in agreement with Mary Louise Pratt (1986:27–50), that some ethnographies are more important and convincing than others because they better convey the authority of "being there." This assertion obscures things a bit since ethnographic authority rests not only on "being there" (in the field) but in "being" in a number of other significant "theres" as well. It makes a great deal of difference where the researcher has been (what degrees, and from which institutions?), where the ethnography is published (major university press, second-tier academic publisher, or vanity press?), and where the ethnographer is affiliated (Berkeley or Podunk?). All of these "theres" are very much interrelated. Geertz's authority depends as much on his tenure at Harvard, Chicago, and Princeton's Institute for Advanced Study as it does on time spent in the field.

In this chapter, I will deal not only with the reception of my work but also with some implications of this reception for the fieldwork process in general. Among the issues to be addressed are (1) native understandings and misunderstandings about the ethnographic enterprise, with attention to the economics of academic publication; (2) how publication influences rapport with informants; and (3) the impact of previous publications on one's ability to continue research on a particular group.

INFORMANTS' UNDERSTANDINGS OF THE ETHNOGRAPHIC ENTERPRISE

The Spiritual Baptists of Trinidad are part of an international religious movement with congregations in Tobago, St. Vincent (where they are known as the Shakers), Grenada, Venezuela, Guyana, New York City, Los Angeles, and Toronto. Earlier studies of the religion referred to these groups as the "Shouters," an appellation many members of the group neither use nor appreciate. Believers most commonly refer to themselves as "the Spiritual Baptists," or, even more frequently, as "the Baptists." This can be confusing for outsiders who assume the religion to be similar to North American Baptist denominations. It actually has much in common with African-derived religious movements such as Cuban Santeria or Haitian *vodun*.

There are about 10,000 members of the Spiritual Baptist faith in Trinidad. Membership has remained about the same over the past fourteen years. Church affiliation is predominantly black and cuts across social and economic lines. During the past ten years, an increasing number of East Indians (who now comprise nearly half the population of Trinidad and Tobago) have become involved in the religion. To my knowledge, there are currently eight white members of the faith: two from North America, two Trinidad natives, and four Europeans.

While a number of elderly Baptists cannot read or write, books are highly valued within the religion, and most church members are literate. At present, all members of the church's denominational hierarchy can read, and a number of higher ranking members have completed degrees at the University of the West Indies (Trinidad) or from universities in the United States, Canada, and the United Kingdom. Spiritual Baptist organizations produce monthly newsletters, numerous tracts, and annual reports, which are widely distributed throughout the island. Many higher ranking members have published tracts, brief histories of their particular churches, and sermon collections. Therefore, most Baptists have very specific notions of what a book should look like.

Informants' conceptions of what a book will be like often lead to disappointment when a book turns out differently. A major barrier is that, even in the most literate of societies, few informants understand the nature and goals of ethnographic research. In my initial stages of fieldwork, Leader Albert DeBique, who was later to become a major informant and close friend, could not grasp the purpose of my study (an analysis of leadership and decision-making processes within his religion). He introduced me to other church leaders—as an earlier generation of informants had introduced Melville J. Herskovits and George Eaton Simpson before me—as a man from the university who was going to "make a history" of the Baptists, and claimed that such a history might serve to attract new followers to the faith and make the Baptist religion more "prestigious and respectable." This is not evidence, however, that Spiritual Baptists consider history to be neutral, objective, and detached. Quite the opposite. Historical study, for the Spiritual Baptists, is a highly charged emotional undertaking demanding skills very different from what academic historians would term "objectivity." Baptists see history as an attempt to uncover the spiritual "truth" behind the facts.

Baptists understand history at two levels: the material and the spiritual. Native histories by Spiritual Baptists deal primarily with the "founders" of specific churches. Accounts vary widely. Because churches are founded both materially and spiritually, it may happen that the individual credited with founding a church might never have physically set foot in that church. The Baptist church in Los Lomas, for example, is widely believed to have been founded by a leader in Point Fortin who is said to have prayed that a church be founded in the Los Lomas area as early as 1910. The church was not established until 1936; nevertheless, the aforementioned leader is widely considered to be the "spiritual" founder of the Los Lomas church, while the leader who physically supervised and financed the building of the church is seen as playing but a minor role in its formation. Baptists hope that scholarly histories, whether written by Melville J. Herskovits, George Eaton Simpson, or Stephen D. Glazier, will serve to clear up opposing interpretations and provide evidence as to who really founded a particular church.

Like most informants, DeBique did not, and still does not, understand the difference between a dissertation and a book and was highly disappointed when after four years of study I had not produced a "history" that he felt he could show to his bishop. He was anticipating a thick, hardbound book, and a photocopy of my 1981 dissertation simply could not fill the bill. When a hardbound edition of my dissertation finally appeared in 1983, he was pleased with its binding and format, but less than pleased with its content. He did not take exception to my portrayal of church activities and organization. The major source of disappointment was that I did not mention churches and leaders by name. In keeping with ethical standards developed by the American Anthropological Association for the protection of human subjects, I had jumbled churches, names, and events in order to give informants a degree of anonymity. Since a major purpose of Baptist history is to get at the truth behind events, names of churches and pastors are of primary importance. DeBique and a number of other Baptist leaders said that they found my 1983 volume worthless as history.

However, DeBique was quite impressed with the photographs appearing on pages 73–77 of the Greenwood hardback and Sheffield paperback editions, in which he and his church were featured prominently. The inclusion of these particular photographs are largely a matter of happenstance. I did not select them as representative images after culling through hundreds of pictures. I have taken nearly 500 photographs of Baptist churches over the years, but the vast majority are color slides, which do not reproduce well when transformed into black and white glossies as required for publication. I had run out of color slide film and had been forced to use black and white film when I studied DeBique's church. This is why his church is disproportionately represented among the photographs (but not in the text itself) and why DeBique carries copies of the book with him whenever he goes on mission, although he seldom encourages potential converts actually to read the book. On the other hand, ministers of competing churches point to sections of the book that they believe refer to them and ignore the pictures. A photograph of DeBique and DeBique's church appears on the cover of the 1991 paperback edition of *Marchin'* (to be discussed below). Due to the prominent placement of DeBique's photograph on the paperback edition, a number of Spiritual Baptist leaders have assumed, inaccurately, that I am allied with DeBique in DeBique's recent and vocal opposition to Shango in Trinidad. This is not the case. Nonetheless, I have been denied access to some Shango centers in northeastern Trinidad. This is unfortunate and has had serious consequences for subsequent fieldwork, since DeBique's opposition to Shango is recent (post–1990), and it was DeBique who first accompanied me to Shango ceremonies and introduced me to a number of prominent Shango leaders. In a show of protest, one Shango-Baptist leader openly ripped the cover off his paperback copy of *Marchin'*.

I had never fully considered the potential impact of photographs in some cultural contexts. In relating my experiences with photographs to John Burton of Connecticut College, he reported a similar experience while working among the Nuer. Burton shared with the Nuer a copy of Evans-Pritchard's now-classic 1940 study. They took little interest in the volume until they stumbled upon pictures of cattle. Suddenly, Evans-Pritchard's book took on immense significance, and the Nuer began heated and protracted debates as to whose cattle these were and to what lineage they had belonged. Ethnographic pictures, perhaps even more than ethnographic writings, often have unanticipated and unintended significances when people read, or at least look at, what we have written.

In time, copies of my dissertation did make it to the library at the University of the West Indies, and photocopies of articles I had written were circulated among Spiritual Baptists in Curepe (many of whom were also students at UWI). The hardbound edition, *Marchin' the Pilgrims Home: Leadership and Decision-Making in an Afro-Caribbean Faith* (1983), received limited distribution in Trinidad. Several Port of Spain bookstores carried it; three or four copies were sold at the UWI bookstore, and multiple copies were purchased for the UWI library. A major barrier was the cost. The book sold for nearly $40 U.S., which amounted to well over $100 in the local currency. The "results" of my fieldwork had been priced beyond the reach of most of my informants and laid a basis for misconceptions about the economics of academic publication.

In most fieldwork, it is only a short time before the question—in the words of the late Barbara Myerhoff's (1978) informants—changes from an emphatic "What do you want from us here?" to a no less emphatic "So, what's in it for us?" People outside anthropology (and even some within the field) have considerable difficulty understanding and explaining exactly what anthropologists are supposed to "derive" from fieldwork. A logical assumption for informants— especially if fieldwork is carried out over many years—is that "there must be money in that." Some Spiritual Baptists could fathom that I wanted to study them to get my credential (a Ph.D.), but then why did I come back year after year after earning that credential? My situation is all the more unusual since so many anthropologists have had their initial field experiences in the Caribbean, but comparatively few anthropologists continue to work in the area after completion of initial fieldwork. Another mystery, at least from the informants' point of view, is that natives already possess (or at least think that they possess) much of the information ethnographers seek, and, in a majority of cases, it has not improved their material situations appreciably. How is a foreign anthropologist able to make money on the Spiritual Baptists, when the Spiritual Baptists themselves, despite much hard work and considerable ingenuity, are often unable to make a bare living from their religious activities?

Several Spiritual Baptist leaders publicly stated that I was "trying to get rich off of their religion." They had spent years teaching me the finer points of their faith, and now I was going to become a millionaire, while they would get nothing for their trouble. Efforts to explain that the $100 cost of the 1983 book did not go directly in my pocket were usually in vain. I also emphasized that royalties from my books (as they should materialize) were to be sent to support a Spiritual Baptist old age home in Curepe. A number of Baptists suggested that I was paid for writing articles for the *Journal of American Folklore* and the *Journal for the Scientific Study of Religion*. This is not true.

NATIVE RESPONSES

My work has enjoyed a number of native readers who have responded in very different ways. As noted, DeBique was upset that he and his church were not mentioned by name. His response was typical of a number of other leaders as well. Although I did say that I would attempt to preserve anonymity of informants in the finished book, none of my informants expressed an interest in having their identities disguised or had any idea why such a practice might be advantageous to them. From their perspective, they were all highly public men; everyone in Baptist circles already knew who they were and what they had done (negatively and positively) for their churches. My book might afford them some recognition, but disguising their identities could not spare them from controversy.

Rank-and-file Baptists responded positively to my general ideas about leadership and leadership decisions within their faith as expressed in the book, but found it difficult to believe that I could publish a book about something "dat everybody already know, mon." Most Spiritual Baptists are already aware—as I had elaborated in Chapter 5 of *Marchin'*—that their leaders overspend in order to enhance their own positions and that leaders of visiting churches make more money from pilgrimages than do leaders of host churches. Sometimes a Baptist who had read Chapter 4, on church organization, would make a particular point of telling me that his or her church does not operate like that, then quickly add, "But I know thems dat does." I received little commentary concerning descriptions of church ritual (Chapter 3). One member implied that my descriptions of a typical Baptist worship service made his religion seem uninteresting. "If services were dat dull," he protested, "no one would ever come."

In addition to personal reactions by Baptists, there were also reactions to my work by native Trinidadian scholars. Elements of nationalism play a part in these reactions, as does the peculiar role of the nonbeliever in a proselytizing group. When the *Trinidad Guardian* published a 1980 editorial calling for a study of the Spiritual Baptist faith, it was doubtless hoping for a native Trinidadian to undertake such a project. After all, the works of Herskovits and Simpson were already well known by that time. By the same token, when the Spiritual Baptists call for a history of their religion, they are hoping for a believer's history that will serve to vindicate or enhance the position of their own church or leader within the faith. Any book by an outsider is potentially disconcerting, and a book by an unbelieving outsider is doubly so. Whenever an outsider and un-believer has spent so long in research, has had access to so many high ranking church officials, and possesses so much information, he or she is unlikely to receive a positive reception. Since proselytizing is a major activity within the faith, to have had someone like myself who has expressed such a keen interest for a long time remain unconverted constitutes a crisis of major proportions. How could I have seen and heard so much and remained "unconvicted"? Native scholarly reactions (for example, local newspaper reviews) have dealt more with who wrote the book than with its contents.

As John Wengle (1988) astutely notes, there is a peculiar psychology to ethnographic fieldwork. The ethnographer desires to be the unseen knower, the fly on the wall, the unobserved observer who comes away with the "real" story, while at the same time hoping to be noticed. At another level, ethnographic work constitutes a cry for recognition: not only "being there," but "I was there" (Pratt 1986: Nash and Wintrob 1972). It is with such ambivalence that I—like any ethnographer who has made a long-term field commitment—approach native publications that utilize ethnographic contributions. One seeks validation, ap-probation, and recognition from native scholars who often resent one's position as an outsider. The question is, is it more painful to be criticized or more painful to be ignored?

In 1987 Reverend Eudora Thomas published her long-planned history of the Spiritual Baptists in order to "set things right" and to counter the works of unnamed "academic sociologists" who purported to know about her religion. Her book, which was published simultaneously in Trinidad and in upstate New York, is unusually accurate and insightful concerning her particular denomination (the smallest of four competing Spiritual Baptist denominations in Trinidad). Thomas does not refer directly to my work, but does follow identical organization, including similar descriptions of ritual activities interspersed with disparaging mention of "foreign-born, university-educated sociologists who are not Spiritual Baptists and therefore are not qualified to pass judgment on Baptists' activities." The works of my predecessors Melville J. Herskovits, Frances Henry, and George Eaton Simpson are also criticized indirectly and without citation.

I incorporated Reverend Thomas's insights into subsequent writings on the Baptists and have cited her in several publications. Previously, Thomas had never acknowledged my writings (or the writings of any other social scientists), but *Marchin' the Pilgrims Home* (as well as the works of Herskovits and Simpson) is to be listed in the bibliography of the forthcoming revised edition of Thomas's *A History of the Shouter Baptists in Trinidad*.

It is unclear whether Thomas's acknowledgment of my book will have a positive or negative impact on my interactions with other Baptists who are not members of her denomination. One consideration is that many Baptists do not think that a woman can or should be a leader, let alone give herself the title "Reverend" and draw attention to herself by publishing a book. While *Marchin'* emphasizes diversity within the faith (especially with regard to sex roles), Reverend Thomas chooses to ignore variation and insists that the Spiritual Baptist faith is a uniform religious movement that promotes sexual equality.

Marchin' the Pilgrims Home also inspired eight senior theses at UWI (four by Spiritual Baptists and former Spiritual Baptists) that deal with aspects of the religion as depicted in my books and articles (some citing me, others not); and the book has been quoted at length twice (without citation) in articles in the *Trinidad Guardian* and on a locally produced television show, "Guyal."

Caribbean Studies theses are doubly interesting inasmuch as many are written by Trinidadians who themselves have been members of Spiritual Baptist congregations. In addition, these students have usually read the published social scientific accounts of the religion and are both willing and able to assess these scientific accounts from an insider's perspective. Where better to initiate such a dialogue than in the Caribbean, that most "modernist" (Manganaro 1990) of places, once at the center and now at the periphery of world events, where ethnic and cultural pluralism is taken for granted, literacy is high, and most everyone is from someplace else? As Michel-Rolph Trouillot (1991), himself a native of Haiti, asserts, there are few peoples in the world less appropriate to fill the "savage slot" than natives of the Caribbean.[2]

A most remarkable senior thesis by Hazel Ann Gibbs-de-Peza provides a comprehensive and detailed examination and critique of all previous Caribbean Studies theses addressing the Spiritual Baptists and Shango. Gibbs-de-Peza, whose late husband was a prominent Baptist leader, describes the content of UWI theses submitted between 1969 and 1988 and offers criticism from a believer's point of view. On balance, Gibbs-de-Peza's comments are well taken, and along with the interesting theses by Denyse Gonzalez (1987) and Franklyn Farrel (1982), provide a valuable corrective to the growing literature on the religion. Gibbs-de-Peza's is also the only post–1980 thesis that does not cite *Marchin'*.

Of course, I am hardly the sole purveyor of information on the Spiritual Baptists. In a number of important respects the Baptists have become prominent and self-reflexive members of the Caribbean mainstream. They have been the subject of an excellent and internationally acclaimed novel, *The Wine of Astonishment* by Earl Lovelace, of which the Malick folk performers are currently in the process of preparing a local stage adaptation (with talk of an off-Broadway production); and have been incorporated into popular music, for example, "Socca Baptist" (1980) by Blue Boy (Austin Lyons) and "Bahia Gyal" by David Rudder (1989). While Blue Boy's treatment of the faith was clearly derisive ("What to them suppose to be spiritual; to me, it was just like bacchanal"). Rudder's "Bahia Cyal" cites the Baptists as an example of the Pan-African spirit, emphasizing commonalities between Spiritual Baptist "adoption" and Somba rhythms. In addition, a number of Spiritual Baptist leaders and myself are negotiating with the Smithsonian Institution to bring out "Spiritual Baptist Music of Trinidad" (Folkways, 1980) in a compact disc format.

As noted, the revised paperback edition of *Marchin'* appeared in early 1991. The cost (under $9 U.S. or about $36 in the local currency) is more within the reach of members of the faith, although distributors in Trinidad report that the strongest initial sales have been to tourists. This may be because the major distributor has two large stores at the airport and one at a shopping arcade frequented by cruise boat passengers. Bookstores have already ordered another 150 copies of *Marchin'* for distribution during the 1993 Carnival season (not an impressive order by American publishing standards, but impressive for a Trinidad bookseller).

No formal attempt has been made to market the book in the interior of the island. Since the Spiritual Baptists are predominantly a rural religion, this would seem a potentially fruitful marketing strategy. Informal distribution networks exist among the Baptists themselves. DeBique has provided his friends with multiple copies of the paperback edition and carries it with him whenever he travels on Baptist business. Some Spiritual Baptists have sold copies of the book that I have given them (at higher than retail prices) while "on mission" to villages in the interior. I have noticed paperback copies of *Marchin'* in a small number of Baptist homes.

Local sales of the paperback edition, as anticipated, have been mostly to tourists and academics. But local sales are not the only measure of a book's impact. The book has also become a symbol of factionalism within the church (some denominations supporting it, others rejecting it). It has become a symbol of "respectability" (e.g., as noted for Leader DeBique, the publication of a book with his photograph on the cover is an indication that he is an important Baptist leader; objectively, he is of marginal importance within the church hierarchy). And as noted previously, some Baptists see the book as an example of foreign exploitation—an occasion to protest being yet again defined and analyzed by an "outsider." I am not the only author to be criticized. Similar charges of exploitation have been raised concerning Reverend Thomas's publication, and she is both a native and an insider. All of this hubbub, of course, greatly complicates day-to-day fieldwork activities and makes it more difficult to gather certain types of data relevant to my ongoing research. On the other hand, recognition—even negative recognition—can open some doors. It has been a source of new information on church economics, ritual, and family lives to which I otherwise might not have had access. For example, one leader took exception to my treatment of church economics and opened his financial records to me in order to "set things straight."

CONCLUSION: WHITHER ETHNOGRAPHY?

The so-called end of traditional ethnography and the rise of experimental genres may have been greatly exaggerated. Sometimes it seems that there are actually fewer experimental ethnographies published than books (like Clifford and Marcus's) expressing the need for such experimentation. Sanjek (1990) and Van Maanen[3] provide representative bibliographies that attest to this point. Moreover, much of the experimental work comes from the same "there" (Clifford, Fischer, Marcus, Crapanzano, and even Geertz were all trained at Harvard), and when Third World peoples do ethnography it tends to be of the more traditional sort. Also, ethnography is but one aspect of cultural anthropology, and (at least in the United States) cultural anthropology is but one subfield of the larger discipline of anthropology. Due to the demands of their subject matters, multivocal representations do not hold much sway in linguistics, biological anthropology, or archaeology.

One possible reason for the decline of experimental ethnographies, ironically, may be the decline of ethnographic authority itself. In *The Predicament of Culture*, James Clifford (1988:26) skillfully charts the struggle that took place at the close of the nineteenth century to establish the ethnographer—as opposed to the traveler, the missionary, and the administrator—as the "best interpreter of native life." This battle was won to a degree, but only to the extent that ethnologists (and other comparative researchers) came to rely almost exclusively on trained ethnographers. Missionaries and administrators continued (and continue) to rely mainly on their own in-house productions. Clifford's argument assumes an ethnographic hegemony that may never have existed, even during ethnography's salad days.

In the late twentieth century the sheer volume of ethnographic production cannot but have an impact on ethnographic authority or the lack thereof. During my 1976 fieldwork, there were four professional social scientists and two UWI undergraduate students conducting research on the Spiritual Baptists. Colleen Ward, a cross-cultural psychologist who was working under psychiatrist Michael Beaubrun, visited many of the same churches I did, and we shared many of the same informants. Alfrieta Parks was finishing fieldwork for her dissertation at Princeton, Frances Henry was beginning a restudy of Shango-Baptists, and James Houk had begun fieldwork toward his master's thesis at Tulane. This is a far cry from the situation in the 1930s when Melville and Frances Herskovits could conduct several months of fieldwork in one small village (Toco) and write a definitive report representing the entire island of Trinidad which would not be critically reevaluated for nearly twenty years.

This competitive situation may force ethnographers to become less experimental. After all, as Marcus and Fischer (1986:140) point out, the best known advocates of experimental approaches are generally in secure academic positions with relatively little to lose or gain. A possible trend in the 1990s might be more seamless, traditional narratives, not so much as ethnographers attempt to come to terms with the native and accommodate a diverse readership, but as ethnographers attempt to come to terms with one another and establish their ethnographic authority, their own ''theres.''[4]

There is an aspect of what John Lofland (1987) terms ''New Columbus'' theorizing in all of this. Lofland contends that once a previously unknown world has been mapped out, fieldworkers who venture into that territory are faced with the new and different—but no less challenging—intellectual tasks of correction, specification, and elaboration. The ''New Columbus,'' if he or she is to be successful, must perform elaborate intellectual and stylistic gymnastics, not so much to convince potential readers that ''I was there'' as to convince an audience that it makes a difference that ''I was there'' at all.

Ultimately, ethnography is both art and science. Replication is impossible (''you can't step into the same stream even once''), and, as Sanjek (1990:403) admits, ethnography's validity is served by, but does not require, extensive fieldnote documentation (also see Hammersley 1992:124–27; Kirk and Miller 1986). Michael Agar (1980:92) compares ethnography to jazz. He offers a quote attributed to jazz great Miles Davis, who advised prospective jazz musicians to ''know your horn, know the chords, know all the tunes. Then forget all that, and just play.'' In jazz there is considerable turn-taking, and I suspect that competition among ethnographers and the desire to represent multiple voices may give rise to a situation in which each ethnographer (stranger and native) makes a brief bid for ''authority,'' only to yield the spotlight to another player (sort of an Andy Warhol ''everyone is famous for fifteen minutes'' phenomenon). Of course, the greatest risk is that some players, because they haven't touched base at the right ''theres,'' may not even get their full fifteen minutes in the spotlight.

NOTES

I want to thank Caroline Brettell, Candace Slater, Jeff Ehernreich, and Lydia Degarrod for helpful comments on earlier drafts. An earlier version was written while I was a participant in the 1992 National Endowment for the Humanities summer seminar "Images of the Amazon" held at the University of California, Berkeley.

1. To illustrate his point, Roger Sanjek cites Levi-Strauss's nostalgic statement in *Tristes Tropiques* that there is "no more thrilling prospect for the anthropologist than that of being the first white man to visit a particular native community" (Levi-Strauss 1955:325–326). He also points out that such romantic Western self-inflation and the racist and sexist conventions associated with it were dying—if slowly—by the 1930s, but quickly adds, "The last gasp of Western middle-class/white/male and female ethnographic hegemony is still to be heard" (Sanjek 1990:39).

2. African-American sociologists and anthropologists have had a long tradition of research in African-American communities. Among the first were Allison Davis, St. Clair Drake, and Arthur Fausset. Among the most notable is Zora Neale Hurston. It is illuminating to compare Hurston's career and those of Boas's other female students (D. Gordon 1990).

3. Van Maanen (1988), an organizational sociologist who teaches at the Massachusetts Institute of Technology, provides a most useful, witty survey of narrative conventions associated with ethnography. He divides ethnographies into five basic types or styles: the matter-of-fact, the realistic report of classical ethnography, the self-absorbed confessional tale, the dramatic vignette of the impressionistic style, and the literary tale. He then attempts to assess strengths and weaknesses of the various types.

4. Fellow Trinidad researcher Kevin Birth suggests that if ethnography is to be accountable it should be framed in a "this-is-fact" mode. He correctly points out that "even the subjects of an ethnography, if they read it, cannot say it is a distortion if the ethnography makes no claim to truth" (Birth 1990:556). For examples, a Trinidadian who has difficulty with V. S. Naipaul or a Spiritual Baptist who dislikes Earl Lovelace's portrayal cannot logically complain on the grounds that these novels are not factual. In practice, natives, like all humans, do complain about such things.

Part II

POLITICIZED TEXTS: INSIDER, OUTSIDER, AND ETHNOGRAPHIC AUTHORITY

3

INVOLVEMENT, DETACHMENT, AND REPRESENTATION ON CORSICA

Alexandra Jaffe

In the last ten years, anthropology has become increasingly reflexive, and has turned its analytical gaze on the social and political contexts that inform both the collection and production of knowledge in the act of fieldwork and in the writing of ethnography. Books such as Fabian's *Time and the Other* (1983), Said's *Orientalism* (1978), Clifford and Marcus's edited volume *Writing Culture* (1986), and Van Maanen's *Tales of the Field* (1988) all emphasize that distance between observer and observed is, in part, an ethnographic fiction with which the anthropologist maintains control and authority over his or her "subjects." In his review article of recent works on Australian Aboriginals, Myers (1986) writes that the narrowing of the gap between "us" and "them" is a function of the modern condition, and is a central part of both the anthropologist's and the community's experience (p. 138). Myers suggests that reflexivity is not just an approach toward analysis and writing, but also an essential condition of interaction with the people we study, who are often sophisticated consumers and regulators of anthropological products.

This chapter examines the ways in which these issues of power and representation affected my research experience as well as some of my writing about my research on the island of Corsica. It is also an attempt to explore the particularities of a reflexive ethnography of Western Europe and to suggest how they may contribute to current concerns with the philosophy and practice of fieldwork and ethnographic writing in anthropology.

Learning about the extreme delicacy of the balance between involvement and detachment when anthropologists study people like themselves has important methodological, ethical, and theoretical implications. On a personal level, it provides us with a humble perspective on our own identities as ethnographers, and forces us to make the connection between what we do professionally and what we live in our own cultures. This kind of reflexivity amounts to a recognition of the political dimension of anthropological practice, and contributes to the goal elaborated by Marcus and Fischer of realizing anthropology's "potential for developing a distinctive cultural critique of American society" (1986:4).

My argument is that studying a less "alien" culture can intensify the reflexive experience of the ethnographer. The experience of writing about people who read what we write and then talk and write back to us undermines our ability to construct an unproblematic Other, and hence, an unproblematic self. This is in fact a significant break with a tradition that is revealed in the structure and style of ethnographic writing. As Van Maanen (1988) points out, there is still a tendency (with some notable exceptions) for anthropologists' descriptions of self-involvement to serve very traditional purposes of establishing their authority by charting the difficulty of their steps toward understanding of or integration in the alien culture. More often than not, as Van Maanen also points out, "confessional" narratives are separated from the main text or turned into separate works altogether (for example, Rabinow 1977 or Messenger 1989), further emphasizing their marginality to the author's conception of the central analytical or descriptive task. Thus the transformation of the ethnographer's persona is kept firmly in the past, leaving the professional persona of the writing present intact. The experience of fieldwork changes how the anthropologist understands the subjects of study, but not how the anthropologist understands him- or herself, or anthropology as a discipline.

Doing fieldwork in a complex Western society can, I think, contribute to our reflection on all of these things. In my case, it exposed the impossibility—and the extraordinary temptation—of authoritative, "imperialistic" ethnographic discourses. This impossibility was brought home to me by the nature of my involvement in the culture I studied. This involvement was required because of the social and political immediacy of academic representations of language and culture in a place in which these issues are hotly contested. But as Myers points out, even though we are "never wholly other" from those we study, we cannot "pretend to total identification with them and only subscribe to their local understandings" (1986:52). So I am also going to talk about difference and detachment, about the ways in which I did not and could not belong, from either my own or from the Corsicans' perspective.

DEFINING THE SUBJECT: THE EXOTIC AND THE FAMILIAR

In the early eighties, French tourists were invited to visit Corsica, "la plus proche des îles lointaines" (the closest of the faraway islands). My professional motivations to study language and culture on Corsica were marked by the lure of both the familiar and the exotic. As Rogers (1991:6) points out, the "marginal" still exercises a considerable attraction to anthropologists of Western Europe. This is because it allows us to define a community. One reason I chose to work on the island of Corsica was that its geographical, cultural, and linguistic peripherality in France provided some ready-made cultural boundaries and conflicts of identity. Since the late 1960s, Corsica has been the site of a strong regionalist movement. Corsican cultural and political activists have used the existence of the Corsican language as a primary reference for authentic cultural identity, and its decline over the last fifty years as a symbol of the negative consequences of French domination.

Thus I deliberately selected a fieldsite in which "otherness" was both a given of my research and politically salient for Corsicans themselves. Even though I took the boundaries of the community to be permeable, shifting cultural artifacts up for dispute, the practice of enquiry about boundaries implicitly lent authority to the notion of Corsican cultural and linguistic autonomy.[1] As a consequence, it was often possible for me to engage with Corsican intellectuals in a discourse that gave the appearance of congruence between my fieldwork and their personal and political cultural interests. This perception of a shared discourse cannot be reduced to political opportunism on their part, naïveté on my part, or false consciousness on both sides. This was because those intellectuals were also *not* marginal; they had been trained in Paris, Montpellier, Rouen. Thus, to use Pierre Bourdieu's term, we conducted our professional lives in a similar intellectual "habitus."

Nevertheless, this perception of similarity was at times exaggerated (on either side) and led to some of the misunderstandings and disappointments that I describe here. This is because my value as an outside, non-French observer made me the focus of a number of conflicting sets of interests. On the one hand, I vindicated the undervalued culture in dominant terms. These terms included such ideals as scientific objectivity and the perfect congruence of linguistic and cultural boundaries. On the other hand, in filling this role, I also represented "the system," and provoked doubts and uncertainties among Corsicans about their ability to control symbolic capital in the dominant marketplace. In other words, my presence evoked two powerful and contrasting theories of knowledge. In one the politics of knowledge was foregrounded; in the other, it was backgrounded. As a result, our interactions were marked by a constant and shifting interplay between involvement and detachment.

In the following section, I discuss some of the conceptual and methodological implications of doing research in Europe. I then examine the changing nature of the way that Corsicans and I conceptualized my role as an ethnographer by looking at examples of changes in our approaches to the politics of representation. My own case is illustrated by three texts that I produced for various Corsican audiences, and the Corsican side by their reactions to my linguistic survey project.

THE RESEARCH IMPLICATIONS OF LACK OF
CULTURE SHOCK

To begin, I would like to discuss some of the ways in which doing fieldwork in Europe shapes expectations about practice and identity. The surface intelligibility of European institutions and social organization attenuates, perhaps even hides, the perception of difference. But this intelligibility is not just an illusion. As an American in Europe who had lived there before, I very quickly developed a real, minimal social competence. I am not talking about professional competence, for getting my research under way was no easier on Corsica than it would have been anywhere else. But there was a certain ease of everyday social integration; I found that after a month or two, I lived a recognizable version of my "ordinary" life; I had shopping routes, newspapers, habits; I went to the university, read books in the library, talked to other graduate students and teachers.

One of the ways in which the surface intelligibility of Corsican life affected my expectations about my fieldwork had to do with what Briggs writes about in *Learning How to Ask* (1986). I arrived on Corsica armed with a great deal of familiarity with the issues surrounding the social status of the Corsican language from my previous six-week visit to the islands, and from an abundant literature on language, ethnicity, and nationalism in Europe, I came with a list—an entire questionnaire—of all the right questions, and discovered to my disappointment that asking them did not seem to get me very far. In effect, the surface intelligibility of the culture dulled my senses to the degree of subtle understanding that is prerequisite to being able to ask questions that are relevant both to the ethnographer and to the people being asked. This sort of understanding cannot be rushed; it can only be accumulated with time.

Learning how to ask also had to do with paying one's dues. The general questions on my original list were in fact too easy to formulate from the outside; asking them demonstrated only a superficial commitment to learning about the island. The questions I learned to ask very often had the explicit rhetorical function of demonstrating that I had done my homework and put in enough time to have a right to ask the obvious questions.[2] The same was true of language, although I was not surprised by this. Much was made of the "extraordinary" effort and ability I displayed by learning to speak Corsican. But the explicit message—"you didn't have to, you should be commended for it"—masked a very different one, which was that if I had not learned any Corsican, I would ultimately have been kept at a certain distance.

In a very different culture, the mechanics of survival are preoccupying. As a result, anthropologists go through a fairly long and painful period of adjustment during which they accumulate cultural knowledge, competence, and sensitivity. Because I quickly dealt with the mechanics of survival in Europe, I found it very hard to let simply "being there" take its course. I think that doing ethnography in Europe illuminated for me the subtlety and complexity of learning not only to ask, but learning how, and what, to learn.

Another of the obvious research risks of a lack of culture shock is that it gives us a premature confidence in our ability to understand familiar social institutions, whereas in fact their meaning, role, and social weight may be significantly different than in our own society. This was dramatized to me very near the end of my fourteen months on the island, when I had the misfortune to hit a cow on a road at night. I knew that it was illegal to let a cow roam, and was incensed to discover that my insurance company would not pay the damages unless I could positively identify the cow (by producing the tag from its ear) so that the insurance company could hold the owner responsible. I was even more furious that the local police claimed that they could not possibly locate the owner. After making several completely useless protests, I was lucky enough to have another minor accident, which allowed me to arrange for the cow damage to be repaired by the husband of an acquaintance, who owned a car body shop. This was as close as I could get to the way that Corsicans dealt with such problems. They did not expect the law or the police to exact social justice; this was carried out by friends and family and the long-term power of informal social control. My neighbor told me that he had recuperated damage costs from a similar accident two years after it happened by commiserating with the owner of the offending cow about the animal's unfortunate limp. The incident did not tell me anything new about Corsica, but it did tell me something about myself: my assumptions about the judicial system were modeled on my image (and limited experience) of this system in the United States.

Similarly, my expectations about the academic community were modeled on my limited experience as a graduate student in American institutions. I was acutely aware of the political dimension of all academic activity on Corsica. But because I was able to link political conflict in the academic world with particular party politics, I was able to view it as an "exotic" dimension of Corsican life that was separable from the core of academic practice. And it was true that Corsican scholars represented political pressure as an "outside" force that was sometimes an obstacle to the pursuit of "pure" knowledge.

This model of academic practice broke down for me when I met with resistance in the institution to a survey project of mine that had initially been received with great enthusiasm. My surprise and disillusionment stemmed from my failure to understand the ways in which the study of Corsican culture by Corsicans differed in its social goals and constraints from what I was doing as an anthropologist. I attribute this failure in part to an unreflexive transference of expectations about the academic environment from the United States. My graduate training had been "reflexive," and hardly empiricist. But even though I had been taught to distrust analyses in which the observer claimed complete separation from the "facts" she described, I still held on to ideas about the superior academic value of "pure knowledge" inherited from the "model of technical rationality" that has been influential in all American social science (Schoen 1983:27).

Some of the implicit models of fieldwork I describe allow American graduate students in anthropology to separate the practice of social science from the practice of social life, and to see their identities as anthropologists as being essentially—perhaps preferably—apolitical. The current public debate over "political correctness" has perhaps increased sensitivity to these issues, but I believe that European researchers are socialized much earlier about the political context and consequences of knowledge. On Corsica, they were also constantly reminded of the political and social repercussions of their work. The university was not the "same" institution on Corsica, despite outward appearances.

Some of my retrospective discoveries about learning how to ask, learning to recognize subtle differences, and learning to take the politics of knowledge and representation seriously may seem obvious, and my failure to anticipate them simply naive. But I will argue that this naïveté is also, in part, a function of graduate education, which (at least for my generation) did not stress the politics of anthropological practice in the field, despite the emphasis on the politics of writing ethnography in the late eighties.

POLITICAL COMMITMENT: AMBIGUOUS RIGHTS AND DUTIES

At the same time that I underestimated the politics of knowledge, I became involved in the politics of practice. The politicization of language and culture encouraged—perhaps even demanded—a certain level of involvement. A certain level of linguistic and cultural advocacy was one of the unspoken conditions of my participation in a circle of cultural and linguistic militants who had a political agenda.[3] I cannot say that members of the intelligentsia, or the "culturels" (as they often called themselves), would not have talked to me had I kept my opinions to myself, or even if I had openly challenged their ideas about the cultural value of the Corsican language. But I think that there would have been a polite limit to the kinds of conversations I could have had, the level of intimacy I would have been offered. This points to the particular nature of the ethics of involvement in the anthropology of Europe and, in particular, in the margins of Europe. I saw taking a position as not only a social, but also an ethical, imperative. It was implied in what and whom I chose to study: a threatened minority language and its speakers in a linguistically centralized state. As Moore (1967:242) points out, "The license we are given by our subjects to collect a great deal of information—much of it confidential—entails in our case an almost explicit bargain with them that this information be used discreetly and in such a way that they will collectively benefit."

By "taking a position," I do not mean abandoning all efforts at analytical neutrality, but recognizing the junctures at which intellectual expression is political and nondisclosure impossible. What this meant, for me, was that I made no attempt to hide my basic sympathies: I was (and am) a proponent of linguistic diversity. I wanted to see the Corsican language survive. Some of these sentiments were personal; they had to do with my affection for Corsica and Corsicans. There was also a professional/academic underpinning to my advocacy that had to do with my understanding of the powerful role of language in the experience and expression of culture. On a less generous note, I think it is also necessary to point out that my dedication to the cause of language was also tied up with my sense of professional identity. The importance of language was a given, a precondition for the fieldwork I was carrying out.

On the other hand, I also viewed language as only one among many ways of articulating cultural identity. That it often became a primary symbol of identity was, for me, an interesting sociohistorical phenomenon. I understood it as a phenomenon that had shaped the intellectual tradition to which I belonged, but I did not have direct, experiential knowledge of the importance attached to language in crises of cultural identity.

The accessibility of European culture made my social integration relatively easy, and allowed both Corsicans and myself to cultivate social expectations that made us both insensitive to the ways in which the politics of representation might divide us. These conditions made the ethics of my involvement in language activism quite ambiguous. I felt that I had a right and an obligation to express my opinions and observations. I also felt that I did not have a warrant to meddle. But the line between meddling and making a contribution was not always easy to define. I was not always able to think of the level of involvement that was required of me in my contacts with Corsican intellectuals as virtual or partial. For example, after I had been there about a year, I remember reading in the paper, after the fact, about a (relatively open) meeting that had taken place on language and culture which all my "colleagues" had attended. I was annoyed and hurt that no one had told me about it. My annoyance, of course, made me aware of the quite reasonable limits on my membership that this implied. But the edge of my foreignness had been sharpened at a moment when I least expected it and least desired it.

THE ANTHROPOLOGIST'S POLITICS: THREE TEXTS

In the course of my stay, I either volunteered or was solicited for articles for three publications (in the following sequence): a university journal, a weekly regional magazine, and a document put out by one of the Regional Assembly's consultative councils. In my decisions to write, and in my selections of language and tone, there is evidence of conflicting impulses and motivations that I still find morally ambiguous. These requests forced me to draw—or to blur—the boundaries of membership and involvement.

My initial reaction was to avoid publication. Part of this reaction was based on completely selfish research motives. I had become aware that I had the very ephemeral advantage of being an unknown; everyone was still talking to me, and I did not want to take the risk that was built in to the act of writing on Corsica of alienating potential contacts. My sense of the research value of non-alignment in a highly political (and very small) social network had been reinforced by my reception at the Corsican Studies Institute, where I had heard and read about several research projects on language and culture being impeded because of the politics or presumed politics of the researchers.

Eventually, however, I did feel an obligation and a desire to write for both the popular and academic audiences. In the academic piece, I wrote about the issue of involvement and how it complicated both Corsicans' and my analyses of the question of language on Corsica. I alluded to the "smallness of island society . . . the impossibility of anonymity," and addressed my readers: "Like all of you who write, I am not writing in a vacuum: I see you, my readers, your names, your faces. What is true for a foreigner has even more weight for the islander; the fact that everyone knows everyone makes it very difficult to find an equilibrium between analytical detachment and political involvement" (Jaffe 1989:17). In this article, I pursued my claim to involvement in two ways. First, there is my reference to the social and political restraints that frame all writing about language in the restricted community of Corsican letters. Second, I centered my essay around the analogy between the tension of analytical detachment and political and social involvement in Corsican intellectual life and the same issues in the practice of anthropology. In doing so, I made a claim of legitimacy for two audiences—a wider anthropological community as well as the local intellectual one. In the local domain, I attempted to persuade Corsicans of both social and academic legitimacy by asserting a brotherhood of shifting and ambiguous experience and identity.

The subject matter of the article was the debate over linguistic purism that had surfaced in the "cultural" crowd and caused a considerable rift among pro-Corsican linguists. Although I did take some risk in regard to some of the people implicated in the controversy, my article was, as I now see it, quite cautious. I restricted my examples to public documents (letters to the editor, etc.) that everyone had already read; in other words, I guarded my knowledge of nonpublic events. In doing so, I entered into the politics of disclosure that I saw operating in the small world of the Corsican intelligentsia *as if I were one of them.* I had felt the smallness of the social universe in which this piece would be read, and did not stray too far from the "party line" of those I most sympathized with.

The piece I wrote for the weekly magazine was not solicited. My motives and my assessment of the audience are also complicated, and somewhat ambiguous. The article discussed my language learning process, and stressed the pleasure of the oral, a pleasure that, in Corsican discourse, was intimately associated with the value of local identity. I remarked how nice it was to be able to say, "indè noi, si dice cusi: . . . " ("in our [village, region] we say it like this: . . . "). This celebration of the oral was meant to resonate with Corsicans' experience and understanding of the social value of the language; it was meant to encourage them to speak the language. However, the form of my message carried a different, highly political message. Writing in Corsican was far from neutral, for literacy in Corsican is extremely limited and its value highly contested on the island. The implicit, and perhaps the stronger, message of this article was: "I learned to read and write Corsican; so can you." While it is linguistically ("scientifically'') true that any Corsican can learn to read and write the language, it is not the case that Corsicans do so under the same circumstances as nonnative ethnographers. My article did not take into account what I knew at the time about the social complexity of the factors that have made literacy inaccessible or undesirable for many Corsicans. In other words, I suppressed my knowledge of social subtleties in favor of my understanding of linguistic processes because a linguistic representation of the situation suited my polemic goals. In effect, in this article, I did exactly what I saw my Corsican colleagues doing every day. They were, in many cases, just as aware of the social complexities of the issue of language as I, but their first priority went to social action, to convincing the Corsican-speaking public not to let the language die. I believed, as they did, that the social marginalization of Corsican literacy was an obstacle to the survival of the language, since it meant that people were likely to reject formal Corsican language education. At the same time, many Corsicans resisted the idea that the oral language was threatened enough to warrant any popular effort to teach children to speak the language outside of the school. The consequences, which I could see before my eyes, were that children were simply not learning the language.

My assumption of entitlement to political expression in this piece stemmed, in part, from the sense that I had developed over the course of almost a year of fieldwork that I had paid my dues in the militant community. My knowledge of Corsican had been overdramatized in my personal interactions with some members of the Corsican intelligentsia; it was also appropriated by them in the public domain for political purposes. The foreigner who spoke Corsican was the ultimate propaganda weapon to shame Corsicans who did not speak the language and incite them to learn it. The circumstances of my public display were, on occasion, embarrassing. Insofar as this embarrassment was personal, and contributed in some positive way to the ''cause'' of the language, I considered it an obligation. But ultimately I chafed over the fact that my public presentation of self and the nature of my contribution to the promotion of Corsican were taken out of my own hands. I felt that having suffered this repeatedly also conferred some rights on me, in particular, rights associated with the representation of my own linguistic experience. Here, I looked at rights and obligations both as an outsider and as (temporarily) an insider.

In retrospect, I cannot claim any superior insights about what kind of representation of me as a speaker or writer of Corsican was the most efficacious for the promotion of Corsican. I also cannot adequately untangle my own mixed set of motives, which range from the self-serving to the more noble. The article certainly suffered from the same narrowness of vision as did the public displays of me as a speaker. There is also some ambiguity about the audience. The magazine had a wide circulation representing a cross-section of Corsicans and a variety of linguistic competencies and attitudes. But by writing in Corsican, I automatically alienated most of the people who might have been persuaded by an appeal based on the value of speaking. In doing so, I participated in one of the unavoidable paradoxes of minority linguistic activism, which is that language symbolism is inevitably out of sync with popular practice. Anthropologists studying minority linguistic movements have been quick to point out this disjuncture, which, like the disguise of invented traditions as "natural" and inevitable dimensions of culture in ethnic nationalist discourse, is implicitly cast as a kind of false consciousness.[4] The point is that these totalizing and necessarily reductive discourses are not unique to "them"; they are equally pervasive—and perhaps equally unavoidable—for us.

My final piece of writing was a translation. I volunteered to do the English version of a trilingual (Corsican-English-French) report on language written by the Council of Culture, Communication, Education and Quality of Life (CCECV),[5] a consultative body attached to the semi-autonomous Regional Assembly. I do not consider this work ambiguous in its intentions or meaning. It was a purely symbolic act for all concerned, for it was almost certain that nobody but me would ever read the English version. What it represented for me was a desire to contribute something to a group that had suffered an outsider's gaze with courtesy and grace. The symbolic function of the English text was to provide a powerful linguistic counterpoint to the agonistic, binary relationship that has characterized Corsican-French relations. This was not something that I thought up; rather, my presence suggested the possibility to the panel, and I willingly carried out the plan.

I was also attracted to the project because of the form and ideas of the document. It was a poetic and abstract piece of writing called "Lingua Matria," which attempted to create a new language symbolism that would encourage personal and institutional commitment to the spread of the Corsican language. The concept of *lingua matria* was meant, first of all, to replace the symbolic hold of the idea of Corsican as a "mother tongue," since the primary language of most Corsican children was French. The author made the point that to categorize Corsican as a "mother tongue" was to discredit claims to authentic cultural identity by non–Corsican-speaking Corsicans. The concept of the lingua matria, on the other hand, emphasized the legitimacy and authenticity of the community's claim on language based on its right, as a People, to make autonomous cultural decisions. This kind of claim could not be discredited by lack of linguistic competence; in fact, it was a strong argument for teaching the Corsican language. The idea of the *lingua matria* was meant to counter the argument that had surfaced in recent debates in the Regional Assembly over compulsory language education that one could not teach a mother tongue. These ideas appealed to me not only because I believed they took into account the tangled web of Corsican practice and ideology, but also because they were highly reflexive and approached the issue of power in a way that fit in with my general academic orientation.

THE POLITICS OF REPRESENTATION: A CORSICAN PERSPECTIVE

I would like to return to the survey project I mentioned earlier, for it illustrates some of the ways in which Corsicans' and my own notions of membership, involvement, and the control of social meaning evolved over the course of my fieldwork. In collaboration with the sociolinguist at the University of Corsica, I developed a fairly standard short questionnaire on linguistic practices and attitudes. In the beginning, it looked as though I had the great advantage of political neutrality in a society in which political alignment closes as many doors as it opens. In the recent past, the Corsican Studies Institute's ability to conduct sociolinguistic research had been hampered by the presumed association of the institute with the nationalist party and, in particular, with the extreme military underground arm of the nationalist movement, the FLNC.

Thus I held out the promise of access to the population unimpeded by political alignment. Many people said that it would be a real benefit to have "an outside point of view" on the issue of language, without, I think, considering the possibility that this point of view might contradict their own. In fact, I think some of them saw me as a sort of surrogate investigator, as a way of extending their access to information. In their initial focus on *la politique politicienne* (party or public politics), Corsican researchers failed to consider the politics of knowledge and representation. My novelty, paradoxically, made it easier for them to believe I was one of them, or at least that I was neutral in a way that served their purposes.

I do not mean to suggest that no thought was given to the potential for the outsider's point of view to be uncomfortable. My sociolinguist colleague had noted in his own writing that the symbolic and ideological value of Corsican was not only politically contested, but also more robust than actual linguistic practice. He noted that this made all sociolinguistic research and interpretation problematic (Thiers 1986:47). This is because the lack of congruence between expressed ideology/attitudes and practice was a matter of political concern for all those who were involved in the promotion of the language. It was political because issues of competence and values could be marshalled to support any number of conflicting viewpoints in the debate over language planning. Those who gained the upper hand in this public debate could influence state and regional policy, the allocation of resources for Corsican language education, teacher training, money for the institute, and so forth. It was serious business.

It is clear that any numbers about Corsican linguistic attitudes or competence could be used as propaganda by either side of the debate over officialization or education. If I had listened more carefully to the story I was told not long after my arrival about the Swiss sociolinguist, I could have better predicted reactions to my enterprise. J. Grob spent four months on Corsica at the university doing sociolinguistic research. She had administered a questionnaire/interview to about thirty people and written a *licenza* (master's thesis) based on her findings. I read the thesis and decided that she had concluded too much from too little data, but that the ideas were interesting and the work good, for its level. I would never have guessed, if I had not been told, that an article version of this thesis created an absolute uproar. She submitted it, as requested, to the institute journal, *Etudes*

Corses. While nobody argued with her observations about the practice of Corsican, the editor took great exception to her conclusions about "attitude"; Grob implied that Corsicans' attitudes were a significant obstacle to the language planning process advocated at the institute. The editor refused to print her article in its original form. Grob refused to retract. Finally, it was printed with an editor's caveat at the foot of the offending page.

The key factor in this incident was that Grob's discussion of people's attitudes was seen as discrediting the assertion of the *cultural* strength of the language. Proof that Corsican is alive and well justifies a lack of social and political intervention on its behalf. Proof that it is moribund can be taken as evidence of either a social or a cultural malaise; the former justifies intervention, and the latter does not. From the perspective of the linguistic activists, it was important to tread a fine line in the portrayal of the practice of Corsican; given their political goals, the language had to be represented as a living, vital part of Corsican culture, and the process of "elaboration" as at least partially successful, with *social*, not cultural, shortcomings, which could be remedied by the implementation of various institutional measures.

As time went on and I became more and more a part of everyday life at the institute, students and faculty had the opportunity to reflect upon me as a social actor. This familiarity ultimately led them to consider the implications of my foreignness. It was then that they realized that their initial enthusiasm about having an "objective," outside point of view was not just a myth, but a myth to which other people would subscribe. In other words, my outsider status gave me an upper hand in the production of knowledge that was inherently political. They were understandably annoyed that I could enjoy both an outsider's authority and an insider's view of their lives (and dirty laundry) without being subject to the kinds of social sanctions that regulated their lives within the community. I could pretend to belong and to be involved, but the fact remained that I could leave; I did not have to live out the consequences of my academic positions on a daily, personal, and permanent basis as they did. As a result, many of the students in the program withdrew their support from the production of information which they no longer saw as neutral, but as a manipulable weapon in the arsenal of someone whose agenda they could not predict.

At the same time, I saw support erode at the weekly magazine. I had approached the journalist who was my initial contact about printing my questionnaire. He was enthusiastic; in fact, my offer came at a time when the magazine was contemplating hiring an independent organization to conduct a phone survey on a number of current issues, including language. He not only got his editor's approval, but told me that the magazine wanted to precede the questionnaire with an interview-style introduction to me and my work (which I could write). I wrote it, attached the photograph they had requested, and waited. Despite numerous calls over the next few weeks to the magazine office, I got no response.

Finally, the journalist told me that the editor had some misgivings, which he would not specify. I asked if we could meet to discuss them, and suggested that

I could first send the editor a letter, since by this time I had a good idea of what those misgivings might be. Unfortunately, I sent this letter the day before a three-month postal strike began. The magazine was seriously crippled by the strike, since they were unable to make any mail deliveries; given the tension it created, I decided not to press the issue of the questionnaire right away. Then, one day near the end of the strike, I saw the reporter at a literary meeting in Ajaccio, where I was sitting with his cousin, an anthropologist. Although I did not say anything about the questionnaire (I had already written off the idea that it would be printed in the magazine), he squirmed visibly in our presence. Finally, he said, "Look, I'm sorry, but you know that given the present political situation, [the magazine] just cannot afford to print the results . . . who knows what we will find. . . . "[6]

Understandably, I was extremely frustrated and annoyed by these setbacks. Part of my frustration stemmed from the fact that support was being withheld from me based on an attribution of symbolic power to me that completely contradicted the feelings of impotence and dependence that I was experiencing.

This led me to discredit the motives of the editor and the students. In a private monologue, I told myself that they had acted inconsistently. They ought to want to find out whatever my survey would reveal. They should be willing and able to challenge the survey results and my interpretation of them. In effect, I was expecting the Corsican intelligentsia to react to me as if they participated in the same world of academic discourse as I did. The mainstream academic discourse I implicitly used as a baseline was the postmodern interrogation of the politics of representation. I did not realize, as Bahloul (1991) points out, that my sense of a shared Franco-American intellectual tradition was, in part, an illusion generated by a shared set of texts and ideas. Both Bahloul and Barbichon (1991) emphasize the degree to which the emphasis on deconstruction of models of textual authority (and on the negotiation of meanings and power) is a distinctly American one.

Furthermore, there was the question of how I was to understand the particular circumstances that surrounded Corsicans' reading of power relations and representational strategies. Marcus and Fischer note that the postmodern is characterized by the "loosening of the hold over fragmented scholarly communities of . . . specific totalizing visions" (1986:8). It was easy to apply a distrust of totalizing visions to the powerful in a relationship of cultural dominance; my desire to deconstruct French claims to cultural superiority in their peripheries coincided with the political agenda of my Corsican colleagues.

It was far less clear to me how I should respond to the totalizing discourses/visions of the dominated. My initial reaction to Corsicans' refusal to support my production of statistics about language use and attitudes was to decry their attempt to control the free circulation of ideas and information. In this light, my magazine article can be read as a call for consistency, a criticism of the gap between militant ideology and practice. Neither of these perspectives is illegitimate; they are both part of my trained attention to "strategies of cultural power that advance through denying their attachment to immediate political ends and thereby accumulate symbolic capital'' (Rabinow 1986:252, on Bourdieu's influence on American anthropology).

But the question of representation remains. Looking back on how I felt at the time, I fully recognize the emotional as well as the intellectual appeal of an authoritative ethnographic discourse that would firmly establish the difference between me and them. They would be described as intellectually bankrupt and inconsistent, as unwilling to face up to the disparity between their own ideology and practices, unwilling to admit that they were engaged in the same process of creating totalizing visions that they decried at the center.

Ultimately, this perspective fails to do justice to the lived experience of both the activists and the ethnographer. It does not recognize, for example, that the ironic, reflexive mode is very easy to apply to others and very difficult to apply and sustain about oneself. This is more than evident in the extremely inconsistent degrees of self-consciousness that I displayed in my choice of publications for a Corsican audience and in my reactions to resistance to my survey.

It is also necessary to recognize the ways in which the less powerful in a situation of domination are constrained in their access to modes of resistance. The dominated may recognize that they reproduce the form of totalizing discourses they wish to overcome, but they do so with firsthand knowledge of the power of such discourses. This power structures the cultural history with which they have to deal, and it also defines and limits the form and content of their attempts at cultural and linguistic legitimation. As an example in the Corsican case, it was the French delegitimation of the Corsican language based on its lack of a literary tradition that led Corsican activists to place a great emphasis on literacy and the production of a Corsican literary corpus. The counterposition taken by the "Lingua Matria" document was to refuse a total dependence on external criteria of value. It was a difficult position, because it failed to establish completely clear cultural boundaries or to establish some concrete criterion for the definition of Corsicanness. The "mother tongue" concept did draw those clear lines, and was evidence of the persistence of dominant ideas about language and identity. In this kind of social context, the power of totalizing discourses and visions was too great to be passed up by people who wished to effect social change.

My experience of powerlessness was therefore not relevant to the context. It was situational, not structural. There was no denying that any statistics I might produce from a survey would have both authority and a life of their own that neither I nor anyone else could completely control. This combination of power and uncertainty compounded some of the risks I have sketched above. The perception that there was much to lose and little to gain from my survey was not unwarranted.

In the long run, the questionnaire setback forced me to reduce the scope of the survey and to eke out responses by establishing personal contacts with small groups. I used friends and acquaintances to gain initial access to Scholastic

Parent Unions, to adult education and vocational training classes, to clubs and associations. I presented my project to these groups in person, explaining the larger ethnographic context and inviting questions. This made me more aware of the nature of the social contract implied by all social science research. I had somehow envisioned the questionnaire as a neutral form of interaction that was quite separate from the larger part of my research. It was not. As a result, I have been very careful not to separate the results from the widest possible context of interpretation. At the same time, I recognize that my intentions do not determine the social use to which this work may be put.

CONCLUSION

Doing fieldwork in the margins of Europe has made me acutely aware of the limits of both detachment and involvement—that as an ethnographer, I can neither escape nor completely take part in the politics of knowledge in the community I study. I can, however, recognize the desire to escape as something that I share with my Corsican counterparts. In the latter part of my fieldwork, for example, I shifted my attentions from the university to the primary schools, where teachers were struggling with the practical implications of the theoretical issues raised in the intellectual milieu. This answered my growing desire to balance the theoretical with the practical, to be a part of a practice rather than of a metalinguistic discourse. I recognized this very same tendency among the Corsican intelligentsia. Most of them jealously guarded an outlet for linguistic or artistic creativity; for Corsican talk, not just talk about Corsican. I got an inkling of this pleasure in the process of learning the language; ultimately, my linguistic apprenticeship was the bond that made it possible for me to maintain a link with members of the academic world.

I also made time to do research on topics that were less contentious and political than language. This mirrored a tendency toward "salvage" ethnography that I saw among Corsican ethnologists. I took part in a collective project to trace marriage patterns over the last century, consulting only silent and cooperative civil registers.

This research has also forced me to consider with greater honesty and clarity the ways in which my own professional practice "back home" is fundamentally political, and that it is difficult to escape or renounce totalizing discourses that lend legitimacy to the practice of everyday life. The Corsican militants I studied were far from exotic creatures: they were who I would be if I were Corsican. My small polemic forays, my excesses of involvement/meddling put the whole interpretive/analytical process into perspective. So when I later wrote about the disjuncture between linguistic and social practices and the form of linguistic activism, it was with the knowledge that I too would probably take some of the same paths, misguided from the "outsider's" point of view but emotionally and politically compelling from the inside.

NOTES

1. Handler (1988:7) also makes this point: "The presuppositions concerning bound-edness that dominate nationalist discourse equally dominate our social scientific dis-course."

2. Goldner (1967:251) reports on the importance of learning to ask "insider" questions for the establishment of the researcher's credibility.

3. The strength of these expectations can be seen in the violent reactions many Breton activists had to Maryon McDonald's (1989) account of the language and the linguistic movement. The year she spent at the University of Rennes studying the Breton language was taken as a sign of her political commitment to the cause.

4. Handler, for example, says he refuses to start his book with a historical account because it would only serve to reify the concept of the Quebecois nation (1988:19). McDonald, writing about Brittany, claims that "two hundred years of French educational policy are collapsed into a single oppression of Breton and all its leading figures, long dead as they are, are cited as if they were speaking today" (1989:77).

5. Conseil de la Culture, la Communication, l'Education et le Cadre de Vie.

6. His misgivings turned out not to be unfounded. In 1991 an independent research company published the results of a telephone survey which revealed that the nationalist party had greater public support than had been believed. Not long afterwards, the head of the company received a death threat and made a public announcement that he was out of the political survey business.

4

FIELDWORK IN QUEBEC, SCHOLARLY REVIEWS, AND ANTHROPOLOGICAL DIALOGUES

Richard Handler

This chapter is a response to responses to *Nationalism and the Politics of Culture in Quebec*, a book that I began researching in 1975 and published in 1988. My response is not meant simply to parry criticisms of my book. Rather, I want to reflect on the fact that certain of those criticisms recapitulated the nationalist ideology that my book attempted to deconstruct. In other words, they took for granted an ideology I rejected, and thus were unwilling, apparently, to understand the arguments that I made. But to say this is not to give myself all the credit while damning my critics. For, not only did they misconstrue my arguments, they found the book as a whole offensive. It angered them. And that anger, too, must be a subject for consideration, for it raises serious questions about the moral role of the anthropologist as cultural critic.

In order to develop the arguments just sketched, it will useful to summarize the deconstruction of nationalist ideology proposed in *Nationalism and the Politics of Culture in Quebec*. It will perhaps help to mention the decisive research experiences that prompted me to write the book that I did. First was my experience of the public presentation of what were imagined to be authentic instances of Quebecois culture—from folk dances performed on stage to the legally sanctioned preservation of historic areas in cities. I always had a strong reaction, both visceral and intellectual, to such presentations, a refusal to accept the framed cultural material as being authentic while ignoring—as the audience is supposed to do—the framing devices. In other words, as an ethnographer, it seemed to me that the machinery of staging folk dances was just as cultural as the dances being staged. It was all culture, modern culture, and it was all fair game for an anthropological analysis. But if it was all culture, then in what way was Quebec different from the hundreds of other modern situations in which an imagined pristine culture is objectified and marketed for mass consumption? The answer, of course, was that Quebec wasn't any different, at least not in the ways in which it went about constructing its difference.

The second research experience that shaped my book concerned the way in which anthropologists and other social scientists wrote about Quebecois nationalism, and about ethnic and nationalist movements in general. It seemed to me that the terms that anthropologists used to construct their notion of "a" culture were the same terms that Quebecois nationalists used to construct their vision of their national culture. Upon reflection, I realized that this is hardly surprising; after all, nationalism and anthropology have common origins in Euro-American romanticism and rationalism of the past three centuries. But it nonetheless meant that social-scientific analyses of ethnicity and nationalism were almost always cast in the same terms that ethnic and nationalist movements used to describe themselves. In other words, social scientists and nationalists spoke the same language. (Indeed, in most parts of the world, social scientists often are among the most prominent of local nationalists.) Given this situation, I decided that I could not use the standard anthropological theory of culture to study nationalism, since that theory was part and parcel of nationalist ideology. I gradually realized, therefore, that I had to write a book that would deconstruct both.

From these research experiences I developed a number of theoretical arguments. I argued that nationalist ideology imagines national culture as a bounded entity made up of or characterized by a further set of entities—"culture traits" like folk dances and old buildings. This ideology "objectifies" culture, I claimed: it construes culture as a bounded object in the natural world, an object that can be precisely described in terms of other bounded objects—the cultural property and attributes that the national culture is said to "possess." I then argued that there is no such "thing" as Quebec culture, precisely because the attempts to objectify it always lead to new constructions of it. In other words, folk dances performed on stage are no longer the dances whose exclusive presence in rural areas or among working classes led intellectuals to classify them as "folk" dances in the first place. Their utility to ideologues may depend on the possibility of presenting them as the real thing, pristinely nonelite and, therefore, authentic, but the act of so presenting them is to rethink them, hence to change them. Culture, I argued, is not naturalistic, and it is not thinglike. It is symbolic, subject to multiple reinterpretations. Thus culture is unbounded and unboundable.

I also argued that a subset of objectifying arguments about national culture depends upon naturalistic or biologistic metaphors. In Quebecois nationalist ideology, the nation is often described as a living entity, person, or personality. With these metaphors, Quebec's history and changing political circumstances can be discussed in terms of a naturalistic rhetoric of life, death, and survival. Cultural productions coming into Quebec from elsewhere, particularly those identified as American or English-language, can be construed as cultural pollution. Pollution metaphors, too, suggest life, death, and survival, and so facilitate naturalistic notions of the Quebec nation. In any case, I stressed that such metaphors *were* metaphors, that is, a way of imagining social realities but not neutral statements of fact.

Finally, I argued that cultural differences do not inhere in bounded cultural objects or cultural groups. Differences are *between*, not *in*—that is, we can say that Quebec is more like France than it is like British Columbia, but to say so is not to say that France and Quebec share the same culture while differing absolutely from British Columbia. Rather, all cultural situations—every moment of every human person's life—are unique. Similarities are not exclusively contained within geographically bounded national entities, just as differences are not necessarily separated by borders. From another perspective, Quebec and British Columbia are culturally quite similar, if you compare them to Bali or Amazonia. Perhaps they are even similar as compared to France. Moreover, Quebec itself is not culturally homogeneous. There are many varying cultural situations within the borders of Quebec. Again, culture is not bounded, and cultural similarity or difference is a function of the particular comparisons that one draws, not of some natural essence that resides *in* the national culture. Notice that, from this perspective, Quebec's current claims to be constitutionally recognized as a unique society are vacuous. Quebec is not a unique society within Canada, for it shares much with Canada, while it is itself internally heterogeneous. There is no such "thing" as Quebec society or culture.

Critical response to these arguments, as revealed in about a dozen reviews of *Nationalism and the Politics of Culture in Quebec*, was mixed. The reviewers divided equally among those who liked the book and accepted, or at least tried to work with, its arguments (e.g., Badone 1992; Cook 1989; Gold 1988; Leone 1990; Molohon 1989) and those who rejected or refused to entertain them (Gagnon 1989; Korovkin 1989; Laforest 1988; Levitt 1989; Waite 1988). Among English-language reviewers writing in Canadian journals were both proponents and opponents of the book. Reviews emanating from French-language Quebec universities were uniformly negative. Here I shall respond only to the negative reviews. As I said at the outset, the two most striking features of these negative reviews are, first, their rage, and second, their uncritical recapitulation of the very ideology that the book deconstructed.

As to rage, consider first that almost none of the negative reviewers attempt to rebut the book's arguments. They neither state its arguments in recognizable terms nor develop counterarguments. In other words, these reviews are not constructed as the rational consideration of ideas that is normal for the academic world. To say this is not to dismiss them as insignificant, or even as invalid, but merely to support my contention that rage, or something other than intellectual analysis, is being expressed in these writings.

Instead of refuting ideas and formulating counterarguments, these reviewers employ a variety of other rhetorical techniques. They say that everyone already knows what the book claims to discover, that there is, in effect, nothing new in it. As P. B. Waite puts it, "The book represents a form of naïveté, greeting the obvious as if it were a discovery" (1988:1726). A particular ploy used to make this point is to mention books that, the reviewers claim, would have spared me the trouble of writing my own book had I bothered to read them. To quote Waite again: "On this subject there is a clutch of half a dozen books already in print (in Canada, admittedly, but in English) that cover the same topic quite well" (1988:1726). In none of this bibliographic argumentation is there any mention of the ideas of the book under review, or, for that matter, of the books listed for the edification of its author.

Another rhetorical technique that, I believe, suggests rage is name calling. This can be divided into attacks on my arguments and attacks on me. As to the first, several reviewers call the style of my work condescending. Others excoriate its "pretentious sociological jargon" (Levitt 1989:377). Still others claim that my arguments are wrong, but without analyzing my errors. As Nicole Gagnon puts it, "His analysis of nationalist thought is neither a description, nor an explication, nor a deconstruction, nor an interpretation: it is a false translation." Gagnon then quotes several passages from the book and summarily dismisses them without argumentation: "Is there any need to specify that these paralogisms . . . are the author's invention and that one would search in vain to find them in the discourse claimed to illustrate them?" (1989:125–126).

As to name calling directed at the author rather than his arguments, some reviewers suggest that I am not a competent anthropologist or ethnographer: "The author's research methods are suspect: he remains an outsider, a tourist in a milieu the ethnography of which he claims to be able to present" (Korovkin 1989:168). Others devote review space to lampooning my trivial errors, like mistakes with regard to the gender of two French nouns (Laforest 1988). In general, it is clear that these reviewers found the book *agaçant*, or aggravating, to use Gagnon ; word: "It is . . . aggravating to see Quebecois nationalism put in the same bag as consumerism, or the work of Fernand Dumont [a major Quebecois sociologist whose nationalist writings are critically analyzed in the book] reduced to insipid mush for a young Narcissus yearning for authenticity" (1989:126).

So much for rage. As for the apparently unreflective recapitulation of nationalist ideology, the theme is epitomized in a sentence by Guy Laforest, who notes that "the deconstruction of nationalism loses some of the radicalness of its outlook when it is mostly applied to a tiny population, attempting to lead a fully modern life in French at the margins of North America" (1988:844). As I understand this remark, it means that nationalist ideology is perhaps worthy of criticism, but criticism ought not to be focused on *Quebec's* nationalist ideology, which is either too fragile or too insignificant to bear the attention. That argument raises an important question, namely, why at this moment in history are mainstream academic disciplines deconstructing minority ideologies? I will return to that question, but for now let me note merely that Laforest's sentence is classic nationalist rhetoric of the type analyzed in *Nationalism and the Politics of Culture in Quebec*. It assumes that Quebec is a bounded social entity, in this case, a "tiny population." It personifies that entity with a metaphor of life. And, finally, it implies the notion of the national struggle for survival.

A more elaborate recapitulation of nationalist rhetoric is found in Joseph Levitt's review. Levitt generally accepts the book's arguments concerning the nationalist appropriation of such cultural "properties" as folklore and heritage. But he draws the line at language:

> The main difficulty with the book is Handler's belief that language resembles heritage property in being just another facet of Quebec culture. Yet while its possession of some heritage property may not prove that Quebec is a unique nation, the fact that it speaks French means that it is a separate linguistic community. The author fails to appreciate what its language means to a people. Individuals can only communicate through their language, and without such communication they cannot live. Not being able to live in French would involve an enormous reconstitution in the lives of Quebecois. (1989:379)

This kind of argument is typical of nationalist writing. Scholarly analysis can always debunk nationalists' claims regarding those cultural features taken to be definitive of their collective identity. Whatever it is that nationalists take to be unique or pure critics can always show to be available elsewhere, as well as "impure" or heterogeneous. The nationalist's response is always the same. They fall back on some other cultural feature to preserve national uniqueness: if not religion, then language; if not language, then a collective spirit or attitude toward life. The process is well known in Quebec, and here Levitt rests his case, as many Quebecois nationalists would, on the French language.

But Levitt's propositions are all contestable. In what sense is Quebec a bounded, "separate linguistic community"? Many languages are spoken within the political borders of Quebec, and Quebecois communicate with the rest of the world in many languages. Strictly speaking, it is not true that "individuals can only communicate through their language." What, in any case, is the meaning of the possessive pronoun in the phrase "their language"? Whose language? Do all Quebecois speak the same language? Can it even be said that all French-speaking Quebecois speak the same language? Phrases like "their language" objectify—to fall back on pretentious sociological jargon—Quebec and make it appear as a unitary entity. Levitt's metaphors of life strengthen that objectification.

At this point, my critics might reply that using the language of nationalist ideology does not automatically invalidate their arguments. But I would argue that one cannot refute an attack on an ideology by simply restating the ideology. As I have suggested, it would be one thing for these critics to attack my arguments and show their weaknesses. It is another thing to ignore them while reproducing, apparently unreflexively, a discourse that my arguments attack.

However, going beyond the validity of particular arguments, I want to consider the implications of an anthropological work that so angers the "natives" that they must resort to name calling and ideological incantation to rebuke their assailant. This is not how anthropology is supposed to work., The stereotypical anthropological project involves coming to understand an alien way of life or thought. The anthropological project is meant to disarm our own Western or scientific prejudices as we go out to encounter "the other" and work to understand the other's culture. There is debate among anthropologists as to whether it is possible to learn to understand another culture from the "native's point of view." Some anthropologists claim that such understanding is impossible, that the best we can do is to construct a sympathetic interpretation of the native's point of view from our point of view. But however accurately, closely, or sympathetically we may be deemed to understand other cultures, our goal is *not* taken to be to criticize other cultures. We are not supposed to laugh at the natives. We are not supposed to say, "These beliefs in rain gods and human sacrifice are foolish and useless, and the natives ought to be taught to disbelieve them." Missionaries, against whom modern anthropologists often define themselves, are supposed to engage in such value judgments. But anthropologists do not. And from that perspective, my work on Quebec seems suspect, for I criticized the worldview of nationalist ideology, the very worldview I purported to study anthropologically.

Now, unless I am to renounce *Nationalism and the Politics of Culture in Quebec*, which I am not yet ready to do, I must find some new way to think about the anthropological endeavor that would permit cultural criticism and anthropological analysis to work together. I can start by suggesting that the insider-outsider distinction is less than helpful in thinking about this problem. To assume that an American anthropologist in Quebec—indeed, any anthropologist in any research situation—is an outsider is to accept the nationalist and anthropological premise of bounded, distinctive, naturally localized cultures. If Quebec culture exists as a bounded entity, then I am an outsider to it. But if culture is an ongoing process of communication, one that is neither naturally bounded nor spatially localized, then a visitor to Quebec who takes the trouble to converse with people there is in some sense a participant in the cultural life of Quebec. This is *not* a function of the visitor's physical presence in Quebec, but of the conversations engendered by human contact—conversations that may well continue after the visitor has left the province. In sum, the cultural life "of" Quebec—even "in" Quebec—is not confined within the political borders of the province.

These arguments suggest a further sense in which a "foreign" anthropologist studying nationalism "in" Quebec is a participant in Quebec's culture of nationalism. Nationalism is a dominant ideology throughout the world, as is the theory of culture which it espouses. Furthermore, the culture theory of nationalists is shared by most anthropologists, who have done perhaps more even than the nationalists themselves to teach the mass publics of modern societies to think naturalistically about national cultures. Quebec nationalists are academics, artists, politicians—all people who participate in an international community of literate discourse, one in which I participate as well. I would claim, therefore, to be "of" their culture in some sense that is not trivial. I claim, that is, the right to speak with these people about our common values and assumptions (though they, of course, have the right not to listen). Moreover, as a participant—not an outsider—in the nationalists' universe of discourse, I claim the right to speak critically about the values and attitudes and worldview of that universe. Indeed, it seems to me that I have a responsibility to be critical of the social and cultural values of the world that I inhabit.

To deconstruct nationalist ideology, then, is not simply to tell the natives that I don't like their ideas. It is to articulate my fundamental disagreement with some of the most powerful values of my own world. None of its critics commented on the fact that *Nationalism and the Politics of Culture in Quebec* opens by quoting nationalist cant articulated by Ronald Reagan. I intended that quotation to remind the reader that however problematic I find Quebecois and Canadian nationalism, I am not unmindful that in my country "of origin" a similar, though perhaps more lethal, nationalism is alive and well.

But the natives' rage suggests that they do not accept my critique as a self-critique. They do not respond to it as an attack on the values of the modern world, values with which both they and I must reckon. They take my work as an arrogant outsider's attack on them. Thus Michael Korovkin writes that "the author's scientific method . . . is not unlike the Popperianism of the early sixties: they (the native Quebecois *hoi ploi*? [*sic*] know in a wrong way because, you see, the new scientific facts are not available to them, while I (the clever positivist *illuminato*?) know better" (1989:168).

Korovkin's response raises a fundamental issue for anthropological cultural criticism. How is it possible to evaluate critically the values that one studies *without* legitimating one's critique by an appeal to scientific authority? Since anthropologists employed by universities enjoy, whether they want it or not, the legitimacy of scientific authority, it is probably disingenuous to pretend to renounce such legitimacy. But perhaps we can use our authority against itself, subversively. The (scientific) analysis of culture—including the culture of science—works by bringing to light values that are presupposed and unavailable for reflection. *That* is the anthropological enterprise—to reveal that human beings live according to culturally constructed values that are neither timeless nor universal nor scientifically correct. When anthropologists study the values of non-Western peoples who have been subjugated by Western power, our responsibility has been to argue that those non-Western values be respected. When, however, anthropologists study modern values, such as the values of nationalism, our responsibility is to deconstruct those values, to refuse to accept them as unquestionable truths about the world. Anthropological analysis of modern culture works by being critical. The job is to make visible—hence available for rethinking—the fundamental yet implicit assumptions that have structured the modern world system and against which many of us are in passive revolt. The point, therefore, is not to proclaim which values are right and which are wrong. Rather, the point is to develop new, critical perspectives on hegemonic values so that we—all of us—can discuss and perhaps revise them.

Korovkin is right to reject authoritative pronouncements about values. A good analysis of Quebecois nationalism should provoke reasoned discussion, not rage, and to the degree that my work has provoked rage, not reanalysis, it is incomplete. (It will, of course, remain incomplete for other reasons as well.)

Although the anthropology of nationalism has increasingly taken a critical turn, the disciplinary mainstream remains, I would argue, unabashedly romantic. The romantic anthropologist buys into the ethnic self-definition of the people he or she studies. Indeed, this anthropologist returns from "the field" with many native artifacts. These have been chosen with an expert's eye. The anthropologist does not buy cheap tourist art, but knows instead how to choose the truly authentic pieces that tourists will neither discover nor understand. This anthropologist is a connoisseur of commodified ethnicity. He or she visits my university and, wearing a suit proper for a formal occasion, delivers a paper on Bongo Bongo rain gods. At the informal occasion held later in honor of the visitor, we find that visitor casually dressed with tasteful Bongo Bongo accessories. Bongo Bongo ethnicity, commodified, has become part of the construction of our modern professional's identity.

Yet does this uncritical acceptance of Bongo Bongo self-definition represent simple respect for the natives? I think not. I think, rather, that the natives have been subjected to a discourse of national and cultural identity. They have, understandably, bought into it, perhaps reworked it, certainly attempted to use it for their own purposes. It is, in any case, the only language they can speak that power will understand. Thus the anthropologist must respect Bongo Bongo ethnicity—but not uncritically. I respect ethnic or national self-definition because it expresses the dilemma that people everywhere face in trying to cope with a hegemonic world system, now several centuries in the making. But I disrespect ideologies that take nationalism as an expression of timeless, universal values. Indeed, to respect those people who must face up to the universe of nationalist values is to speak to them critically about those values rather than naïvely celebrate them. To celebrate the natives' nationalism is the true act of condescension.

5

THE STUDENT OF CULTURE AND THE ETHNOGRAPHY OF IRISH INTELLECTUALS

Elizabeth A. Sheehan

Most of the chapters in this book address the issue of how the communities we write about as anthropologists respond to our texts. My chapter forms something of a prologue to this issue: it describes the difficulties involved in the actual process of writing about communities that anticipate misrepresentation by foreign ethnographers. In such situations, the ethnographer's normal concerns about accuracy and confidentiality are compounded by an, at times, almost paralyzing fear of offending informants and closing off opportunities for further research in the fieldsite. It becomes difficult to sort out one's appropriate ethical concerns as an ethnographer from less noble, but no less significant, concerns about the implications of the finished product for one's career.

In my case, these concerns were heightened by the fact that my research was set in Ireland, a country where American ethnographers' accounts of local communities have long provoked controversy. As the introduction to this book discusses, John Messenger's *Inis Beag* (1969) and Nancy Scheper-Hughes's *Saints, Scholars and Schizophrenics* (1979) have been major targets of this criticism. Each has been challenged by native academics and journalists on the basis of their accuracy and research ethics. Messenger and Scheper-Hughes's informants have also expressed hurt and dismay at finding aspects of their personal lives depicted in print, notwithstanding the fact that some informants agreed with the authors' analyses. In the case of both books, the issue of outsiders' *capacity* to interpret Irish culture has been conflated with that of their *right* to publish what might in fact be true.

By the time I did my fieldwork, in 1986–87, Scheper-Hughes's work had become the main focus of native scholars' criticism of Americanist ethnography of Ireland. (My informal impression was that Sharon Gmelch's book *Nan* [1986], also discussed in the editor's introduction, was generally well regarded by Irish academics.) Although more than six years had elapsed since the publication of Scheper-Hughes's *Saints, Scholars and Schizophrenics*, I found suspicion of American ethnographers' fieldwork and research methods still evident within the Irish social science community. This was of particular significance to me because my research population consisted of Dublin-based university academics, some of whom were the country's leading intellectuals and thus deeply concerned with issues of Ireland's public identity and representation. To make matters worse, I was a graduate student gathering data for my first major piece of ethnographic writing, my doctoral dissertation. Thus, if necessary, my interpretive authority as an outsider could be challenged by my scholarly informants on the most fundamental and chilling grounds of intellectual ineptitude.

My dissertation (1990) examined Irish university academics' participation in the public sphere of politics, social reform, and cultural debate.[1] Part of my fieldwork took place at Dublin's two oldest and most influential colleges, Trinity College and University College Dublin (UCD), institutions which over time have had close links with Ireland's national-level political and intellectual life. As such, many of their faculty members move within intersecting spheres of influence based not only on their position as educators but on their access to government, state agencies, and the media. Interviews with academics and administrators across a wide variety of disciplines in each college were supplemented by participant observation of campus social life and debate. From these academic settings, my research then extended to observation and analysis of academics' activities and statements in the public sphere of political, social, and intellectual debate. My methodology was closely linked to my theoretical stance: that intellectuals, under certain circumstances, constitute observable social groups acting to influence the world around them and to promote interests both self-serving and socially meaningful. Ireland seemed an ideal place to explore this thesis, given the long association there between culture and politics as well as the active participation of Irish intellectuals in national political life from the colonial period to the present.

Underlying my enthusiasm for my research project, however, was my awareness that those I wrote about would also be, in some instances, the same people authorized to critique the publications resulting from my research. It is not unusual for outsider anthropologists to have their ethnographic analyses challenged by native scholars or journalists, as the introduction and several chapters in this volume discuss. Handler, for example, describes how his sympathetic effort to deconstruct the appeal of nationalist ideology in his book, *Nationalism and the Politics of Culture in Quebec* (1988), was met in large part by his critics' reiteration of Quebecois separatist identity rather than by an effort to examine the logic of his analysis. In my case as well, some of my academic critics would also be my informants, the very people written about. How would *they* separate their roles as critics and subjects, as disinterested scholars and as individuals deeply concerned with what I said about them and their colleagues? How would I, as an ethnographer hoping to write honestly but also fairly about what I had learned, separate my feelings of resentment and exclusion as a questionable outsider from my genuine fascination with my informants and my compelling desire to describe the complex world of ideas, politics, and gossip they inhabited?

This chapter discusses these problems of sorting, editing, and self-censorship in the writing process, while trying to explore the personal and scholarly bases of the decisions I eventually made as I wrote. Inevitably, local suspicion of my discipline and research motives, combined with the fact of my informants' notoriety and influence, affected many of the decisions I made about how to write up my data, what information to include and to leave out, and how to connect the public lives and opinions of those I studied with the more private information about them I inevitably gained access to. Some of my reflections on this experience have been affected by the passage of time and by the subtle changes in self-perception that have accompanied my transition from graduate student to professional anthropologist. Return trips to Ireland since completing the dissertation have also deepened my understanding of at least one aspect of my writing difficulties, as I will discuss near the close of this chapter. Still, it is only recently that I have begun "circling to return," in Irish poet Seamus Heaney's phrase, to the central issues and questions that first attracted me to Ireland. This chapter constitutes a step in that process.

THE CONTEXT OF CRITICISM

In the years since her book was first published, Scheper-Hughes has discussed her own complex and evolving responses to the ethical issues raised by her fieldwork and by her informants' responses to it (1981, 1982a, 1987), while also responding to specific criticisms of her methodology and research conclusions (e.g., 1982b). One point she makes (ibid.) in her discussion of this case is the role the Irish press played in stimulating public interest in her study and in the ethics of sensitive research by outsiders. Although criticism of Scheper-Hughes's work and more generalized concern over foreign ethnographers' research in Ireland was expressed by some native anthropologists (see, for example, Kane 1979 and 1982, as well as Blacking et al. 1983), it is likely that the average Irish person's familiarity with the book was derived from mass media sources. As in the case of many other books written about Ireland by outsiders, *Saints, Scholars and Schizophrenics*'s greatest interest to Irish people may have been the opportunity it provided them to reflect on what non-Irish observers think of their culture.

My own experience in Ireland in the mid–1980s showed that while Scheper-Hughes's name and book title were well known, few beyond her fieldsite and the Irish social science community had a clear idea of what she had written, where she had done her research, or what was "wrong" with it. This did not prevent many of the Irish academics I met, who may or may not have read the book, from trying to engage me in debate over it and the author's merits. Further, like some kind of ethnographic Elvis, Scheper-Hughes was reported to me as having been sighted in villages and pubs all over the west of Ireland, notebook in hand, long after she had left the country. My point is that the mythic element of stories about exploitative outsiders can easily overtake the reality of the actual research as well as informed analyses of it. It certainly discourages open-minded interest in reading the actual text.[2] Inevitably, these stories of victimization that are "good to think" become the framework within which any future ethnographic research in a country is evaluated.[3] Also inevitably, they become part of the psychological baggage successive ethnographers of such fieldsites carry around in their heads as they face up to the act of writing.

It is crucial to understand, however, that Irish social scientists' concerns about Scheper-Hughes's work were framed within the wider context of reaction against an ethnographic tendency (termed by some Irish anthropologists the "Americanist" tradition) toward viewing modern Ireland as a declining and debilitated society, a sociopathological culture made up of alcoholics, chronic depressives, and sex-starved country folk. Wilson (1984) has reviewed the trajectory of this bias in Irish ethnographic studies, although it by no means represents the major portion of research done in the country, by both native and foreign ethnographers, in the past twenty years. More profoundly, Irish scholars and intellectuals are appropriately sensitive to negative portrayals of their society, long a victim of misrepresentation and at times near-genocidal social policy by British colonial administrators. If the cold-blooded government agent is no longer around to trivialize and condemn Irish culture, perhaps the Yank with a tape recorder and a research grant raises his specter. Awareness of this deeper historical experience of distortion and betrayal is also something the would-be ethnographer of Ireland carries in her head, forcing her to sort out the distinctions between the political and scholarly responsibilities of the ethnographic endeavor.

PUBLIC LIVES, PRIVATE INFORMATION

Any effort to write ethnography requires the anthropologist to return repeatedly to the circumstances, events, and moods of one's fieldwork. We reread field notes, transcribe tapes, pore over diaries that reveal more about ourselves than our research, and are reminded by scraps of paper that fall out of books of the transitory nature of our once-brilliant insights. More crucially, the dilemmas that arise in writing ethnography are linked directly to the specific politics of each exchange between ethnographer and informant, observer and setting. Without giving in completely to what Geertz (1988:130) has termed the "pervasive nervousness" of the postmodern effort to explain the Other, we must still acknowledge that the process of translating the complexity of other people's lives and cultures into a seamless narrative takes enormous hubris. At times it resembles a form of fiction writing, when we suppress what we know or force these insights to fit a hypothesis we have nursed too long to abandon.

But what about the more specific, and less hermeneutical, dilemma of deciding what is *safe* to write? For me, this dilemma operated on several levels: my junior academic status; my hypothetically imperialist impulses as an American outsider; my need to protect the intellectual property of my academic informants; and perhaps most seriously, the implications of writing about a well-established and self-protective national bourgeoisie.

I will deal with the last issue first, although it must be stressed that my various levels of otherness and the anxieties they produced were closely linked and came into play in most of my fieldwork encounters. Some of my informants were very prominent individuals, including a former prime minister, the current president of the Republic, and an archbishop, all of whom were members of college faculties at the time of my fieldwork. The thought of ruffling their feathers by connecting their words and actions with my own analyses was unsettling, to say the least.[4] Quite a few were journalists and media personalities involved in public debates about Ireland's postcolonial condition and the country's vulnerability to foreign economic and political forces. Despite my sympathetic stance on these issues (which became, in fact, major themes in my dissertation), was it not presumptuous of me as both a low-status outsider and a "privileged" American to comment on how Irish intellectuals framed their arguments about these issues?

Others among my informants were academic culture brokers whose professional influence derived greatly from their ability to attract fee-paying American scholars to Irish conferences and summer schools. My research, which explored in part the mass-marketing of Irish intellectual culture and its relationship to Ireland's economic dependency, certainly would not sit well with those who preferred to maintain easy and collegial relations with their American clients. This old boys' network had also been remarkably successful in marginalizing anthropology as an Irish Studies discipline, emphasizing instead the literary and historical aspects of Irish culture that appeal to so many foreign scholars. Did I want to help perpetuate this academic marginalization, and ensure my own, by offending those in charge of brokering Irish-American intellectual exchange? Those of my informants whose public profiles were not so high had other, less-evident access to power which impinged on my freedom to write. Brothers of bishops, sons of civil servants, confidants of cabinet ministers, they slowly revealed to me an inbred world of people who had known each other since college, married each other's sisters, and slept with each other's spouses.

It is easy to advise leaving out the scandal and questionable data in writing about one's research population, but I wonder how many anthropologists who do *not* study powerful people feel the same moral compunction? It is of more than passing interest to an ethnographer to know that a number of a country's now middle-aged academics, writers, judges, and politicians were members of the same university cohort and have all been involved with the same woman (even now I write this in a way that obscures what I really mean). The personal (but well-known) lives of these people are none of my business from an ethical standpoint, but they are from an ethnographic one, given the social and institutional linkages they reveal within a generation that wields significant power over the country's political, judicial, and intellectual spheres. And what does this situation say of the women who marry or are born into this social group? My dissertation does not include this story, nor any vague allusion to it. Instead, I opt to attempt to convey the closed world of the Dublin professional classes in more general descriptive terms. As an anthropologist, presumably committed to "fact" and to protecting informants, I am acutely aware that I have less freedom to write than the average newspaper columnist who chooses to imply, or state outright, information I must suppress.

Leaving aside sex, let's consider another famously delicate topic: religion. How can I write—or not write—that an extremely high-ranking Irish politician described an equally influential churchman to me as a "drunken lunatic"? This is Ireland, remember, a country where the struggle to separate church and state is of vital sociopolitical concern. Further, the comment was made by a Catholic politician (and former university professor) during the time of a national debate about reproductive rights, an issue around which academics and intellectuals have mobilized on both progressive and conservative sides. I *did* include this quote in my dissertation, but obscured it in the same manner as it is written above. I deeply regret not being able to identify the individuals involved (although I recognize that most Irish people would know to whom I was referring), because the story helps convey the complexity of public and private stands on moral issues in contemporary Ireland, so often portrayed in simple black and white terms by non-Irish commentators.

The writing decisions described above refer mainly to the problem of making ethnographically meaningful connections between publicly and privately available information. All ethnographers face this problem and try to resolve it in ways that do the least damage to their informants and to themselves. I want to emphasize, however, that "gossip" takes on different significance when one's research population consists of people with real power. Social sanctions against gossip, about what kind of information meets this description, as well as proscriptions against repeating it, are in large part middle-class conventions that serve the interests of those with the most to hide. With powerful or influential informants, the most important gossip is not about marital or alcohol problems; it is about backroom deals, political compromises, and that old standby, the gentlemen's agreement—decisions and actions that may affect the lives of many outside the inner circle of those who have access to this information. It is extremely difficult for the ethnographer of elites, or, as in the case of most of my informants, well-placed professionals, to know the extent of her responsibility to protect informants in such instances; even more difficult to write honestly about the issues they involve without seeming to violate a social contract portrayed as universal but often invoked to protect a privileged few.

PUBLIC LIVES, PRIVATE IDEAS

It is a cliché to say that knowledge is power, but in the case of informants who are intellectuals, knowledge is also capital, symbolic and otherwise. Here too the boundaries between public and private forms of information become confused, merge, and cross over to opposite sides in the exchange between anthropologist and informant. As a result, ethnographic writing about academics and intellectuals raises serious issues of intellectual attribution. Published work and public statements remain private property, not only within the terms of scholarly convention, but also as part of an individual intellectual process that extends beyond the finished book or paper. As intellectuals, many academics create their lives through their work, and their work through their lives. Interviews with such informants can provide exhilarating insight for the ethnographer (Yes! Yes! *This* is what I mean!), brought to a sudden halt by the realization that the ideas you are now thinking—and thinking of writing about—are not entirely your own at all but the product of a mutual intellectual exchange. How do you correctly ascribe ideas that are offered within the context of an interview but which may also be the basis of new works, new publications? How do you separate the public thinker from the private, honor his confidentiality and intellectual property, and still offer a meaningful analysis? I might add that this process can work both ways, but with less ethical difficulty for the informant. I was both flattered and dismayed to see some insights of mine appear in the *Irish Times*, unattributed, under the byline of an academic I had interviewed a few days earlier. He had no need, as had I, to sort out his ideas from my own in a setting which was, for him, just an interesting discussion with another academic.

Another unique issue concerning intellectual property arises when one is writing about those who earn their living in large part through their ideas. I confronted a version of this during an interview with a professor who was a prolific scholarly writer as well as a frequent contributor to national publications. I had hoped to gain this man's views on what I perceived as neutral and unproblematic topics: his intellectual development and perspectives on his discipline. But these topics were not to be so casually discussed by him, given that he intended to write about them himself and to place his own interpretations upon them. With the life history method, anthropologists can be said to write the book for their informants. Intellectual informants want to write the book themselves. They are aware of the capital in their ideas and experiences, and many rightfully limit your access to these and to your writing about them, not because they are too personal, but because they are too valuable.

It is appropriate for academics to protect their property, but this desire may take extreme forms. One very cautious informant I interviewed requested attribution for all her intellectual statements and confidentiality for many of her personal ones (this academic's concerns about speaking to me were so great that she asked to see not only my standard letter of introduction from my university, but my personal identification as well). I was stymied, however, by the nature of her requests for confidentiality and attribution. Some of her intellectual observations were, in my opinion, in the public domain and not hers to control. Further, I already knew some of what she had offered as confidential information from other sources, who had not imposed any constraints on my use of this material. I tried to resolve this problem by receiving confirmation of what I had been told from yet another source, without indicating my prior knowledge of it, but I am not sure if this absolves me of my original pledge of confidentiality to my informant. Given the sensitivity with which she viewed the information she gave me, I would still be violating her understanding of our agreement by repeating it. Ultimately, I ended up not using any of my interview with her, perhaps, in part, because I was so irritated by what I felt to be her exaggerated sense of self-importance.

In some cases, my concern about repeating information received from informants derived from their own fears of being identified. Like other ethnographers, I always ascertained before and frequently after interviews whether or not the individual wished to be quoted for attribution, quoted without attribution, or used merely as a background source. My status as an outsider to the local academic community often seemed to give people greater freedom to express their private frustrations or personal grievances toward individuals or the institutions that employed them, but I realized there might be a morning-after effect in many of these cases. One academic, for example, wrote me a note the day after our interview telling me he didn't really mean to call his colleagues blithering idiots. (Subsequently, I didn't either.) The fact remains, however, as with all fieldwork, that we learn much more than we can tell, and that this larger body of knowledge informs what we write. Even with the best intentions of protecting our informants' privacy and intellectual property, as well as ourselves, time and distance can blur the distinction between what is safe to write and what is not. And in the case of an influential informant dealing with a foreign or junior scholar, it is likely that any charge of indiscretion will be laid at the ethnographer's door, not the informant's.

THE INFORMANT AS MULTIPLE PERSONALITY

Anthropologists frequently draw on the narrative device of splitting up a single informant's identity, presenting quotes and extracts from life histories discretely in order to preserve anonymity and confidentiality. This practice has obvious negative implications for the clarity and force of one's argument, but is generally viewed as the lesser of two evils. (The alternative device of merging several individuals into a single, composite character may have great literary appeal, but seems to me to be profoundly problematical.) But strategies for writing meaningfully about public figures whose activities and influence extend into several different domains become even more difficult to devise. Much of the value of telling the person's story, or stories, derives from his unique status or insight; nonetheless, this type of informant has the right to expect the same kind of ethnographic discretion that would be granted a less public figure.

The case of one individual provides a particularly vivid example of the difficulties I faced in sorting out and still making sense of my informants' overlapping professional, political, and personal identities. His case also lays bare the subtext that guided many of my day-to-day writing decisions: the danger to me of repeating or even suggesting any information that could be construed as actionable under Ireland's fairly stringent libel laws. This individual had recently been the center of a well-publicized controversy about his appointment to the chair of a major department at one of the colleges I worked at. His story was worth telling because it demonstrated the continuing concern among Irish intellectuals that native scholars maintain control over key areas of Irish scholarship (another dimension of the postcolonial condition, as the original, but eventually rejected, candidate for the job was an Englishman). At the same time, the professor involved was a leading authority in his field, and thus an important source of information for me about a discipline (which in this discussion I cannot identify) that has tremendous influence in Irish political and intellectual life. Further, he was a close personal friend of the then prime minister, a circumstance which may have influenced his appointment to the chair, and which encouraged some of his critics to view this professor's scholarly biases as helping to serve the prime minister's political agenda.

All of these facts were important and highly revealing of the links between Irish academia and party politics, and this one individual offered the perfect device for exploring these links. I could describe the events and issues surrounding the debate about his academic appointment, but could not identify him for fear of offending him and treading too close to the edge of libel. This was not because the public facts about the case were dangerous for me to repeat, but because my arrangement of them in narrative form required interpretation and inference on my part. My discussion incorporated the perspectives of unnamed colleagues critical of his appointment, as well as published comments by the man who didn't get the job about the ethics of the hiring process. I was well aware, however, that I did not have access to all the facts involved. Thus my discussion, no matter how accurate it might have been, could be challenged on the basis of incomplete information and damaging innuendo. No doubt any Irish academic reading my dissertation would recognize the situation as I eventually described it. What I did in writing about it in an obscure manner was simply protect myself, at worst from legal threats, at best from this influential academic's undying enmity.

But I still had the problem of writing about this person in his other role as leading scholar. Even here, however, his identity had to be fragmented. In the dissertation he becomes several people, not by the questionable device of pretending he was really a number of different individuals, but simply by my failing to inform the reader that "one professor," "another commentator," and so forth who appear throughout the dissertation are actually one person. Consequently, this single individual is discussed as the unnamed center of the appointment controversy, as an anonymous example of the links between scholarship and party politics, as an attributed commentator on his research discipline, as an unattributed commentator on his colleagues in this discipline, and as a published source on his research specialty. If it was legal fiction to write up my data in this way, it was also, of necessity, legal ethnography.

THE ETHNOGRAPHER AS MULTIPLE PERSONALITY

As noted earlier, my diverse forms of otherness often coalesced in my interactions with informants, as well as in my subsequent effort to find a voice in which to write about them. Ironically, my two most contradictory identities were often linked in informants' attempts to categorize me. On the one hand, I was a needy student, asking them to share their knowledge, insights, and life experiences with me so that I could advance to their professional status. On the other, I was an American anthropologist, one of those "blow ins," in the local phrase, who breeze through Ireland for a few weeks and then go home to win fame and glory by writing some crackpot study of Irish dipsomaniacs. My interpretive authority could thus be challenged on two very different levels: my student status, and my questionable research motives as an American ethnographer.

In retrospect, I believe that my identity as a junior scholar had more significance to me than to my informants. This was in part the result of my long, and often demeaning, socialization as an American graduate student. In Ireland, by contrast, graduate students are generally treated as professional academics, probably because the number of people pursuing advanced degrees there is so much smaller and because many established scholars do not themselves have doctorates. Also, having started my academic career rather late, I was in my early thirties by the time I did my fieldwork. This meant that many of my informants were actually close to me in age, a situation that usually led to their treating me as a colleague. However, older academics (men in particular) seemed caught between treating me as an adult and as one of their undergraduate students. That I was married, information they frequently tried to elicit from me, may have allowed some of these men to define me as a grown-up, albeit one whose advanced age as a graduate student somehow suggested that I had missed the academic boat.

However, my being a female also probably emphasized my junior status with some informants. Like most academic institutions, my two fieldsites functioned (one might say, survived) on sexist principles. Female heads of departments were few at the colleges I worked at, and women tended to be clustered in the younger, lower status, and less well paid end of the faculty spectrum. I was also told by a woman graduate student in sociology that in Ireland the social sciences, having their academic origin in the field of social work, are considered a female and therefore less prestigious scholarly domain. Being a woman social scientist and a graduate student may have facilitated my work with older male academics by making me appear less threatening and thereby inducing greater cooperation. However, this "benefit" was accompanied sometimes by an irritating paternalism on their part and by an expectation of malleability that undermined my self-confidence, both in the field and later.

Of greater significance to many of my informants, and ultimately to me as I wrote my dissertation, was my status as an American anthropologist. As noted earlier, few interviews I conducted began without a discussion, initiated by the informant, of Scheper-Hughes's work and its merits. To me, this seemed an effort not only to establish where I stood on her work but to warn me of my own vulnerability to future criticism. Most of the academics I met were cordial and cooperative, but a few (all of them social scientists) snubbed me or used my citizenship and discipline as an opportunity to lecture me on American imperialism. The closer I got to "home," that is, to academics most likely to share my theoretical and disciplinary interests, the more distance I often felt in my personal exchanges with them.

Unlike Jaffe (this volume), who describes how many of her scholarly informants initially assumed that her political and intellectual motives for studying the Corsican language were similar to their own, I found that very few of the academics I met (with the important exception of feminist scholars) assumed that I was there to support their cause, whatever that might be. On the contrary, I was often subjected to the third degree about my research motives and methods. While this interrogation was often placed within the context of a general discussion of the politics and ethics of interpreting other people's cultures, it was likely that my informants were also disturbed by the fact that they themselves were the subject of ethnographic study. The hypothetical "plain people of Ireland" they claimed to be protecting were also themselves. This disingenuousness allowed them to have it both ways in deciding how to deal with me: if I could not be dismissed as an ignorant student, then perhaps I could be dealt with, and shamed, as an exploitative outsider.

Yet I was in many ways similar to my informants, as well as sympathetic to some of their political and social causes. I was an academic, and thus, like Jaffe, I experienced little culture shock in my university fieldsites. Further, I was Irish-American, a fact that meant less to my informants (swamped as they are every summer with Midwesterners looking for their roots) than to me. I felt that I could not presume to speak "for" Ireland, either during my fieldwork or later as I wrote about it, yet I felt a strong degree of personal affinity for the country and its people. I wanted at all costs to avoid romanticizing Ireland in my discussion of it, but felt in doing so that I would be betraying my own emotional ties to it and the realities of my family's historical connection with it.

These multiple identities placed me on tenterhooks during the writing process. *I* had often felt victimized by the elitism and exclusivity of my research population, but it was clear that, once I was beyond the field, my informants saw

me as having some power over them. Further, as suggested above, I abhorred
the thought of writing either some winsome account of the "Celtic personality"
or another reverential treatise on the "Irish genius" for poetry, literature, and
verbal wit (hard to avoid when writing about Irish intellectuals). I had to decide
for whom I was writing: the community of American anthropologists whose
responses to my work would be most important to my career, or the Irish
academics who had shared their time and thoughts with me, and perhaps expected
an inappropriate degree of discretion and dissembling on my part in my subsequent effort to write about them.

My solution to this dilemma was both practical and emotionally satisfying, if
not original. In my mind, I wrote for those with whom I most identified, those
whom I saw as fighting for political and social causes I supported, and, although
I did not quite realize it at the time, the younger scholars I had met who also
felt marginal to the structures and politics of Irish academia. In other words,
like many ethnographers, I created heroes and villains. My intent with the finished
product, however, was not only to describe objectively those I feared and in
some cases disliked, but to highlight in positive terms those whom I considered
allies and, in a few instances, friends.

This brings me to a final point about my fieldwork and writing experience,
one I did not fully appreciate until after I had finished my dissertation. During
my fieldwork, and in the period following when I was writing up my study, I
did not reflect much on the implications of my male-dominated fieldsite for my
sense of discomfort as I wrote. I was aware of a latent sense of grievance toward
my male informants' seemingly effortless self-confidence, but saw these feelings
largely as a reflection of my own insecurities—as a late-starting academic, as a
person from a lower-middle-class background, and as an often stereotypically
tongue-tied female. It wasn't until I returned to Ireland in 1991, during a time
when Irish women activists and scholars were engaged in an aggressive public
critique of Ireland's male political and intellectual establishment, that I realized
how much I had internalized, and personalized, the second-class status of women
in Ireland. With all my "book" understanding of Ireland, I had made the as-
tounding ethnographic error of not realizing that I was living part of the daily
experience of the average Irish woman, and had carried these feelings home
with me to my computer along with my fieldnotes and tapes.

ADVICE FROM ABOVE

The possibility exists that advice on how to write about sensitive material can
be drawn from colleagues, dissertation supervisors, and other ethnographies.
Yet the tradition of "studying down" in anthropology encourages a view of
informants and their communities as victims to be protected at all costs from
the external forces that control their lives. But if we are to face power, as Eric
Wolf (1990) admonishes us to do, we must study it from all sides. Unfortunately,
at this point our rules of conduct become less clear. There is little guidance

available on how to write about powerful informants. Discussions of elite research rarely even raise the issue, unless the elites studied can be defined clearly as "evil" and the anthropologist can thus align himself with said elite's victims. In a subtle manner, this is what I did myself, but I am not entirely comfortable with this decision. This is because my relationship to my informants was much more complex than that of the clear outsider, if such an ethnographic entity still exists. I was in one sense a colleague studying across, in another a student studying up, and in yet another a social scientist studying down.

My experience of seeking guidance back home, as a dissertation writer, on how to write about influential informants in a contentious fieldwork setting was not particularly rewarding. Several of my graduate student cohort were in a similar position, having studied political and economic elites in different countries, and they remained perturbed and ambivalent about how to resolve this issue throughout the length of the dissertation-writing period. In some cases, these feelings may have even prolonged the writing process (I can hear experienced dissertation supervisors snorting at *that* suggestion).

Perhaps because most of our professors had themselves studied the powerless, or because they were far removed in time from the initial terrifying effort to write ethnography, our requests for advice were not taken very seriously. "Just write it and fix it up later," one impatiently advised us. Change names, obscure locales, use unattributed quotes. Protect your informants *and* yourself, they said. But this advice presumes an epistemological split between fact and interpretation, between public and private knowledge, which derails the ethnographic endeavor from the start. Especially in the case of well-known and influential informants, active in the public sphere, it is absolutely essential to devise strategies for drawing these varied sources of data and insight together into a coherent whole. If we cannot write about the powerless without moving from the bottom up, how can we write about the powerful without moving from the top down?

CONCLUSION

I will close this discussion by noting a final irony in my struggle to sort out what I could and could not write about my informants, one which also points out some of the frustrations of writing ethnographically. By a strange coincidence, each of the colleges where I conducted fieldwork has in the past few years provided the setting for an Irish murder mystery. The one about Trinity College (Gill 1989) involves the stabbing death of an English professor; in the UCD novel, appropriately called *Publish or Perish?* (Forrest 1991), a professor of genetics gets a bullet in the brain. The Trinity novel was written by a professional detective story writer, and is one of a series featuring his trademark inspector. Yet the book is no doubt based on real Irish academics and their quirks, embellished by insights into college life available to any Trinity graduate or member of Dublin's intelligentsia. The UCD novel was written by a college faculty member, under a pen name, and is thus even more specific in its personal characterizations and description of the gossip, backbiting, and pettiness of UCD's academic culture. As the paperback cover states, "A Dublin university, plagued by staff rivalries, calls in the Murder Squad."

The catharsis writing these books may have granted their authors is of course not available to me (not to imply that I actually wish to *murder* any of my informants), but reading them has led me to reflect on the novelist's freedom to state hard truths and likely possibilities under the guise of fiction. As Messenger (1989) points out, and as we know ourselves from our surreptitious reading of cheap novels and tabloids, the fictional account or blind gossip item is often more likely to be considered true than the "scientific" effort to record reality. I know that attempting the latter, or some postmodern version of it, is the ethnographer's task, but who among us has not considered the sheer liberation of abandoning scholarly detachment in favor of the novel, in our case, the roman à clef?

I am well aware that the issues and concerns I have discussed in this chapter have deeply influenced my own attitudes toward publishing. Since finishing my dissertation in 1990, I have slowly crept up again to my data, my field experiences, and to those I met in the course of my research. My first article written about Ireland dealt mainly with the abstract difficulties of fieldwork with academics and intellectuals (1993, in press); the second analyzed a national political debate that took place during my fieldwork (1991). The third concerned the architectural and intellectual traditions of the colleges where I conducted my research (1992). These have been followed by a general analysis of "Irish academic types," an article in revision as I write, and now by this discussion of the difficulties of writing ethnography about specific people. The next project is clear: dissertation to book, author to authority, victim to villain?

NOTES

1. Although my research took place in the Republic of Ireland, it also addressed political and social issues concerning Northern Ireland and Anglo-Irish relations in general.

2. A few years ago, the proprietor of a New York bookstore devoted to books of Irish interest told a friend of mine that she refused to carry Nancy Scheper-Hughes's book. Informal censorship leaves a long and convoluted trail.

3. I want to make it clear that while I have used Scheper-Hughes's published comments on this case in my discussion, the opinions expressed here are entirely my own and in no way reflect her more informed views on this matter.

4. Nonetheless, here is a warning to all would-be office-seekers: beware the lowly student with a tape recorder. In May 1990, the deputy prime minister of Ireland granted an interview to a UCD graduate student in political science. The interview was taped, with the permission of the politician, and included discussion of an incident involving a potentially unconstitutional effort made by this individual to involve the then president of Ireland in a political matter concerning the prime minister's office. By the fall of 1990, the deputy prime minister was himself a candidate for the presidency, and seemed to have a substantial lead over his two opponents until the graduate student produced his

taped interview. The unconstitutionality of the candidate's actions, acknowledged on the tape, was not so damaging to his campaign as was his subsequent denial to the media that they had ever taken place. Partly as a result of this incident, Mary Robinson, a progressive lawyer and human rights advocate, won the election and became Ireland's first woman president in November 1990.

Part III

MEDIATED TEXTS: ISSUES OF REPRESENTATION AND IDENTITY

6

WHOSE HISTORY IS IT?
SELECTION AND REPRESENTATION
IN THE CREATION OF A TEXT

Caroline B. Brettell

In a 1961 essay on anthropology and history, Evans-Pritchard (1962:177) stressed that the traditional history of a people is important because "it forms part of the thought of living men and hence part of the social life which the anthropologist can directly observe." "We have to distinguish," he continued, "the effects of an event from the part played in the life of a people by the memory of an event."

Although the meanings of the past and of history are of long-standing interest in anthropology, in recent years they have received renewed attention as subjects of investigation. Various ethnologists have explored how "the past" or tradition is invented, redefined, recreated, remembered, or incorporated into the present (Appadurai 1981; Behar 1986; Bloch 1977; Borofsky 1987; Eisenstadt 1973; Handler and Linnekin 1984; Handler 1991; Hobsbawn and Ranger 1983; Linnekin 1983; McDonald 1986; Sahlins 1985). Even historians, in their adoption of anthropological concepts and perspectives, have explored the ways in which memory is shaped, recalled, imagined, distorted, omitted, or reorganized (Thelen 1989:1120; also see Breen 1989, Lowenthal 1989). They emphasize how memories of the past are constructed for purposes of individual, group, or cultural identity (Thelen 1989).

A good example of this approach is provided by Hanson's (1989) extremely influential but controversial article on the making of the Maori.[1] Hanson argues that Maori lore, rather than being an authentic tradition, is a cultural invention of Europeans, including anthropologists. And yet he also points out that the Maori have not only accepted this invention as historical fact, but have incorporated it into their social movement of Maoriness or Maoritanga. As a result, they resist the efforts of latter-day anthropologists to determine the truth about the origins of their myths and lore. The past, from this perspective, is appropriated for particular purposes, and establishing what is true is of less concern than what is believed to be true.

In a similar vein, Fienup-Riordan (1988), writing about the production of a feature film focusing on the Apanuugpak story cycle of the Yup'ik people of Nelson Island in western Alaska, points to discrepancies between the anthropologist's understanding of history and that presented in the film. She tells us that the people of Nelson Island rendered their past in a particular way to the scriptwriter. As a result, "the tradition . . . , which may well appear to be old, is really quite recent in origin and has in fact been intentionally invented by the Nelson Islanders to establish continuity between their present political position and a suitable historic past" (1988:452). Reflecting on the problem, Fienup-Riordan not only draws an analogy to the Mead-Freeman debate, but also concludes that anthropology misses the point if it simply dismisses a particular rendition of history as inauthentic or inaccurate.

This latter point was also taken up at an Association of Social Anthropologists of the Commonwealth (ASA) conference on history and ethnicity that dealt with how the present creates the past. Some of the participants asked whether it was the business of anthropologists "to tell people under study that they were wrong" (Chapman, McDonald, and Tonkin 1989:9), to which others responded that it was a sad state of affairs when anthropologists could no longer assert what was true and what was false. Beyond these questions of truth and falsehood, issues of selective memory were also raised. Collard (1989), for example, explores, in the context of a Greek village, why certain historical periods and events are remembered while others are ignored or forgotten.

It is within this framework of the meaning of the past and the selective way in which it is remembered and represented that I have cast my account of a confrontation between the ethnographer and the people she has studied. The contested text that I discuss is not written but oral. More precisely, I deal with the impact and outcome of a keynote address that I gave at a meeting of members of the Illinois Center for French-Colonial Studies. The address was delivered at the Kankakee County Historical Society in Kankakee, Illinois, a town about seventy miles south of Chicago. To the east and south of Kankakee is the small rural community of Frenchtown (a pseudonym), a community where I had been conducting both historical and ethnographic research.[2] Frenchtown was settled in the 1850s by French-Canadian immigrants from the province of Quebec, and many descendants of those original settlers were in the audience for my lecture.

THE LECTURE

My lecture, titled "Habitants of the Prairies: French-Canadian Immigrants in Illinois," dealt with the history of settlement and particularly with the charismatic priest Charles Chiniquy, who was largely responsible for bringing between 900 and 1,000 French-Canadian families to Illinois in the middle of the nineteenth century. In my naïveté, I assumed that a lecture about history would be straight-forward, neutral, and unproblematic. The outcome was far from that and became an ethnographic lesson in the meaning of the past and of a founding hero to a local community.

When Charles Chiniquy died in 1899, his obituary in a local newspaper began, "Kankakee County has never conferred citizenship on so picturesque and notable a figure." With the exception of Abraham Lincoln biographers, who inevitably come across the pamphlet by Chiniquy in which he accused the Jesuits of mur-dering the Civil War president, most historians of America would not even recognize the Chiniquy name.[3] And yet the obituary characterization was no exaggeration. In the late 1850s and early 1860s the eyes of the international Catholic Church and of various Protestant denominations were turned on the French-Canadian settlements in Illinois and the schism that Charles Chiniquy had instigated there. All the religious tensions of this period when Know Noth-ingism was at its height were played out on the prairies of Illinois among a group whose very ethnic identity was rooted in Catholicism.[4]

As I rendered my version of the history of their community and the life of its founder, I skirted some of the more controversial aspects of Chiniquy's biog-raphy. I made little reference to the accusations of sexual misconduct that had surrounded him since his days at the Nicolet Seminary in Quebec. I did allude to his ability to enthrall, almost hypnotize, his audience; to his claims to having converted more than 200,000 French-Canadians in Quebec to abstinence; to the scandals in which he became embroiled soon after his arrival in Illinois (a lawsuit for slander, and the accusation that he had deliberately burned a church and absconded with the funds sent to rebuild it); and to his heated confrontation with the Irish Catholic Bishop O'Regan of Chicago, a confrontation that eventually led to his excommunication and conversion to Presbyterianism.

I went on to discuss some of the causes of French-Canadian emigration during the mid-nineteenth century and told my audience about the reactions—both pro and con—in the Quebec press to a letter that Chiniquy had published to encourage French-Canadian habitants to join him in the American Midwest. I described *les Tondeurs*, the group of Frenchtown residents who, under the leadership of Chini-quy's brother Achilles, organized themselves into a kind of vigilante group to intimidate Father Chiniquy's opponents; and I quoted from letters written by worried parishioners to the Bishop of Montreal in which they asked whether they should continue to receive communion from a priest who had been excom-municated—an act, by the way, that Chiniquy ignored for two years as his battle with Bishop O'Regan of Chicago continued.

I discussed the possibility that many of the letters written in support of Chiniquy and published in various French-language newspapers in Quebec may have been penned by the renegade priest himself. But I also spoke of the famine experienced by the French-Canadians of Illinois in 1858 and 1859 and of the funds that

Chiniquy raised, particularly among East Coast Presbyterians, to alleviate their suffering. Although I mentioned that many people at the time suggested that Chiniquy had grossly exaggerated this suffering (they even doubted the existence of a famine), I was able to document the extensive mortgaging of property and chattels at the time, a good indication of economic difficulties.

I went on to talk more specifically about the process by which Chiniquy and his supporters became Protestants, contextualizing the monetary response of East Coast Presbyterians to the plight of the French-Canadian schismatics in the Midwest with reference to a larger fear about the growing Catholic population in this region—a fear explicitly outlined some years earlier in Lyman Beecher's book *A Plea for the West.*

In 1860 Chiniquy and his followers formally allied themselves with the Presbyterian Church, having worshiped for two years as "Christian Catholics." In that year, the United States Census recorded close to 12,000 French-Canadian immigrants in Kankakee and Iroquois counties. I drew on this census to present my audience with a demographic and socioeconomic portrait of the first generation of settlers in Frenchtown and the neighboring satellite communities. These were the direct lineal ascendants of many people who were sitting in the room listening to me.

I then told my listeners that by October 1860 the minutes of the Chicago Presbytery (the overseeing body of the First Presbyterian Church of Frenchtown) reported "evils in the French Church of Frenchtown which the session of the Church now constituted are unable to redress." Certain elders, including Chiniquy's brother Achilles, were charged with immoralities. Achilles, who admitted to an "addiction to the use of profane language," agreed to withdraw from the position of elder. But the damage was done, and in February 1861 approximately 140 parishioners of the First Presbyterian Church of Frenchtown petitioned the Chicago Presbytery to be permitted to establish a second church under the leadership of a Reverend Monod who had stood in for Chiniquy while he was absent on a lecture tour. The Chicago Presbytery agreed to the separation, but not before Chiniquy's attempt to diminish Monod's character in a series of letters to church officials.

I then recounted Chiniquy's continuing problems with the Chicago Presbytery and the accusations that were leveled against him. Although initially cleared of these, he eventually decided to withdraw his church from the Presbytery of Chicago (claiming that they had "more Jesuitism than the Roman Catholic church"), and to join a presbytery in Canada. I quoted from a Canadian official who tried to communicate to his American colleagues a means by which to contextualize and comprehend Chiniquy's character and behavior.

I ended my lecture with a description of the reunification of these two Presbyterian churches in 1888, a second demographic and socioeconomic profile of the population of Frenchtown in 1900, and a discussion of the celebration of the patron saint's feast and the healing miracles that were reported between 1904 and 1909 that served to revive Catholicism in the area.[5] I closed by commenting on the stereotypes that have been developed to describe the French-Canadian immigrant experience in the United States—stereotypes that emerge largely from studies of New England factory towns; and I shared my hopes of correcting these through an examination of the experience of those who went to Illinois.

The floor was then opened to questions. I do not recall them all, but I was inevitably asked to develop my passing reference to sexual misconduct. Put on the spot, I attempted to give a balanced view, stating what the accusations were and when they arose, and ultimately concluding that it would be very difficult to prove their veracity. At one point, I was asked a question about the conversion itself. I launched into a comment about how significant and important this change was, and I emphasized even more strongly the roots of French-Canadian identity in religion, language, and customs (the basis of ethnic *survivance* or survival in Quebec until World War I).[6]

Prodded by this questioner, a member of the Center for French-Colonial Studies (i.e., not a resident of Frenchtown), I emphasized the evangelical fervor of Charles Chiniquy and the powers of persuasion that he must have had in order for so many of his parishioners to follow him into schism and to let go of an important piece of themselves (their religion) in the process. I recall pausing for five seconds as I debated in my own mind whether to move the discussion to another analytical level—was this the right audience? Perhaps mistakenly, I decided to "go for it," prefacing what was to follow with the observation that I hoped it would not be taken in the wrong way.

I told the audience of my interest in comparing Chiniquy to other charismatic leaders who had influenced people to make dramatic changes in their lives, or to do things that in a less heated moment they might not otherwise do—"like a Martin Luther," I said, making reference to a comparison that was made during Chiniquy's lifetime by Protestants, and, since I had been thinking and reading about it recently, I added, "like a Jim Jones."[7] Low but audible gasps came from a few corners of the room, and after the questions were over some residents of Frenchtown came up to challenge my comment about Jim Jones. I tried to explain further the way in which I was drawing the comparison—that I was not equating religious conversion with drinking poisoned Kool-Aid, but rather examining the influential relationship between a magnetic individual and a group of his followers. The evening wound down, and I went back to my motel room considering whether I should have said what I did, but at that point I was not concerned enough about it to lose any sleep.

THE OUTCOME

A few weeks after the lecture I received a letter from the minister of the First Presbyterian Church—the church that Chiniquy stripped of its Catholic symbols when he made it into a Protestant church. Although the building is not the original one, on the lawn outside, displayed in a glass case, is a piece of stone from the original building as well as a fragment from Chiniquy's own house, a structure that burned in the late nineteenth century. Inside the church is a bronze bust of Chiniquy, the father and founder of the First Presbyterian Church. Enclosed with the minister's letter, which I will return to shortly, was a newspaper clipping reporting on my lecture. The headline read "Anthropologist Sheds Light on Chiniquy," and set off in bold type in the middle of the first column was the sentence, "As a social scientist and anthropologist, Ms. Brettell says she can't help but compare this dynamic, yet powerful figure of the 1850s to the following Jim Jones had more than a century later."

The minister had marked several parts of the article with an orange highlighting pen: the name George instead of Charles (a mistake on the part of the reporter); the bold-typed box; the phrase "accused of everything from land fraud to adultery" (not words I used—adultery was never an issue); the phrase "Chiniquy was a troublemaker among his superiors in the Quebec diocese" (they did indeed think so, and I did allude to it, though never using the word "troublemaker"); the phrase "often made indecent comments against women and regularly preached overly [doubly highlighted] political sermons" (in my lecture I used precisely these words but characterized them as accusations and quoted from a letter from the Bishop of Montreal warning Chiniquy to "watch his language and to use moderation in his predications"); the phrase "created scandal after scandal" (I did mention several); the phrase "violence was rampant (the unsolved gruesome murder in 1898 of Chiniquy's nephew, Emile, and his wife, Victorine, was even linked to the schism)" (violence probably referred to my comment on the Tondeurs, but I never mentioned the murder that evening); the word "documented" with reference to the miracles of the early twentieth century (I used "reported" and "recorded"; the minister inserted a question mark in the margin); the phrase "Chiniquy, who continued to uphold his reputation as a womanizer," followed by the unhighlighted "eventually married Euphemie Allard in 1864" (I cannot find any place in the text of the lecture where I used the word "womanizer"; I may have made some reference to the marriage to his housekeeper in response to a question); and finally this paragraph: "He really did possess some commendable traits," she added, "especially his desire to educate his parishioners, the majority of whom were illiterate" (this is probably a direct quote taken from an interchange in the question and answer period—in the margin the minister wrote "O.K.").

Although the minister had been in the audience that night, although I had sent him a copy of a more extended article dealing with the history of Frenchtown and of Chiniquy, and although some items in the newspaper account came from old clippings in the *Kankakee Daily Journal* newspaper files rather than from the lecture,[8] he chose in his letter to reprimand me. He recognized the mistakes and some of the places where my opinions or more careful wording had been turned into historical fact. He acknowledged that a "parenthetical conjecture" (is parenthetical the word I would choose?) had been "blown out of proportion." Yet, he considered it unfortunate. "Presbyterians," he wrote, "will certainly not like the feeling that their Church here was based on the fanaticism of one who actually confused himself with God, as Jones did, and encouraged mass suicide.''

Using the newspaper account as a reference text, he labeled my characterization of Father Chiniquy "flat and distorted." "Accusations and rumors make good press," he claimed, "but they remain just that"—a point I carefully emphasized, though it was clearly not picked up by the newspaper that way. He thought that my description of Chiniquy's abstinence efforts in the years before he emigrated to Illinois was biased. (I did make the unfortunate and insensitive choice of the phrase "rabid advocate"). "From a much different perspective," he observed, "Chiniquy was way ahead of his time . . . and groups like MADD are just now catching up with him." He concluded his letter in the following way:

Certainly he was a rebel; certainly he was a charismatic personality in the sociological sense; certainly he was prone to exaggeration at times. Perhaps he sometimes was guilty of indiscretions or even scandalous behavior. But accurate history must attempt to view him as a human being and in many ways a moral and spiritual leader of his day—to see some reason for his views and some good in his life. It seems to me unbalanced to seem to believe every charge made against him, and then to turn around and believe without questioning the "documented" healing of the relics of St. A. I hope your book promises a more well-rounded view. Judging from his picture (see attached) that would be more true to life.

I was very upset by this letter, not only because this minister had been extremely supportive in helping me gain access to individuals in the community as well as to church documents stored at the Presbyterian Historical Society in Philadelphia, but also because it was apparent that I had clearly offended him as well as some other local residents who had traveled back to Frenchtown with him that night. However, as the days went by and as I formulated my response to his letter as well as a letter to the editor of the newspaper, I realized that what had happened provided some important lessons. It is to these that I would now like to turn.

THE LESSONS

In the preface to the paperback edition of her book *Saints, Scholars and Schizophrenics*, Nancy Scheper-Hughes (1979:v) calls the reactions of the people studied to the ethnographer's description and interpretation of the meaning of their lives an important source of ethnographic data. For me, this was indeed the case, because I learned in this one experience what the past really meant to at least some of the residents of Frenchtown, and particularly to the man who several generations later had succeeded as pastor of the church that Chiniquy had created. The past is a cultural possession, and I was naive in thinking that I was on safe ground in talking about it. Although I was not violating any personal confidences and thereby breaking specific ethical codes that are frequently and thoroughly discussed in the pages of the *Anthropology Newsletter*

C. Chiniquy. From *Fifty Years in the Church of Rome* by
Father Charles Chiniquy. Fleming H. Revell, 1886. Used
by permission.

and elsewhere, what I had done was to challenge a local interpretation and the local construction of a founding hero whose kindly demeanor sings out to present-day Frenchtown Presbyterians from his photograph.[9]

My references to the accusations of his moral weaknesses and my characterization of the kind of influence that a single individual can have over a collectivity, because they were not fully comprehended, were, to use Scheper-Hughes's word, "shattering." When the questions were posed, after brief hesitation, I chose not to ignore the warts either, and as a result I undermined the privilege of a community to manage its own history and its own identity. My oral text immediately became public property, and the accusations that interested me because they were part of a discourse and rhetoric of schism were turned, on the one hand, through journalistic mediation, into historical facts that I believed, and on the other into historical untruths that I was perpetuating.

If I was sensitized through this experience to the meaning of the past, I was also made aware of how the past shapes life in the present. The minister's comments about the "documented" miracles as opposed to the undocumented "facts" about Chiniquy's life are particularly revealing in this regard. The distinction is his, and it signifies that the rifts between Catholics and Protestants that tore this community apart in the mid-nineteenth century are still with them, if more subtle, and this despite repeated emphasis from both Catholics and Protestants on how the past was behind them. Annual ecumenical services are held in Frenchtown as evidence of this harmony. And yet, when pushed on the question residents admit that such services have special meaning in their community because of its particular history.

However, perhaps the most egregious error I made was in drawing comparisons that were incomprehensible, if not irrelevant, to local residents. Howard Becker (1964:273) has observed that the people who are the subjects of ethnographic fieldwork become very upset when something that is unique and special to them is treated as an instance of a class of events or objects. This is precisely what I was doing in trying to explore Chiniquy as an example of a charismatic leader with the ultimate purpose of addressing and understanding a rather abstract process. As hard as I tried, I was unable successfully to communicate precisely what I intended by introducing the case of Jim Jones.

Ultimately, this failure to communicate stems from the difference between the way our respondents understand and frame something and the way it is framed within ethnography or social science. In part, it is this difference that, as the introduction to this volume points out, explains the conflict surrounding the publication of *Small Town in Mass Society*.[10] But, more important, the failure to communicate emerges from the fact that we rarely define our respondents or informants as our primary readers. In our writings we are, in general, addressing ourselves, and while I hesitated for five seconds to consider the fact that my audience was other than my professional colleagues, I did not imagine the seriousness of the outcome. Indeed, I fully considered neither the presence of the media nor the possibility that my text would be highlighted in a particular way when it was re-presented in the newspaper. If selective memory reshapes history, selective reporting can reshape a text, and often does so for readership appeal.

Recently, several anthropologists, writing within a reflexive mode, have drawn our attention to the issue of audience. In her effort to reconcile two different versions of the history of the Yup'ik Eskimos, that of the filmmaker and that of the anthropologist, Fienup-Riordan (1988:451) concludes that there are different agendas. "Both of us," she writes, "must have the support of our peers for our work to succeed. To find backing for his film, Hunsacker [the filmmaker] had to convince the Sundance Institute that his script had broad dramatic appeal, not that his facts were correct. On the other hand, I must convince research agencies that there is something "special" but not necessarily of "universal appeal" about the Yup'ik people that merits detailed inquiry."

Lederman (1990:89) observes that once we leave the field our commitments tilt toward our professional community and away from the field community. Our presentation of material is "constrained by common anthropological idioms," or what Karp and Kendall (1982) refer to as the rhetorical forms of the discipline.[11] Anthropological texts are written "so as to exclude all but the committed fellow professional from the exclusive circle of understanding" (Spencer 1989:16). While this tilting toward our colleagues and away from our informants is easiest when our fieldwork site is located far from our professional world, Marilyn Strathern (1987a) has observed that the problems are the same for the ethnographer who does research in his or her own backyard. The anthropologist at home is, in her view, a writer "not so much for those he/she studies, who may well challenge his/her versions, but for colleagues, the main readership. For the ethnography is always to be compared and brought into relationship with a body of shared knowledge, and the contrivances of method and theory" (Strathern 1987:26). This body of shared knowledge is clearly foreign to the experience of the people we study.

Until we fully address and explore the question of for whom we are writing, and how we write for whom we write, we will not resolve the problem of the misunderstandings that are generated when those we write about read what we write, hear what we have to say, or read some mediated version of what we have written or said. Nor do I think that this problem has been eliminated by those who engage in the production of experimental ethnographies, for it is highly likely that these texts, unless they are truly coauthored (as is, for example, McBeth's in this volume), are inaccessible to those whose voices they presumably represent, as are more conventional ethnographies. Conversely, those texts that leave the anthropologist out can be puzzling to Western readers who may need a more omniscient interpretive voice to help them make sense of what they are reading.[12] The question we are left with is whether a single ethnographic account can ever successfully satisfy the diverse readership of late twentieth-century anthropology.

Renato Rosaldo (1989:50) has suggested that ethnographers "should take the criticisms of our subjects in much the same way that we take those of our colleagues. Not unlike other ethnographers, so-called natives can be insightful, sociologically correct, axe grinding, self-interested, or mistaken.'' The response to my oral text contained all of these elements, and in responding to it, perhaps with some self-interest, I too have gained insights which I hope are not mistaken. Joan Larcom (1982) has recently observed that a 1934 book by A. B. Deacon titled *Malekula: A Vanishing People in the New Hebrides* has been used by the people of the area as the final source for disputes about the past. Whether the written text that I produce will be used in the same way remains an open question, but somehow I doubt it.

CONCLUSION

I began this chapter by making reference to the relationship between anthropology and history, to a renewed interest in how the past is given meaning in the present, and to the way in which different representations of the past can become a contested arena. I want to explore this latter issue a little further in this conclusion in relation to a debate over text and the interpretation of history that emerged in the national press during the spring of 1991. This example demonstrates, I think, that the problems outlined here extend far beyond the production of ethnography.

In March 1991 an exhibition titled "The West as America: Reinterpreting Images of the Frontier 1820–1920" opened at the National Museum of American Art in Washington, D.C. This exhibition was a revisionist reading of westward expansion, a reading that toppled the heroic concept of Manifest Destiny and replaced it with an antiheroic history of capitalist exploitation and destruction. This new interpretation was evident not in the pictures hanging on the walls, but in the lengthy wall texts and catalogue that accompanied the show. The furor that erupted was not about images, but about the written word that mediated those images.

For many who saw the exhibition and read the texts, or who read about it in one of numerous media accounts, the experience was as shattering as those recounted in this and other chapters in this book. In the guest book accompanying the show, the famous historian and former Librarian of Congress Daniel Boorstin used epithets such as "perverse, historically inaccurate, and destructive" to describe what he had seen (cited in the *Village Voice*, June 25, 1991). An article in the *Washington Post* (March 15, 1991) claimed that the exhibition "amounts to a jeremiad against American idealistic art and westward expansion, seen through a politically corrective lens." Several months later a writer to the same newspaper said that to attack "a nation's founding myth is tantamount to burning the flag" (*Washington Post*, June 8, 1991). *New York* magazine reported on June 17, 1991, that the museum, thinking that it was "simply mounting an exhibition about current historical thinking," instead "touched on one of America's fundamental myths of origin and stepped into the midst of an acrimonious debate about the nation's future.''

While not all the comments were negative, and while some readers of the wall texts observed that the exhibition raised healthy issues for debate, the more generous assessments were overshadowed by a Congressional crowning blow. Robert McCormick Adams, the head of the Smithsonian, was called into the office of Senator Ted Stevens of Alaska, a man powerful enough in his position on the Appropriations Committee to cut off funding from an institution that he claimed should be ''a place where we really demonstrate the truth'' (quoted in the [Baltimore] *Sun*, June 9, 1991). Stevens warned Adams not to politicize the Smithsonian. The irony is that Senator Stevens was basing his attack not on his personal experience of the show, but on the press accounts. Again, it was the texts about the text that mediated and generated response.

What are the lessons to be learned from this lengthy debate in the national press (for indeed it reached as far as Chicago and Los Angeles, and the two museums that were to receive the show after its venue in Washington—Denver and St. Louis—cancelled their commitment, in some part due to the controversy)? Clearly, people have strong feelings about their past and the way that it is presented. As Verrey and Henley (1991:80) suggest, to challenge this representation is to ''undermine the meaning of an icon and run the risk of losing support or having our research devalued by the community.''

As history increasingly becomes an integral part of ethnography (Ortner 1984), anthropologists must be sensitive to the way that they write about it. Furthermore, while we may be intrigued by a turn of phrase such as the ''invention of the past,'' convinced by a framework that reconsiders the benefits of capitalism as it developed through time, or attracted to a mode of analysis that ignores the details in order to evaluate the structural relationship between a charismatic leader and his followers, our readers may not be. Indeed, they may be as offended by these approaches as they are by seeing in print things they considered private, uttered in a moment of confidence between friends rather than between anthropologist and respondent. Those who produced the text for ''The West as America'' thought they were providing a more truthful history, and they may indeed have introduced a set of voices that have hitherto been unheard, but perhaps they have fallen short in exploring questions of the ownership of and audience for this history. The questions of ''whose history is it?'' and ''for whom?'' remain both crucial and fundamental.

NOTES

1. For aspects of the controversy see Langdon (1991), Levine (1991), Linnekin (1991), and Hanson (1991).

2. This research was generously supported by the National Endowment for the Humanities and the Social Sciences and Humanities Research Council of Canada.

3. Lincoln defended Chiniquy in the 1855 slander suit brought against him.

4. A fuller account of this history can be found in Brettell (1985).

5. See Brettell (1990) for more detailed discussion of these miracles.

6. The influence of the Catholic Church began to erode after the war and especially after 1960. Language and culture, of course, are still the basis of French-Canadian survival in Quebec today. For a discussion of *survivance* see Wade (1950).

7. Jim Jones was the pastor of the People's Temple. In November 1978, having led his parishioners to a settlement called Jonestown in Guyana, Jones convinced over 900 of them to commit mass suicide by drinking poisoned Kool-Aid. See Hall (1989) for an analysis of Jones and the Jonestown suicide.

8. I know this because I had examined them myself some months before. In the article there is a reference to Chiniquy once leading a crowd in tearing down a brewery. I am not aware of the incident and therefore certainly made no mention of it.

9. Although the minister did not wish to sanitize Chiniquy fully, such a process, as Roseberry (1989) suggests, does occur, and itself carries meaning. For additional discussion of the conflict between local history and that collected and interpreted by specialists, see Verrey and Henley (1991).

10. In his evaluation of the reception of this text, Becker (1964:273) writes that the relationship between the social scientist and those he studies contains elements of irreducible conflict emanating from the differences in approach between the scholar on the one hand and the layperson on the other.

11. Hanson (1991:450) pursues the same line of thinking in pointing to the use of the word "invention," as in "the invention of tradition," as a rhetorical device that catches the attention of readers. He evaluates its advantages as well as its dangers, particularly the danger of being misunderstood by those who feel that the authenticity of their actions is being challenged. To most people, he observes, invention means made up and therefore not genuine. This meaning is imputed even if it is unintended by the anthropologist.

12. Spencer (1989:156) criticizes Crapanzano's *Tuhami* and Dwyer's *Moroccan Dialogues* (1982) for precisely this reason.

7

WHEN THEY READ WHAT THE PAPERS SAY WE WROTE

Ofra Greenberg

In October 1989 my book *A Development Town Visited* was published in Israel (in Hebrew). The book contains an account of my experiences in Kiryat Shmona, a community where I lived and conducted research for five years. Kiryat Shmona was founded on Israel's northern border in 1950, largely as a result of a government policy promoting the geographical distribution of the population. It was settled by new immigrants from North Africa, Iraq, and Hungary, and was given the status of "development town" on the strength of its location and the composition of its population. This entitled both the municipality and its citizens to various government dispensations.

Within a few years, most of the inhabitants of European origin (Ashkenazis) had moved to the center of the country. By the 1980s, 90 percent of the population of 15,000 was of oriental origin, characterized by a low educational level (half the population had only an elementary education), negligible professional training, and low average income. During the period under study, families there were receiving welfare support at a rate 50 percent above the national average, partly a result of the high proportion of families with four or more children. Most of the inhabitants defined themselves as being religious, or at least as adhering to Jewish tradition.

At the outset of my research I was interested in the utilization of traditional medicine by immigrants from oriental countries. While attempting to investigate the extent and nature of this activity, I also looked into the characteristics and quality of the established medical services. Since Kiryat Shmona is situated far from the center of the country and has a predominantly low-income population, modern, private medicine was all but nonexistent. Virtually all medical services were provided by Kupat Holim, a medical insurance organization belonging to the labor federation.

I discovered early on that a large segment of the population was utilizing the services of practitioners of traditional medicine. Residing in the town were several folk healers who employed a variety of techniques which included charms and combinations of herbs. They treated a diversity of physical, emotional, and social complaints. A considerable proportion of their patients simultaneously sought help from conventional physicians for ailments beyond the scope of the folk healers, such as heart problems or cancer. Some were treated by both folk and conventional medicine for the same complaint (e.g., depression, infertility), with the conventional practitioners utterly unaware that their patients were receiving treatment from folk healers. Use of folk medicine was concealed from establishment figures such as teachers, nurses, and social workers, since patients were apprehensive of their hostile and dismissive attitude toward such "primitive methods."

In due course, I broadened the scope of my observation to include the operation of the other social services, in particular the welfare and educational agencies. The findings revealed a predominantlty passive population supported by a variety of social services. Moreover, this population demanded greater practical and financial support from the services than that provided for by the formal regulations and criteria (e.g., a demand for a full subsidy for children attending a summer camp rather than the 75 percent subsidy that had been offered). By contrast, in the realm of folk medicine—a sphere of activity whose existence is not recognized by the authorities—people acted independently, with initiative and even mutual assistance.

After the publication of my book I was interviewed by a young journalist from a small left-wing newspaper. Her review grossly distorted facts and displayed a complete misunderstanding of the book's contents. According to this journalist, the people of Kiryat Shmona were depicted by me in a venomous manner, as being cruel and generally obnoxious. I quote from her article:

Upon reading the book, only a masochist would want to visit the place. Kiryat Shmona, according to Greenberg's description, is a horrible town. The residents' outlook on life and their attitudes are fundamentally flawed, they are selfish and evil, public office holders are corrupt, the doctors and teachers are the worst imaginable. . . . During the five years she spent in Kiryat Shmona, Greenberg found innumerable negative traits among the town's residents, which she proceeds to enumerate one by one. First and foremost is the irritating tendency to change one's place of work. As if possessed, they leap this way and that, until at times it seems as though all of Kiryat Shmona is in a mad spin. (*Hotam*, November 10, 1989, p. 8)

She continues: "They don't know how to organize their meals or their lives so as to ensure that all the family is satisfied and healthy." In support of each such claim a quote is produced from the book, removed from its context and often distorted, as in the following phrase: "the greengrocer, a cunning and avaricious young man." This did not appear in the book, and neither did the following supposed quote: "The shoppers slice the cheese themselves with their filthy hands."

This journalist referred to a 1949 newspaper report about North African immigrants. (I have not checked its authenticity.) This report claimed that "we have here a people primitive in the extreme; their level of education is pitifully low, and worst of all, they are unable to absorb anything of intellectual value." She then added her own observation: "Forty years on, Greenberg does the same thing, the only difference being that she cloaks her argument in rational explanations." Purporting to quote from her interview with me, the journalist records a question she did not ask, and an answer I did not give: "One gathers from reading the book that the residents are worse than the establishment?" . . . "That is what happens during the initial period there, they behave atrociously towards outsiders." . . . "It seems that you have difficulty accepting the residents of Kiryat Shmona because you feel superior to them."

In her article, the journalist somehow connected the presentation of "the bad people of Kiryat Shmona" with the analysis of weakening family commitment. She is scornful of my analysis of the effect of social factors on the behavior of the members of the community, maintaining that I am suggesting that their inhuman behavior stems from their evil character. In fact, my analysis of the disappearance of family commitment does not imply any criticism of the local people. In the book I present in a neutral way the social conditions (in particular the proliferation of welfare services) that induce the general passivity of town residents toward their lives, expressed here in the evasion of family responsibilities and the expectation that the authorities will intervene. This pattern of behavior constitutes a surprising finding, considering that we are dealing with a traditional community characterized by binding family ties in its country of origin and during the initial period of settlement in Israel.

The journalist concluded her review by portraying me as an arrogant, privileged individual who observes the "natives" from a superior viewpoint, "like the traditional European anthropologist who investigated the native Africans, and who enjoys describing their backward and cruel world." She emphasized my affiliation with the veteran sector of Israeli society, my European origins, my secularity, and my academic education, and underscored the extent to which these attributes make me quite different from the people I studied. It was thus easy to characterize me as a European colonialist, invading the lives of the natives out of sheer curiosity.

This newspaper article was soon brought to the attention of the people of Kiryat Shmona, and they reacted angrily. I was attacked in the local newspaper and received several telephone complaints. In fact, the furor in the town eventually caught the attention of the national radio. A publication that would otherwise have reached only a circumscribed and mainly professional readership became, with the help of media exposure, a news item broadcast throughout the country. The controversy died down only when the editor of the local newspaper curtailed the publication of further letters. However, it had gone on long enough in print to ensure that almost everyone in the town had heard about the issue.

In this chapter I describe and analyze the reactions of the investigated population to the book's contents, paying particular attention to the role of the press in mediating the reading of my ethnography as well as in defining me, a native anthropologist, as a foreigner and an outsider.[1]

HOW THE COMMUNITY RESPONDED

Direct Responses

The stream of reactions was not monolithic. People responded differently to the publication, in general according to their position in society. In addition to the townfolk, responses came from friends and acquaintances, from public figures and politicians, and from professionals. Some responses were direct and others were indirect. The first direct response came through a phone call from an indignant acquaintance from Kiryat Shmona. Born in the town, she worked for the welfare services with senior citizens. "Ofra, what have you done to us?" she exclaimed. "How could you sling mud at us like that, after we accepted you so warmly?" I was surprised and embarrassed. Although the journalist had promised to send me a copy of the article as soon as it appeared, she had failed to do so. I did not know how to reply to this caller. Once I had managed to obtain a copy of the newspaper from friends living on a nearby kibbutz, I was appalled by what I read.

Some days later, the local Kiryat Shmona paper, *Maida Shmona*, printed an article written by the leader of the municipal opposition. This man also had an administrative position in the academic institution where I had taught, and he knew me personally. In the article he wrote: "Ofra, or rather Dr. Ofra Greenberg, who honored us by her presence, resided in Kiryat Shmona . . . and collected incriminatory material about the locals . . . the measure of evil, contempt, hatred, and in particular racism exhibited by one person towards an entire population, is equivalent to a lethal dose of cyanide." Later in his article, he admitted not having read the book, claiming, "The [newspaper] article is good enough for me."

From this point onwards, the episode rapidly developed into a full-scale public furor. People used different mechanisms to direct their criticisms at me. Personal acquaintances used the telephone. A friend who lived in the vicinity of Kiryat Shmona and who had worked with me at the local college was among the first to call. I explained the distortion in the newspaper account and suggested that she read the book, which she promised to do. She advised me to reply to a letter in the local paper, as silence on my part would be regarded as an admission of guilt. I took her advice and my letter appeared. It elicited no direct response.

Several other people called to express their support. These included a secretary at my former college who had spoken to the friend mentioned above; a former student who asked me to send him the book (unavailable in Kiryat Shmona); a volunteer teacher; and a former local journalist who had since moved to Jerusalem. The latter told me that after receiving a copy of *Maida Shmona* from his brother, he had immediately bought the book and read it in a day. He was calling to convey his support, as he could imagine how hurt I must feel. In his opinion, the book portrayed a true, if in part painful, picture of the place. He found in it considerable affection for the local people, and considered the "review" to be blatantly unfair both to the book and to me. He also mentioned that he had persuaded his brother to read the book, and his brother subsequently wrote a letter of support that was published in a different local paper.

In addition to telephone calls, I also received a number of letters, including one from the chief rabbi of Kiryat Shmona, with whom I was personally acquainted. He wrote with sympathy and support that "it is sufficient to photocopy the book's pages, conveying their love; there is no simpler or more relevant evidence. To my mind, the article in the newspaper . . . was an expression of the feeling that 'an outsider cannot understand us,' and A.'s aggressive review was a faithful expression of Kiryat Shmona's complexity, which you have portrayed with a craftsman's hand."

I received another letter from a member of Parliament who had lived in Kiryat Shmona for a while and to whom I had sent a copy of my book. He wrote: "A wave of memories swamped me upon reading the book, and the characters you describe so well—with sympathy, understanding, compassion and warmth—appeared before me again. . . . I believe that this little book, which contains so much warmth and beauty, will find a path to the hearts of Kiryat Shmona's people." This member of Parliament, an active and well-known public figure in Israel, also wrote to the national newspaper.

My husband telephoned two or three friends who worked in the public service in Kiryat Shmona (the director of the urban renewal project, the coordinator of programs at the local community center) to enquire about their opinions. They reported that they had found it very difficult to accept the article in *Maida Shmona*, and that they wished to read the book. Once they had done so (I sent copies), they called back, expressing support and inviting us to visit them. They added that many people in Kiryat Shmona were now hostile toward me. The community center coordinator told us that there had been a number of lively discussions about the book among center employees. After people had read it a staff meeting was devoted to further debate about it.

Indirect Reports

News of reactions reached me indirectly as well as directly. From a neighbor whose brother lives in Kiryat Shmona I received a report of the uproar that broke out after the local publication. The brother added that he would advise me to keep well away from the town. A friend who works near Kiryat Shmona, and who comes into contact with town residents, told of their anger and of the reaction of one man to a suggestion that he read the book. ''I've read the article, and that's good enough for me.'' Another friend who teaches in the Department of Social Work at Haifa University reported a furious outburst from a student from Kiryat Shmona when my book was mentioned during a lesson. She had not read the book.

There were also responses in the local press. The first letter came from a lawyer, a Kiryat Shmona resident of many years' standing who was also a personal acquaintance of mine. He asked me to send him the book and wrote to the paper after he had read it. I quote from his published letter at length.

The reader will find a serious, balanced and fair work of research into the structure of Kiryat Shmona's community, and the institutions that are supposed to serve this community. The author does not refrain from criticism, but likewise does not fail to record the positive aspects of this community. If the research is not entirely objective, this is due to the sense of pain born of love, which is evident in the book.

A copy of Ofra's book is to be found in the library of the college at which A. works, but he has not bothered to read it, preferring to criticize the book, and what is more, also the author (whom he knew personally during her five year stay in Kiryat Shmona), on the strength of a tendentious publication in the supplement ''Hotam.'' This was A.'s first ''foul.'' His second mistake was in failing to elicit the author's response. These two transgressions led A. to produce an amazing collection of unfounded and malicious slander, to which the term ''character assassination'' may be applied as an understatement.

No less serious than the damage caused by A.'s slanderous attack is the general outlook from which it derives. Unfortunately, this outlook is not peculiar to him . . . and is shared by most of those who represent and form public opinion in Kiryat Shmona. According to this outlook, mere residence in the town endows its inhabitants with rights devoid of obligations; the residents, and in particular their leaders, are above all criticism. Should the mirror reflect an ugly image, or the thermometer indicate the existence of a disease, they must be broken! (November 20, 1989, p. 20)

The local paper published three other responses, two of which expressed support from people who had read the book, while the other, from someone who read only the article, was angrily antagonistic. I received a long letter in favor of my book and castigating A.'s behavior, which the editor of *Maida Shmona* chose not to publish on the grounds of lack of space.

HOW THE NATIONAL NEWSPAPER RESPONDED

The discussion in the national newspaper *Hotam* was of a more academic and professional nature than that in the local paper *Maida Shmona*. In one camp were the author, a member of Parliament, a university anthropology lecturer, and the publisher's editor, all of whom criticized the journalist's abuse of press freedom in the form of distortion of the facts. The respondents were the journalist and the editor of *Hotam*.

Whereas the correspondence in the local paper revealed emotions such as anger and hurt, and dwelt upon personal and emotive issues, such as the author's character and qualifications and the accuracy of descriptions of the town, the discussion in *Hotam* focused on general questions, such as the role of the press, or the anthropologist, as a detached and balanced observer. For example, the university anthropology lecturer wrote:

The contents, style, and spirit [of the article] constitute, in my opinion, a crass and disgraceful exploitation of the sacrosanct ideal of press freedom, in the name of which such an article can be published. . . . This is not merely a matter of quoting out of context, or of sarcastic comments with no basis whatsoever in the book, but mainly of the selective and tendentious manner in which the journalist has chosen to convey her own messages. . . . Finally, as a social anthropologist, I protest at the irreversible damage caused by the journalist to the reputation of the discipline. . . . The residents of Kiryat Shmona and of other development towns may, with justification, regard your article as an incitement to a renewal of inter-ethnic conflict. Had Ms. X done justice to the book, she may have discerned its constructive aspects, and by so doing may have encouraged political and social action designed to further the welfare and interests of the residents, who are deprived by the establishment and paid venomous and hypocritical lip-service by the media, of the sort exemplified by the article. (*Hotam*, December 1, 1989)

The journalist replied by alleging that the chapter containing descriptions of interesting and sympathetic characters had been added under pressure from the publisher (a complete fabrication), and that the complaint about quoting out of context was a routine and devious defense.

Finally, the publisher's editor responded by claiming that what infuriated him about the article was "not only its distortion of the book's contents, but also the malice evident between the lines. . . . The journalist from *Hotam* has missed the point of the book. She makes only brief mention of the governing institutions' responsibility for Kiryat Shmona's condition. Ironically, the establishment and its failings are let off extremely lightly by the crusading journalist" (*Hotam*, December 1, 1989).

MAKING SENSE OF THE RESPONSES

Perhaps the most interesting aspect of the reaction of members of the community where the research was conducted is that it was by no means monolithic. People both accepted and rejected the contents of the publication as well as the choice of action taken (or not taken) by government agencies as a result of the conclusions drawn. Their position was influenced by a number of factors including their public role, their level of education, issues of self-image, and their personal acquaintance with the researcher.

Certain local politicians used the event to further their own interests, that is, to achieve popularity by identifying with the "humiliated" public and by berating the "stranger." For example, the mayor of the town, who had his eye on a career in Parliament, added his comment to the original article when approached by the journalist. His reaction was given without reading the book and without checking her version with me. Quoting a Hebrew idiom, he spoke of the good people of the town being maligned by career-minded outsiders who "spat in the well from which they had drunk."[2]

The leader of the municipal opposition, an ambitious contender for the mayorship, also made no attempt to clarify the facts with me. His theme was ethnic prejudice and the lack of integrity on the part of educated Ashkenazis like myself. This theme, a recurring one in Israeli party politics, has been successfully invoked by the major right-wing party to win the votes of oriental Jews. Vidich and Bensman (1958b:4) observe that in Western society no reaction is to be expected when the ethnography deals with marginal or minority groups. In Israel, however, the poor and uneducated oriental population is somehow protected from public criticism, which can easily be construed by interested politicians as ethnic or even racial prejudice.

A few people read the book in order to form their own opinion, but the great majority of the public relied solely on information gathered from newspapers and formed their opinions on that basis. It appears that the higher a person's level of education, the greater was his ability and inclination to examine the facts independently (in this case by reading the book). The more educated individuals in the community were less likely to accept the newspaper account as the truth and more likely to take action beyond the confines of their immediate surroundings—by writing to the local or national press, for example.

There is a powerful relationship between self-esteem and a tendency to defend oneself and protest against criticism. In Israel, the correlation between oriental ethnic origin, low educational level, and low income has given rise to a paternalistic attitude on the part of the establishment toward the oriental communities. One of the by-products of this attitude has been low self-esteem among many of the uneducated oriental Jews who have no confidence in their ability to exert influence and to bring about change, and who therefore took no action with regard to my book even when they could have responded. This pattern of inactivity was evident in many aspects of life, some of which are discussed in *A Development Town Visited*. The general lack of active response upon reading the article in the local paper is symptomatic of this syndrome.[3]

On the other hand, when those suffering from low self-esteem imagine that their weakness is being pointed out, they are apt to react strongly. In the development town under discussion, many of the public officeholders had little formal education. The leader of the municipal opposition, who held a senior administrative position in the college although lacking a complete academic education, was quick to ridicule my doctor's title as well as my discipline as part of his defense of himself and his community.

While responses differed depending on factors such as public role and level of education, there were nevertheless a few issues around which objections were fairly uniform. One of these was my discussion of family ties and obligations.

Not every issue will arouse the same intensity of objection, and they will vary from one culture to the next. In Israel, the family is clearly a sensitive topic.[4]

The role of the family in the national myth has, over the years, undergone several changes that have been bound up with the complex pattern of relationships between Ashkenazi and oriental Israelis. In the initial period of statehood, emphasis was placed by official ideology on the individual's commitment to society, whereas the importance of family attachment was considerably muted.

Later years brought with them a change in official attitudes toward the culture of oriental Jews in general, and toward the place of the family in that culture in particular. This change was due to complex sociopolitical processes. An accumulation of sociological knowledge stressed the importance of social continuity for the successful absorption and social adaptation of immigrants, and explained the central role played by the stability of the community and the family in the process of social integration. In a parallel development, political changes brought the "attitude toward oriental Jews" to the forefront of party political struggles, with the main right-wing party successfully turning it into a major election issue. The primary argument was that the time had come to respect once again the neglected honor of oriental Jews by, among other means, fostering their special culture, and by respecting their traditions.

As a result, there has been a revival in the value attached to the family. Whereas during the early years an effort was made to "modernize" the oriental Jews, recent years have seen a glorification of the "good qualities" of oriental ethnic groups (as a result of both social consciousness and political manipulation). Among the components that form this romantic-nostalgic idealization is the extended, warm, supportive family. This image plays its part in the newly acquired ethnic pride among some of the orientals. To question its validity in public discussion is unacceptable, although in private many orientals admit that reality falls far short of the ideal type. Nevertheless, a description perceived to be critical of an important component of the recently established community pride (in this case also ethnic pride) causes an emotion-laden response.

As Brettell points out in the introduction to this volume, sensitivity on the part of an investigated community to its public image has been noted by other anthropologists following reactions to the publication of their research. Scheper-Hughes, for example, reports that people do not object to the distortion of reality, but rather to seeing it in print. They are willing to accept her writing about them—even if it is critical—as long as it is not widely published, even though this is intended to benefit them.[5] Conversely, criticism of public institutions such as schools or a health clinic is readily accepted because responsibility is easily assigned to outsiders, in particular to government offices and officials. It is, in short, the violation of self-image, that brings about the stormiest reactions.

CONCLUSION: THE PRESS AS MEDIATOR

Newspapers played a leading role in shaping the response to the publication of *A Development Town Visited*. Most of Kiryat Shmona's residents would not have heard about the book's publication had it not been for the appearance of the article. Without the journalist's subjective and tendentious interpretation there would have been no public outcry.[6]

Anthropological literature provides us with several examples of the manner in which the press magnifies the resonance of a research report, selectively publishing certain sections in an endeavor to provoke the interest of readers. Renato Rosaldo (1989:63) describes the reactions to his research among the Ilongot in the Philippines, while Gmelch (1992) had a similar experience in Ireland. The account extensively reported in the introduction to the present volume of the Italian media representation of Schneider's work strikes a familiar note, as does Wrobel's (1979) account of his treatment by the Detroit press.[7]

The conflict between the anthropologist and the journalist arises out of a discrepancy of interests and a different professional ethic. First, the journalist is guided by a goal of drawing maximum attention to his product. In some cases this is achieved by distorting the facts in order to create a more sensational effect. Second, his professional ethic allows him to make value judgments on the material he presents. Some journalistic ideologies (e.g., "new journalism" [DeFleur and Dennis 1981]) go so far as to encourage the journalist to express his own subjective opinions. Many journalists thus find it difficult to understand the complex approach of the anthropologist, who can respect the people he or she researches while at the same time describing and analyzing their behavior from a neutral perspective. The anthropologist does not make judgments, whereas the journalist in many cases does. The work of the anthropologist is thus evaluated according to journalistic criteria. This results in misunderstanding.

The press is often perceived by the public as a representative of society and its product as a reliable reflection of reality. The question of whether a certain event really did take place (in our case, whether the book actually contains derogatory material) becomes largely irrelevant. Most people will not bother to read the original book or article, as they "know what is written there already." The information that sticks is that put out by the media.

The media's version of the "truth" becomes the issue under discussion as the publication galvanizes an aggregation of individuals into a community under attack, seeking to defend its honor. The debate takes on a life of its own beyond the control of the ethnographer, and around issues (in this case the role of the family in Israel and the status of various ethnic groups) that may not even have been central in the original text.

What happened after the publication of *A Development Town Visited* is yet another instance of how the press shapes reality. As early as the 1920s Lippmann (1922) was aware of the communication media's ability to create their own version of reality. Consequently, people do not react to objective reality, but to an environment perceived through the media. More recently, theoreticians (including neo-Marxists) have discussed the "constructing of reality." According to them, the mass communication media necessarily present a nonobjective picture of reality and thus affect the moral and ideological perception of what is "really going on." For example, if a certain unusual phenomenon is presented from the conservative viewpoint of social consensus, the coverage will tend, indirectly, to denigrate the deviant phenomenon, thereby affirming the existing consensus (Cohen 1972). This "spiral of silence" theory (Noelle-Neumann 1974) maintains that the communication media not only form the image of reality, but actually intervene to play a part in forming reality itself by urging people to action or to passivity on the strength of distorted information. They thus bring about a result that would otherwise not have occurred (for example, people who do not bother to vote because they have been led by the press to believe that theirs is a lost cause). The press, in short, is a powerful factor influencing what happens when the people we write about read what we write.

NOTES

1. It would be possible to expand the discussion of the responses by including readers from outside the community, such as friends and fellow professionals. Here I focus primarily on the community in which the research was conducted and its variety of responses.

2. Criticism of me as a stranger and an outsider, although I am an indigenous anthropologist with shared citizenship, religion, and language, was very powerful. I was defined as an outsider because it was then easier to oppose my analysis, and to define it as emanating from ulterior motives for personal advancement. Evans-Pritchard (1968:173–174) describes the role of the mediator among the Nuer. This role is performed by a person belonging to one certain lineage who derives his authority from being an "outsider" (belonging to a specific lineage). To the outside observer, the mediator seems hardly to differ from other Nuer people, but from within he is an outsider. I find my position as "stranger" to be quite similar.

3. It is interesting to note that none of the town's inhabitants wrote to the national newspaper, although several had promised to do so. The sense of social distance proved decisive; the townfolk did not feel sufficiently at ease or confident to contact the strange, "far-away" newspaper.

4. I had been apprehensive about objections that readers might voice with regard to my presentation of this topic, but I never imagined the intensity of the reactions. It must, however, be emphasized once more that the majority of those reacting in this manner had read only the commentary mediated by the press.

I admit to having had some misgivings about writing on the subject of a lack of family commitment, knowing that this would be a sensitive issue in Jewish culture in general, and among oriental Jews in particular. I was naive enough to believe that anyone reading the sociological explanations of this process would not regard my presentation of the phenomenon as an allocation of blame. Whereas the press's distortions came as a complete surprise, I could have foreseen that most of the local people would not read the book, but would merely seek a short summary of its contents, and would therefore have taken offense in any case. I was consciously thinking of a specific readership, made up of professionals and a slightly wider circle of interested general readers.

5. As an aside, I must admit to harboring some faint hope that the contents of the book would gain the attention of public authorities, who would then amend their policies in such a way as to bring about changes in phenomena such as apathy and lack of

commitment. Unfortunately, I can report no such change of policy. What remains is the sense of humiliation and betrayal among residents.

6. Unless a local politician had learned of the book's publication, bothered to read it, and then used it to further his aims, I consider this an unlikely possibility.

7. I find a good deal of similarity between my experience and that of Wrobel, beginning with the quotes taken out of context, which lead the innocent reader to believe that the author was "blaming the victim," and continuing with the way in which other communications media took up and broadcast the issue. His reactions to the publication are also familiar, including the use of personal contacts to get friends from the community he researched to read the book, thereby gaining their understanding and moral support.

Part IV

COLLABORATIVE TEXTS: ETHICS, NEGOTIATION, AND COMPROMISE

8

IS ANONYMITY POSSIBLE? WRITING ABOUT REFUGEES IN THE UNITED STATES

MaryCarol Hopkins

Enter the side yard through a gap in the chainlink fence and walk down the concrete, past the blue bike rusting and fenderless, past the torn overstuffed couch, past the refrigerator, to the backyard. Step over the puddles and the milky water gushing from a pipe protruding from the side of the house. The two-year-old and three-year-old, in pink lace dresses but no underpants, grin their greeting as they look up from their delight in the cool mud. If you pause, you will have a dancing-eyed beauty in your arms, a kiss on your cheek.

Step up, carefully because the steps have sunken and parted from the house, out of the August heat into the dark cool of the kitchen. Shoes are heaped in the entryway, an electric skillet and wok are on the floor, a ricepot and dishes tower precariously on the small bench that serves as table and work-counter. The faucet runs steadily because it can't be turned off; flies cover the food and dishes because there are no screens on the windows. At the far end where the stove sits, the floor angles downward rakishly so that pots skid to the back of the stove, and the floor no longer meets the wall, so daylight, and perhaps other things, seep in.

Just beyond, we find sixteen-year-old Ly in the only other room, the bedroom she shares with her mother, four brothers, and three sisters; her father and other siblings died of disease or starvation or overwork. The beds are neatly made, the green peeling paint on the walls is posted over with school awards and pictures of Buddha, and the dresser is arrayed with incense, candles, and vases of flowers. Profusions of flowers in pink, fuschia, turquoise, and gold fill the room. The doorway is framed with flounced organza, and a curtain of sparkling beads creates a sense of separation between the two rooms. Crepe paper, tinsel streamers, and multicolored Christmas lights festoon the walls and doorways, looping around photos of the father and other ancestors. The high-pitched notes of Asian singing and strings rise in the air amid the sweet and pungent smells of incense and cooking spices.

I am taking Ly to McDonald's for a job interview, and for the occasion she has chosen a floor-length taffeta skirt of bold Christmas plaid—red, green, black, and white—and a fuschia, blue, and pink plaid ruffled blouse. She sews with skill, and has added lace flounces of various colors to the skirt. Spike heels and many gold necklaces and barrettes complete her outfit.

"Do you have your Social Security card?" I remind her.

"No, my Mom have."

Mom is "out," and may have been for the previous day too, Ly not knowing where or when she might return. I have stressed the importance of the card to her for several days, and I am annoyed that she has neglected to get it. "What about the kids?" She hustles them into the house under the supervision of five-year-old Pia and locks them in with a key; they cannot stay outside, because the neighbors throw garbage, chairs, and epithets at them.

En route, I explain to Ly that she must try to look at the interviewer. She laughs and says yes, their teacher at school has told them about that, but she assures me she could never do such a thing. When we arrive, she has no idea how to answer the questions on the application form—she's not clear which name is her last and which her first, doesn't know her phone number or the name of her school. She doesn't know the word "hobby," and when I suggest she answer the question about "interests and skills" by saying that she has had lots of experience working with children, she prints out simply, "wt chldrs."

Now, Ly is not a dull girl. She gets straight As in her classes in English as a second language and has earned many awards at school, including a citywide art contest, the entry for which hung for a time in City Hall. But she didn't see her picture there or even know it was there. In fact, she does not know that a four-year college scholarship awaits her if she keeps up her grades, though her teachers and minister know. No, Ly is in fact quite a bright girl, strikingly beautiful, and probably has more potential and more possibilities open to her than most of the girls in her community.

But she hasn't been hired by McDonald's. She is dismissed from the interview with a "We'll call you," while we see other young people filling out tax forms and receiving information about the training program. We both know the call won't come. As consolation I offer to take her out for pizza. "No, rice; need rice to grow. Only rice make you big and strong." She attributes the interview failure to her small stature and youthful shape. At four she still could not walk because of malnutrition, and now at sixteen she looks twelve and weighs only eighty-two pounds ("American girls so BIG, you know?"). So we go for rice and soda pop, and talk of her probable upcoming marriage. Her mother, trapped by illiteracy, lack of English, lack of urban job skills, and three preschool children, has arranged a marriage for her. If Ly is unable to get this job, she may help the family best by bringing a son-in-law into the household to help her mother with the tremendous financial burden of raising the seven younger siblings. "I don't want, but what can I do? She my Mom."

Anthropologists have always been faced with the conflict between the search for knowledge and the moral responsibilities that knowledge, particularly knowledge about people for whom we have come to care, brings. In recent years four trends have developed in anthropology that particularly affect the way we carry out and present the results of our research, and that must cause us to look even more closely at those moral responsibilities. One of these trends has been a turn, for various reasons, toward research closer to home. While one cause for this shift may certainly be funding, another is the deliberate effort to distance ourselves from the stigma of an earlier generation now often accused of "studying down" or, worse, being a part of the colonial process by studying only cultures unable to defend themselves from such study—a kind of anthropological colonialism. Whether studying American drug addicts, college students, day-care centers, lesbian families, and refugee communities really removes us from similar culpability is an important ethical issue, but a slightly separate one from that which I am raising here. This shift toward research within the United States, often quite close to our own environments, has several consequences which in turn result in important ethical problems.

First, this close-to-home research means that the project has the possibility of being more long-term, as well as more sporadic or intermittent, and thus the fieldwork may come to interweave with our everyday lives—families, work, even friends may occasionally become enmeshed with our field community or its members. It also means that we are often researching cultures or subcultures that are literate and that may therefore eventually read the studies produced.

A second current movement is being led by feminist anthropologists, who urge that we consider our informants as audience (Caplan 1988) and write only what will be acceptable to them, while others (Kaplan 1988; Iamo 1988) have urged that we write only what will actually benefit the community under study.

During this same period, there has also developed the postmodernist concern with our writing, with the poetics of anthropology. Anthropologists as early as the Boasians have been attentive to their literary craftwork, but in the past decade works by Marcus and Fischer (1986) and Clifford and Marcus (1986) have rekindled and focused this concern. We are urged to write "thick description" (Geertz 1973), to attend to the art of the telling (Van Maanen 1988); we are reminded that the great contribution anthropology can make to the social sciences is our ability to "richly contextualize" (Pitman and Maxwell 1992:768) our findings.

And finally and most recently, the American Anthropological Association (AAA) has been revising the Principles of Professional Responsibility (generally referred to as the "code of ethics"). Although the general intent is not radically changed from the principles fieldworkers have followed for nearly two decades, the code under recent consideration is more emphatic: "Anthropologists must respect, protect and *promote* the rights and *welfare* of all of those affected by their work" (American Anthropological Association 1990; emphasis mine). In addition, several recent books have addressed themselves to this issue of ethics in fieldwork (Punch 1986; Fluehr-Lobban 1991) and in anthropology in general (Cassell and Jacobs 1987).

RESEARCH AT HOME

It is not merely these circumstances and mandates individually that are problematic, but the constellation of them, and most particularly their effects on our long-held and strongly felt belief in the protection of informant anonymity, which presents bewildering ethical dilemmas for anthropologists.

The vignette recounted above is based on my ongoing research in a small community of Southeast Asian refugees, and I expect the reader can begin to see some of the problems of public presentation of this material. The issue of anonymity is so elemental in anthropology that anthropologists do not even have to explain that we have used pseudonyms for individuals, clans, and villages. Does one use a pseudonym for the ethnic group too? Sometimes this has been necessary (Mead 1932), and it may not affect the usefulness of the research. But the people among whom I have done research have a distinctive history and to call them simply refugees, or even Southeast Asian refugees, does not allow for a complete explanation. It neglects the very important factors of their traumatic recent history and also of their richly artistic, technologically simple, and somewhat isolated traditional culture, all of which have had great impact on their adjustment to life in the United States. At times early in my research I called them Eskimos, as they have Eskimo cousin terminology, and also because doing so caused me to be constantly mindful to protect their anonymity. But really to tell their story would clearly identify them.

Perhaps this would not even be a problem if I didn't also locate them, but in truth these people are not in California or Minnesota among thousands of compatriots. Their isolation as a small group of a few hundred in a conservative city, lacking an ethnic association or even a temple, is part of the problem at hand. To provide these details so crucial to the usefulness of my research, I may at some point be forced to disclose their ethnic identity and perhaps the city. It would seem that I can at least follow anthropological tradition by protecting specific institutions and individuals; however, by naming the ethnic group and describing the city, I will have identified the specific community, and this is problematic because the community is so small that once it is identified specific individuals will become easily recognized by a few details of their lives—only a very few have professional jobs, only one is blind, only one has twins, and so on. In addition, most of the community knows which families I spend most of my time with, and so will identify my writing with those particular families. Szklut and Reed (1991) discuss this issue, recommending that anthropologists consult with the informants in this matter, but also acknowledge the possibility of informant factions exploiting the knowledge itself or the opportunity of decision making. They also warn that once a community is publicly identified, that revelation cannot be retracted when the ethnographer wants to publish more sensitive material at a later date.

Other obvious difficulties with anonymity arise if our children become friends with children in the informant community or if informants visit us in our homes and offices and see us in our ordinary daily social life. Do we introduce them to friends and colleagues, some of whom might read our work? The informant population might actually be eager for this—interested to meet other Americans who might be helpful, or just curious to see the anthropologist as a more whole, more real person. But have we not then breached the privacy of that informant whose home or activities are described in our pages? Are we still culpable even if the informant herself seeks these face-to-face meetings with our American colleague-readers? Does her enthusiasm in this constitute "informed consent"? How capable is a nonliterate informant of giving informed consent in a situation such as this?

Another ethical angle arises here if the anthropologist examines the broader community context in which the informant community lives. To understand an immigrant or refugee culture one must examine its interaction with other social institutions, particularly those which seek to facilitate refugee adjustment and from which the refugees indeed solicit such aid. Concurrent with my participant observation in refugees' homes, temples, and communal events, I also did fieldwork in the schools and social agencies that serve their community. It is equally difficult to protect the anonymity of these groups, because there is in fact one elementary school, one high school, one church, one social agency, one clinic, upon which these people depend. While for the most part the individuals involved are sincere and kind, their lack of training, inadequate funding, or the organizational structures in which they work may render many of their efforts ineffective. I could explain this point in the same detail I used to describe my morning with Ly, but the risk is greater: those individuals and their supervisors are indeed quite likely to read what I write. Some occasionally ask, "When do I get to read that?" How do I describe in clear detail the "terrible teacher" I watched, and the stories told to me about her by a community member (who is qualified to know and judge), when all the other teachers and social workers know her? This problem is not really new; it harkens back at least to Vidich and Bensman's (1958a) study of Springdale noted in Brettell's introduction to this volume. Furthermore, the anthropologist who writes too much or too clearly has often been refused permission from officials to return. What is new is the trend toward research that is more ongoing than in former years, and closer to home. As a consequence of this shift we cannot so easily "exit the field," or avoid officials or situations we have exposed.

FEMINISM AND ETHNOGRAPHY

At this point this may seem a hypothetical issue in my work. Neither Ly nor her mother is likely to read this chapter, and none of what I have written about is likely to present them with any serious legal problems; none of it is going to have direct, tangible repercussions such as the loss of a job, house, or political power. But there is a constraint, a moral constraint, because if they were to read it, or if their friends were to read it, I would choose my data and my words more carefully. Ly and her family, like most in their community, do not have jobs, houses, or political power to lose, but they do have pride. Feminist anthropology asks us to consider our subjects as audience, or even as collaborators. Erika Bourguignon even warns, "The people whom we study may not only read us but [may] also send their children to sit in our classes" (1988:85). Such a situation is of course even more likely when our research community is proximate to our teaching community. I have described this event taking that into some account, and have avoided many important details about the particular family and about the community's culture in general. But we cannot launder everything; filtered and disguised as this vignette is, I would not like them to read it. They would recognize elements as their own and be embarrassed.

Perhaps we can begin to find solutions by examining the source of such embarrassment. Ly would be embarrassed because she would see revealed the impoverished condition of her home, her inappropriate choice of clothes, her failure at the interview—although my intention here is to illustrate with clarity and detail the inadequacy of city housing and housing codes, the deficiency of the schooling, and the absence of support systems for the widowed mother.

Ly would be embarrassed to read it, and she would be embarrassed to have her friends read it. She wouldn't, at the moment, care whether anthropologists read it. But anthropological writing occasionally becomes a part of a public image of a people. If she were to consider this possibility, Ly might share the sentiments expressed by Warilea Iamo, a New Guinean anthropologist, in her critique of Margaret Mead. Iamo claims that through work such as Mead's, cultures are

perceived as nothing more than these things . . . their dignity and their right as a human being is denied because they . . . no longer can represent themselves or their civilization. . . . [There is] a process of stigmatization which enhances the power of the Western cultural hegemony . . . [and] influences the way in which Papua New Guineans at home perceive themselves in relation to the dominant cultures, in relation to their own kind, and in the way they build their society. (Iamo 1988:58)

Ly, like the generation of Mead's informants, will not immediately be so articulate, but her daughter, like Iamo, may come back to challenge us. And does it lessen our responsibility if no one does complain?

PROMOTING WELFARE

Ly may in fact never care whether anthropologists read such descriptions. But I have a further audience in mind, and work beyond this chapter. My hope is that ultimately my work, an ethnography of that community, and work like it will be read by teachers, social workers, and educational and social planners and officials. It is partly to this end that I have tried to write this vignette without jargon and statistics, to hover in that delicate balance between art and science sought by many in our profession. I have not quite said "this man beats his wife," "so and so gambles," "that family has lice," "this mother is an alcoholic." But I do hope that what I write can present to the ordinary teacher or clinic nurse, in a more immediate and vivid way, the normal circumstances in which these people live and the enormous problems with which they must daily contend. To be useful, my work must reach those whose job it is to help this community and to plan programs for them. But Ly would not like them to see it either. She knows the teacher, the minister, the social worker. Although intellectually she may know that it would be helpful if such people really had a clear picture of all the difficulties faced by her community (and as a whole the community has supported my research for just that reason), she does not want to be the one that is the example.

We have created a dilemma here: protect anonymity, but be useful. Under the old "Principles" the obligation was clear: protection of the informant came first; the production of data was secondary. But the proposed wording, "promote the . . . welfare" of the group, adds a new dimension. In this case, promoting the welfare of the group probably means getting some social and educational changes made, and this undoubtedly will require the exposure and documentation of problems.

Of course there is also the question of just whose welfare it is we are to promote. Who, precisely, is the informant? The welfare of the individual informant and the informant community may well be at odds, as in the vignette above. This is a means-or-ends dilemma: is it acceptable to embarrass the individual informant if the larger informant community will benefit significantly from changes initiated because of the research? How significant does that benefit have to be, and how do we measure community benefit against degrees of individual embarrassment or other psychological harm, or even just the risk of such harm?

These questions themselves engender further issues, because they place the ethnographer in the difficult position of predicting long-term outcomes of such short-term goals as accessible day-care for children, improved schooling, or more efficient health-care delivery, all of which might have long-term effects such as weakening the family or distancing people from their religious traditions—which could in themselves be harmful or not in the longer run. Similarly, it could be argued that different informants might be embarrassed to different degrees by different information. Ly might be embarrassed by the vignette because of her age or particular personality, but her mother or another person might not. To some extent the anthropologist becomes a jury, judging how a "reasonable person" would respond to the work, and must therefore be quite familiar with the ideas and feelings of "reasonable" people in that ethnic group. Of course, this is indeed one of the major goals of an ethnography, but some anthropologists are clearly more gifted at this than others.

THE SUBJECT AS COLLABORATOR

Another issue for contemporary anthropologists to consider is that the people among whom we work often cannot really comprehend the method of participant observation or understand the consequence for themselves of the outcome of our research. I explain to those who understand English (which means primarily only the teenagers) that I am studying them, and writing something like a book, so that Americans will read it and understand their culture better. Generally they like the idea, and most people are cheerful and helpful about interviews—they want the tapes, or they want to see the interview in writing; they ask, when am I ever going to be done? But probably they don't completely understand all that I am doing. For example, I do not take notes when someone is confiding marriage problems or disciplining a child. To do so would not only be rude and clumsy, but would be a breach of the friendship upon which my (and most anthropologists') research depends. It would also probably preclude further such opportunities. It is our obligation to see that our informants have an understanding of what we are doing, just as in other fields researchers are supposed to obtain "informed consent" from their subjects; but can we really convey to a nonliterate community what an ethnography of them will be like? To what extent can they genuinely be collaborators in such an enterprise?

To some extent I have let a few literate informants read bits and chapters—the most impersonal and neutral sections. Some people are either genuinely or politely positive about what they read, but others have been critical:

"Mary, you can't put that in! We don't eat that!"

"Yes you do—that was one of the dishes at the wedding last week."

"Well, we do, but you can't say that. That's embarrassing. Americans will think we're crazy!"

"WRITING CULTURE"

While I make no pretense of being a postmodernist, I do see anthropology's position as lying in that borderland between art and science, and acknowledge our responsibility to portray the cultures we study in the richest possible detail. I also recognize that, like Monet's haystacks lined up along the wall of the Art Institute in Chicago, the landscape I portray may appear different at different times and under different circumstances. What I once saw was desperate impoverishment later came to be rich with color and light and multitextured meaning. Must the anthropologist hold off on publishing the ethnographic landscape until she is certain that all the possible variations have been viewed, so that she can present them all at once?

In fact, the vignette opening this chapter is indeed not the result of a single afternoon, but a composite of many scenes, events and individuals. There is no Ly, no such family, no such house, no such incident, though all of the details come straight from my fieldnotes of actual events, and so in another sense many of the families in this community are "such" families, the houses are "such houses," and the event here described is really rather typical. In her argument for a more feminist anthropology, Pat Caplan says, "An ethnography should not be homological, . . . positivist, or analogical. The name of the game now is aesthetics, pastiche, collage, juxtaposition" (1988:9). What I have presented here is just such a collage, but I wonder if this is the answer, if this is what we mean by ethnography, whether such a rendering makes it ethical (or even merely slightly less unethical), and finally, can such ethnography be science?

It appears that the new interest in "writing culture" (Clifford and Marcus 1986), in the telling of the "tales" (Van Mannen 1988), in "thick description" (Geertz 1973) may be somewhat at odds with the renewed concern for the privacy and "welfare" of our informants; similarly, our wish to include informants more intimately in the research process by sharing with them prepublication drafts will surely jeopardize the anonymity of some other members of the community. These conflicts seem particularly acute for those of us doing research with refugee communities that cannot yet but soon will "read what we write." I present my vignette here not as a solution but as a plea for help, hoping that anthropologists and sociologists may make these critical issues central to our professional dialogue.

9

JUST STORIES OF ETHNOGRAPHIC AUTHORITY

Richard P. Horwitz

Fieldwork for a scholar in anthropology, sociology, or folklore can greatly resemble everyday life for most everyone else. In many ways, it is a simple matter. You visit a setting, register surprises, venture generalizations, contrast them with others you have read or recall, and write it up. You tell a story. Of course, the sorts of generalizations and stories that interest academics are apt to estrange a novice. But when considered in the abstract, the process and the report, both known as "ethnography," could easily be mistaken for a trip to Amish country or Disneyworld and a letter home. Given the resemblance, friends find it hard to believe that ethnography requires training or merits professorial compensation, much less angst-ridden methodology. But a vast, diverse literature on the subject has grown particularly tortured of late.

At stake, supposedly, is how ethnography ought to be done, written, or read in a world that is imperfect enough to demand a response. There is widespread agreement that the world is unjust, but there is little consensus on the reason or the sort of response that fact requires. The arguments often feature cautionary tales about relations between traditional ethnography and the real world, particularly about the ways that ethnographers as authors have tended to ally with ignoramuses or oppressors. This is but one urgency in the debate.[1] So, I ask, how do we form better alliances? If ethnographic stories really are to be worth telling and hearing, what kinds of stories, whose story, should be told? Who decides? How, in short, should ethnography be authored?

Those are, at least, the questions I tend to bring both to the literature and to the field. Reflective ethnographers and informants often claim my attention in the name of other urgencies: affection, science, or liberation struggle; utopian, cynical, or realistic schemes; remedies for some more important agenda, ours or someone else's. Clearly, I cannot respond to all such pressures here. I have three more modest aims. First, I aim to sort out some key positions that claim ethnographers' attention. In particular, I will identify two kinds of stories about authoring ethnography that seem also to distinguish two fairly discrete bodies of literature: "theory" and "ethics." Second, I will outline some compromises between the two that I have found it necessary and desirable to strike while in the field. And third, I will introduce an example from my own field experience that is consistent with the principles of compromise but that remains profoundly troubling. The closing example, then, is also just a story, but it is intended to be a kind of parable, a narrative enactment of problems that defy codified solution even as they urgently invite us to try.

The story begins, though, with a particular version of the problem of ethnographic authority. By "the problem" I mean how can I conduct fieldwork and write it up so as to fulfill my responsibilities to informants, readers, and myself? How can I help construct representations and criticism that these parties can agree to live with, that matter for reasons that at least the perpetrators can defend? In short, how should I contribute to ethnography that is just?

Several feminist scholars, in particular, have placed this version of the problem near the center of a challenge to ethnographic traditions and experimental alternatives.[2] Despite great differences among their analyses, they tend to agree that sexism must be critically engaged in confronting the real world. Substantive recommendations for fieldworkers range from adding gender to the list of standard subjects for hard-nosed research to replacing hard-nosed research itself with less phallocentric designs. Regardless, they converge in using an analysis of gender to integrate a critique of the world and a critique of ethnography. Much of the rest of recent writing about the nature of ethnography and field experience offers very different, even conflicting advice. Nevertheless, nearly all of it can be read/recalled as if it implied an answer to my question—how should ethnography be authored?—or at least recommended a serviceable solution in practice. The solutions tend to be of two very broad types.

First, there is a type characteristic of what we might call "(reflexive, postmodern, rhetorical, ethnographic . . .) theory."[3] This literature is probably the one most immediately implicated in my title. It includes the bulk of writing since about 1970 that has taken as its subject the history, rhetoric, and poetics of ethnography and postmodern representation more generally. Its followers are a diverse lot, though academic colleagues and competitors often consider them a kind of cult. Names such as Howard Becker, James Clifford, Clifford Geertz, Henry Glassie, George Marcus, Frances Mascia-Lees, Barbara Myerhoff, Paul Rabinow, Michelle and Renato Rosaldo, Dan Rose, Dorothy Smith, Stephen Tyler, and Steve Woolgar come to mind. Some are building a simple catalogue of ethnographic strategies; others a new branch of critical poetics, a warrant for culture criticism, or an end to patriarchy and imperialism. Nevertheless, these authors tend to cite each other enough to be considered a school of thought, a loose band of social scientists who read Jacques Derrida (or at least Wayne Booth) and humanists who read Emile Durkheim (or at least Geertz). As one of them recently joked, their scholarship is distinctly "high in fiber, low in content."[4] The joke plays on the suspicion of detractors that theorists produce more pages of professional self-flagellation than of substantive field reports. Narratives outnumber rituals, and tropes outnumber traits.

Despite their differences (including arguments over the reading I propose), I think most "theory" can be read as a set of stories with a single moral, in particular, a moral that counsels ethnographers to "decenter" authority. A common foil is "realism," an omniscient narrator's account of generic others locked in an eternal present: "The Wuba-Wuba prepare for harvest with cross-cousin gift exchange. . . . " Instead, theorists suggest, ethnography should be offered as a negotiated agreement, play, polyphony, or dialogue among the ethnographer, the subjects, and the readers. Or the aim should be an unabashed monologue by an ethnographer/narrator who challenges the reader to beware of authorial artifice. Or the aim should be translation, the subjects' monologue which the ethnographer empowers through inscription. Or the narrator, amid punctuating confessions, should fill pages with elegant, evocative raw stuff, everyday talk and events. By some accounts the result is a representation that empowers its subjects; by others one that deconstructs itself. In any case, one can usually infer that there is a more or less "correct" way to narrate ethnography that can be built into the narrative itself.[5] In theory, decentered authors are a preferred response to monopoly capitalism, patriarchy, and postmodernism.

A second set of solutions and recommendations comes from the literature on "fieldwork ethics."[6] In this case, too, differences of opinion can be extreme, and some participants would likely object to the norms that I read into it. But also in this case it is easy to posit a school of thought and a creed. Most professional associations have an ethics committee and endorse a written code. For example, the membership of the American Anthropological Association has approved "General Principles of Professional Responsibility," and the AAA newsletter and sundry essays provide Talmudic commentary on their application in the field.[7] Some of these rules are now among the federal regulations that bind scholars as employees of tax-exempt educational institutions in the United States.[8]

Of course, many of these codes, commentaries, and regulations have nothing to do with authoring ethnography, but some of them quite explicitly do. Most codes feature directions for identifying and adjudicating potentially conflicting interests of producers, subjects, and consumers of ethnography. For example, authors are required to protect their subjects by assuring that participation is informed, voluntary, and anonymous. Readers are due a full, candid account of what the ethnographer has learned. And at least in anthropology, given a conflict among these parties, the subjects should prevail.

As commentators note, conflicts among these standards (including those on how to manage conflict), are, in fact, routine. In a long-term project, for example, how can an informant be at once guaranteed anonymity and be sufficiently identifiable to be allowed later to withdraw from participation? If behavior is only recorded in aggregate in 1990, how can variables be disaggregated in 1995 to remove a case? How can one informant receive credit for participation when his close associate demands anonymity or when, after publication, he changes his mind? How can rights of readers be protected when they are not party to the contracts binding fieldworker and subject? What happens to the public's right to know or the ethnographer's right to speak when an informant insists on a self-serving lie?

Such contradictions are hardly news to fieldworkers. They are part of day-to-day life, grist for yet more commentary and insufferable meetings of Human Subjects Review Committees. In the end, you do the best you can. If successful, you muddle through and no one notices. If not, someone feels wronged, maybe even hauls you into court. No matter how such challenges are resolved, when viewed in terms of ''ethics'' the author is considered a singular, responsible being. Although ideally decentered in theory, authors are powerfully centered in the literature and jurisprudence of field ethics.

Yet, there are important bridges between the works that I place in two piles, theory and ethics. Both tend to affirm that authoring ethnography is a valuable, socially complex act. They tend to share a cautionary flavor, emphasizing potentials for abuse of authority either through failure to share knowledge with readers or failure to protect the interests of subjects. Both grudgingly acknowledge the importance of practical circumstance and the limits of norms and regulations for preventing abuse.

But in one fashion or another, these two literatures should be distinguished, not only because they bind different sites, authors, and audiences, but also because they tend to address different challenges. For theorists the key circumstance is present postmodernism or phallocentric, imperial decadence. Authority appears to be an arbitrary sign, a narrative trick that an ethnographer plays on readers or that ideology plays on authors to nab their trust. Theorists, then, aim to unmask the tricks so that readers and writers will not be so easily duped by hegemonic discourse. Codes of ethics, on the other hand, tend to treat authority in more modernist terms. Authority is earned in the closing of a standard, implied contract between ethnographers, subjects, and readers. Ethical commentary, then, aims to help these three parties better know, name, and arbitrate specifiable interests.

Practically speaking, then, the two literatures conflict in the ways they counsel an ethnographer to act as narrator and researcher. For example, how often should she use ''I'' or quote from ''natives''? Should an informant be translated, paraphrased, or identified? Whose interpretation comes first or last? That is, how should various parties control what appears in print? Generally, theorists look to ethnographic texts for an answer. We can know that authority is earned (or they might say "properly disavowed") versus abused when the text displays the right/avant garde versus wrong/canonical narrative strategy. For example, trust the ethnography that displays a convincing mix of decentering moves. In ethics, however, process is more important. For example, authority is earned when samples are representative, footnotes are in order, and release forms are signed. Narrative ideals are moot because informants are in control. Trust ethnography that has played by the rules.

Of course, also practically speaking, processes are imagined from texts, and texts can be treated as processes. Informants never have total control, and no one is utterly free to choose a narrative. In fact, at any particular moment the distinction between ethnographer and subject or text and process is difficult and perhaps undesirable to draw. Nevertheless, these differences in emphasis between theory and ethics and their common promise of a just solution give me pause as I set out for the field or face a Human Subjects Review Committee. If only to satisfy the committee and keep myself out of litigation (but also to convince myself that I am not an imperialist ignoramus), I feel pressed to opt for one or the other in crafting a protocol and warrant for authoring ethnography as I do.

In response I have fashioned a serviceable protocol, a compromise. I cannot gloss all of my procedures here, much less their variations or the thinking behind each of them.[9] I can say, though, that particular circumstances have been as important as my reading of the literature. For example, most of my fieldwork has been in workplaces in the United States—shops, farms, factories, offices— and a public university has paid the bill. So I have sparred with hack realists on review committees and with corporate executives whose attorneys are saddled nearby. I often feel torn between my own affections and convictions as well as the demands of diverse subjects. Employers insist that I keep their cover, and employees count on me to blow it, while my own employer hedges, "Do the right thing . . . but don't say anything that will get us sued!" Although elements of my protocol have long pedigrees in ethnography, as a whole it is unusual enough to have occasioned great difficulty in qualifying for "minimal risk" review.[10]

One source of the difficulty is well known among qualitative researchers. Review committees (in consultation with university liability insurance companies) are accustomed to less improvisational designs such as controlled experiments or questionnaires. Their worries increase when they face a person like me, a critic as well as a student of culture who wants to be turned loose, not on some impoverished tropical isle, but in an office tower with its own legal department.

Their worries may also be attributable to my unusual place in the academic bureaucracy. Although affiliated with anthropology by disposition and training (e.g., my mentor at the University of Pennsylvania was Anthony Wallace), my degrees and most of my scholarly commitments are in American Studies, which is an interdisciplinary "program" rather than a "regular department" like anthropology. I am the only member of the faculty at my university whose appointment is entirely interdisciplinary, without even paper ties to a "regular" discipline, meaning among other things an outfit with canonized procedures for protecting human subjects. Each of the social sciences has a "departmental reviewer" who is empowered by a university committee to approve protocols that fit established norms, while humanists tend to proceed without any protocol or review. Since American Studies spans the humanities and social sciences, and since few Americanists have ever engaged in face-to-face research, it is unclear which norms should apply to me or if they should apply at all. My professional association, the American Studies Association (ASA), which has been in existence for about a half century and now counts about 3,000 members, has never endorsed a code of field ethics.

Furthermore, the topics I favor require unusually flexible relations with subjects. Most often I have studied cultural definitions of personhood in the United States, historic and contemporary relations among the fractured and contested identities that Americans engage. These have included studies of the relation between being "ethnic" and "American," between the "real me" and the one who is hired or goes shopping, between "the way I used to be" and "the way I've turned out." Hence, the most telling stories for me, the ones that I aim to elicit and interpret and that I aim for readers to engage, are quite personal accounts of discovering, inventing, altering, or ignoring identities that are negotiated in everyday social life. With these accounts in mind, reviewers may classify my work with journalism or oral history, where sources are best identified. But since I also analyze the way institutions affect accounts, reviewers may classify it with Chicago School sociology or traditional ethnography, where unnamed sources have been the rule.

Although my position and interests may be anomalous, the fieldwork itself is not very mysterious. I generally work a long time, six months to several years, in very unstructured (i.e., casual, friendly) contact with a small number of individuals in settings they call their own. Although I often use a tape recorder and take notes, the sessions rarely deserve to be called anything so formal as "interviews." Informants and I rapidly vacillate between fleshing out details, confessing interests, trading interpretations of everyday life, and getting on with it. Questions and debates are improvised to weigh the significance of daily routines for the individual participant and for others who in varying degrees occupy and affect the scene. Such as they are, those exchanges generate the "data," thoroughly soiled by the occasion, including a drone of evolving explanations for my persistence and for informants' indulgence.

From notes and transcripts, I then draft a single story. The writing process is very difficult to gloss, especially given a variety of forms, ranging from reminiscence or confession to technical report. But most often I begin with a single moment, monologue, or dialogue which seems best to encapsulate what I've learned from one person. I then patch in pieces of other material that should seem "natural" (that is, fulfill readers' expectations of the form) and that should strike the informant as a faithful account of reality. Within those limits, I try to tag interpretations and explicate allusions as a reader may require. For that reason quotations and events may be altered, certainly reorganized and compressed, but the whole account is still supposed to seem true to life from the vantage of the informant, the reader I can best imagine, and me.

I then present the story, with real names, to the informant for review, inviting corrections. We edit the final draft together. These editing sessions have ranged from the most congenial to the most acrimonious encounters of my adult life.

The congenial ones, fortunately, are most common. I am grateful to informants for pointing out when I have made an innocuous mistake, oversimplified complex conditions, or taken a local variant for a defining norm or irony for comedy. The rarer and more contentious affairs center on informants' desires to appear perfect or at least likable from the vantage of every friend and crank that they can imagine in the audience. Theirs is an understandable desire, but one that may also argue both for falsifying the record and for reducing everyone to a flat character.

For example, long after the usual extended discussions of risks and benefits and the signing of a release form, I spent a week fielding late-night, panic-stricken phone calls from a key informant, a manager of a motel with second thoughts about my publishing the strategies he used in getting the maintenance men to moderate their hallway antics: "What if some housekeeper or her husband says, 'You work for *that* guy!?' . . . as if I enjoyed it. You know, even if they're wrong." I countered: "Well, those strategies *are* yours, aren't they? And they're normal with managers, right? What else would you guys be getting paid for? The piece talks about the pressures on you, too. Besides, do you think you and the maintenance men or the housekeepers and their families or, for that matter, academics who will actually read this stuff will be better off if we all pretend that we don't know these things go on?" He responded, "You mean, if they think I'm an asshole, *they're* assholes." "Yeah, I think so," I said. He bought it. Years later we remain good friends, and he tells me that the project was one of the most valuable things he ever did. Yet in this case as in others I have to acknowledge that negotiating with informants can resemble pushing them around. I still do not know what I would have done if he had not bought it.

In such cases I am torn between my respect, if not affection, for individual informants and my sense of professional duty as a critic of the cultures to which they/we belong. On the one hand I aim to please—print what flatters—but on the other to challenge—print what "helps" even if it hurts. A key aim of my protocol is to make the textual representation of that tension not only an object of reflection but also a part of the fieldwork and writing process itself.

Three steps in particular—collaborative editing, favoring end-point versus prior release forms, and using real names—are among the most challenging aspects of my approach. They clearly signal ways that the theoretical literature has convinced me to break with common codes of ethics. They also challenge me to explain some of the implications of this literature to informants. Of course, given my social position and experience as a fieldworker, I still have extraordinary control over the report, and the consent of subjects in no way guarantees their empowerment. But at least I do not begin demanding a blank check. Both the informant and I have a story of what we might learn from each other, a version of its basis, and veto power over the conclusion.

In negotiating a release, I usually have to make plain the difference between facts about which we ought most easily to agree (specific things said and done) and generalizations or interpretations of them about which we might well differ. We have to talk quite concretely about those differences and how they should or should not find their way into print. Clearly, such discussions affect the editing process. In particular, informants may insist that I be a distinct, centered narrator, even, say, if I am working in such a monophonic form as autobiography. For example, one informant was so articulate about tensions in his community that I could edit his own words to highlight a condition that, we agreed, amounted to bigotry among his Middle American neighbors. While they echoed his claim to have been accepted as "one of us," he was also known as "the Jew on Main Street." When, in the name of getting along, he objected to my publishing this contradiction as an experience he well knows, I agreed to serve as the expert narrator who unmasks it. Some of the theoretical ideals, then, begin to break down in practice. In such ways, field experience has shaped my reading of the literature as much as the other way around.

In general, I think the protocol has worked very well, or at least better than alternatives implied in ethics or theory alone. It has helped me and the people I study to learn from each other and to demand the attention of readers for good reason. It is "good" because it is defensible in ways that both informants and I can articulate, including the contractual attention to process suggested in one body of literature and the textual attention to authority suggested in the other. In practical, especially micropolitical terms, I claim that the protocol best enacts the spirit of both.

There are occasions, however, when the compromise has not worked so well. The troubling cases may not be a large share of the whole, but they demand attention.

The most common problems can be traced to particularly large social inequities. There are cases when informants are so vulnerable and my work so easily misappropriated that their need for protection vastly overshadows the face-to-face niceties that the protocol presumes. People on the verge of being fired or jailed should be urged to elect anonymity. They cannot be expected to share the same responsibility for authoring cultural criticism as their employers or prosecutors. For those who are so vulnerable, candor itself can be taken as a kind of arrogance, being "insubordinate" or a snitch, and the sources of reprisal may be too distant for them or for me to anticipate. Conversely, there are cases when informants are so powerful that they may too easily deflect responsibility for their acts. I have not felt compelled to negotiate the "empowerment" of lofty executives by encouraging them to don a disguise. Of course, they deserve protection like anyone else, but they are usually well situated to protect themselves, sometimes too well. They can condescend to candor. So, protocols and theories bend in response to social inequity in the field. That seems to me neither surprising nor unfortunate.

The more interesting cases are not so easily explained and present the most difficult challenge when sitting down to edit notes and transcripts or when negotiating the final draft and release. Here I sketch just one example that suggests the limits of the compromise I have struck. Like those featured in theory and ethics, it is a cautionary tale. It may be a bit frustrating as a conclusion, since it reopens questions that scholarly articles aim, albeit tentatively, to close. I, too, am inclined to argue that I have found a solution that can be codified, considered apart from the conditions that led me to it or that might discredit it, and recommended to others. The argument above begins to do so. But even going as far as I have risks implying that justice ought to be so routinized: procedures can guarantee moral engagement; rules are superior to narratives; statutes are superior to common or case law. On the contrary, such reasoning deflects attention from circumstances that ought to be kept in mind if the practice as well as the data of ethnography are to be responsive to the real world or at least our narratives about it. That is why I close unapologetically with just a story.

In this case, for reasons that will be obvious, I must discard my usual protocol and alter identifying information.

Over the course of about two years, in connection with a much larger project, I got to know a man I'll call Bill. When the interviews began, he was a wealthy forty-five-year-old Euro-American, and president and owner of an entrepreneurial realty development corporation. In this and associated companies I was especially interested in the relations of business organization and practice to autobiographies of participants. How did people refer to their position in or relationship to the organization in explaining the "opportunity" they had to be "themselves"? Most of my prior work was with Bill's employees, clients, and competitors, who led me to guess that he was an egomaniacal, conniving businessman. Although they respected his success and dissociated themselves from local bigotry (e.g., "I've heard he's homosexual, but that has nothing to do with it"), nearly everyone claimed to be his victim. Since I generally liked them, I suspected that I would not like him very much. It would take some effort to give him a fair hearing, and I was determined to do so. I prepared by anticipating ways that first impressions might collude with surrounding lore to confirm a cruel stereotype. For example, I guessed that he would recount his life in the manner of Ben Franklin or Lee Iacocca, a tale of postured humility, desperate origins left behind with common sense, luck, and pluck. So in dealing directly with Bill, I was on the lookout for opportunities to belie that expectation.

But, in fact, despite my invitations to digress, to complicate or at least texture his autobiography, he insisted on the flat, luck-and-pluck version. He had it down pat. In transcripts, nearly every sentence began with a prepositional phrase, precisely locating his strides over adversity to success: "On a Thursday morning in March 1971, I did X. At that time, I felt Y.'' His oral style alone, its jerky robotics, could account for hearers' distrust of his integrity, even if, in fact, it had little to do with his character. In print, where verbal ticks are more annoying, the effect would be worse.

So, in drafting an autobiographical monologue, especially in preserving its oral flavor, I felt compelled to soften its precision. Otherwise, it might too easily lead readers to neglect the difference between oral and written tales or to mistake verbal robotics for defective character. If I didn't at least increase the proportion of "around thens" to "on that dates", I feared it would be boring to read or be taken as a sign that I edited with an axe. To further remind readers about the pitfalls of style, to encourage the possibility of reading against the autobiography, and to implicate my active role as offstage editor/narrator (while getting in an ironic jab on behalf of alleged victims), I also prefaced the draft with a paragraph from a realty trade magazine, raving about Bill in comically pure Chamber of Commerce hyperbole. In fact, when I first gave the draft to Bill I mainly worried that he would object to the preface, either because he caught the implied insult or because he wanted to appear humble.

The worry I had for readers was that they might not learn enough about Bill or people in his position to credit the way they justify their own routines. In particular, I worried that readers might just laugh off the trail of slain adversities that Bill used to plot his course. Such a possibility could not be blamed alone on the smugness of modern readers. In fact, the experiences that were most useful to me in appreciating Bill's position did not appear in the draft.

Bill was gay, and at the time of the interviews he was in a monogamous relationship with a much younger man who, from a heterosexual perspective, played femme to Bill's butch. Although Bill avoided acknowledging his presence almost as steadfastly as local homophobes, his lover was inescapably part of the scene. While we sat in heavy leather chairs in the living room taping Bill's conquests, his lover usually darted about the kitchen doting over canapes.

Such scenes easily undercut the sour expectations with which I began. My initial understanding of his story—a fastidious chronicle of explosive ambition—was very much tempered by an image of him growing up in a small farm-market town in Nebraska, an unlikely place for a gay young man to find much companionship or understanding. Rigidly gendered roles still invaded his love life. His time as an entrepreneur was spent doing business with people, particularly heterosexual men, who spread ugly gossip, framing feelings toward him in terms of sexual deviance. This story, the one I told myself, was also a familiar fable of triumph over adversity but one that came closer to pathos than bathos. It must have been just as formulaic, but it was at least as true and natural as the one that Bill offered, and it was certainly more useful for understanding him.

With that story in mind, Bill's compulsiveness, his rabid search for wealth and security, his manipulation of homophobic associates, seemed far more reasonable, even heroic, to me. But it also seemed to me not my place to broach the subject, at the very least because publishing his homosexuality might hurt him. At the time, in fact, lawyers were threatening to subpoena my fieldnotes in connection with a million-dollar suit and countersuit involving Bill. I did not think his sexuality was relevant, but I had good reason to fear that bigots would abuse documentation that he was gay. In any case, as long as I provided ample opportunities for Bill to talk about coupling, family, varieties of adversity, and contrasting contexts, I felt that I had done all I could. So, in surveying his entire life story, Bill never discussed his sexuality, and I never insisted on it.

After several months, I gave Bill my draft, the tale of luck and pluck, prefaced with an ironic quotation. A week later, he gave it back to me with only two sets of comments. Bill went through the monologue and crossed out nearly all the "around thens" and without benefit of tapes or transcripts replaced every "at that time" almost precisely where it originally occurred. The other comment was from Bill's attorney. On the top of the draft in a note to Bill he wrote, "I like it, but you're even more interesting than this."

Without protest, I changed the draft according to Bill's suggestions, and he signed the release form, agreeing to be identified by name, actually more or less a formality, given his visibility in the setting and others' insistence on being named. We shook hands, and that was the end of our relationship. "His" autobiography was published as planned.

But I still worry about this resolution, this particular exercise of ethnographic authority. I wonder if the preface was too coy. I wonder if I should have argued with Bill about how his precision might read, how the robotic time markers might make him look bad. The comment from the attorney could have been a convenient prompt for suggesting revisions. I wonder if I should have renegotiated agreements with other informants who wanted to be identified (wresting more muscular authority from them) to allow me to deal with Bill more anonymously. I wonder if I should have more openly beckoned Bill out of the closet. Most of all, I wish I could discuss all of this more with Bill. But within a year of publication, both Bill and his lover died of diseases associated with AIDS.

In evaluating the authority of this account, push has already come to shove. I cannot help but feel that the compromise I struck, whatever its theoretical or ethical warrants, helped maintain the ignorance, bigotry, and hysteria associated with AIDS and homosexuality. Of course, these were not among the subjects of my research. Of course, even if I had been more assertive, Bill might have insisted they were none of my business. Of course, nothing I can do will bring him back, and we may well question if a thousand ethnographies, however centered or decentered the authority or however ethical the protocol, could help prevent such injustice or give me less reason to grieve.[11] But his memory makes this story inescapably mine—now, I hope yours, too—to challenge the stories we tell about the shoving match that ethnographers author.

NOTES

This chapter germinated at the symposium, "Writing the Social Text," at the University of Maryland, April 13, 1990, and it flowered in the NEH summer workshop on "Narrative in the Human Sciences'' and the associated conference, July 5–8, at the University of Iowa. I am indebted to colleagues at the symposium, the workshop, and the conference for their support, advice, and tolerance. I especially want to thank the other fellows in the narrative workshop: Mitchell G. Ash, Barbara A. Biesecker, Richard H. Brown, George J. Graham, Mary Francis Hopkins, William F. Lewis, Thomas M. Lutz, David R. Maines, William Monroe, Allen Scult, and workshop directors Bruce E. Gronbeck and Michael G. McGee. None of our work would have been possible without the administrative assistance of Kate Neckerman, Lorna Olson, and Jay Semel, the research assistance of Kevin Burnett and John Sloop, and the example set by associates in the Project on the Rhetoric of Inquiry. Thanks are also due the workshop and conference sponsors: the National Endowment for the Humanities, the University of Iowa (the Project on the Rhetoric of Inquiry, the Office of Academic Affairs, the Department of Communication Studies, and the A. Craig Baird Fund), Drake University (Center for the Humanities), and the Speech Communication Association. I also wish to acknowledge the support services provided by the Center for Advanced Study at the University of Iowa. Further editorial assistance came from Caroline B. Brettell, John Calabro, Marian Janssen, James McLeod, George F. Marcus, Kathleen M. Sands, John Stewart, Margery Wolf, and sundry anonymous referees.

1. For one of many virulent examples of how ethnographers and critics have taken global injustice on their shoulders, see Powers 1990. After a book reviewer who is a linguist chastises him for failing to distinguish aspirated and unaspirated Lakota affricatives, Powers responds, "Lakota speakers, whom I see as one of the major readers of *Sacred Language*, have been raised on orthographies inspired by whims and dictates of missionaries, federal educators, and more recently linguists, each of which has introduced various kinds of orthographies depending on the latest phonological fad of the day."

2. See, for example, Caplan 1988; Clough 1992; Gilligan 1982; Golde 1986; D. Gordon 1988; Haraway 1988; Harrison 1991; hooks 1989; McRobbie 1980; Mascia-Lees, Sharpe, and Cohen 1989; Mies 1983; Minh-ha 1989; Modleski 1986; Reinharz 1992; M. Rosaldo 1980b; Stacey 1988; Strathern 1987b; and M. Wolf 1992.

3. For a brief introduction to recent ethnographic theory, see Clifford 1983; Clifford and Marcus 1986; Clough 1992; Marcus and Cushman 1982; Mascia-Lees, Sharpe, and Cohen 1989; Strathern 1987b; and G. Watson 1987. A basic sampler might also include Agar 1986; Asad 1973; Brady 1991; Clifford 1988; Fabian 1983; Fischer 1977; Geertz 1973:3–30; Geertz 1983:19–70; Geertz 1988; Golde 1986; D. Gordon 1988; Hammersley 1992; Harrison 1991; Herndl 1991; Hymes 1969; Keesing 1989; Langness and Frank 1981; Marcus and Fischer 1986; Rabinow 1985; M. Rosaldo 1980b; R. Rosaldo 1989; Rose 1990; Ruby 1982; Said 1978; Sangren 1988; Sanjek 1990; Shankman 1984; Smith and Kornblum 1989; Stoller 1989c; Tyler 1984; Van Maanen 1988; M. Wolf 1992; and Woolgar 1988.

A multidisciplinary sampler of applications/instances of such theory might begin with Berger 1985; DeBuys and Harris 1990; Glassie 1982; Horwitz 1985; Kennedy 1980; Myerhoff 1978; Narayan 1989; Rabinow 1977; Rose 1987; Stoller 1989b.

4. The joke/admission/accusation comes from a dialogue between an anthropologist and a sociologist set in 2089 by Paul Stoller (1989a:17). Clearly, Stoller is playing with a familiar caricature of contributors to recent ethnographic theory.

5. Such inferences are in many ways easiest in the literature that is less avowedly "theoretical" and that resists generalization across time and space (e.g., in Clifford's essays on the history of rhetoric of particular ethnographies). Often this literature identifies

stock moves and the ways they bespeak the particular context in which the fieldwork was completed and the temperament of the author. The common denominator or residue of a series of such analyses is often alleged to be the inherent potential of the form, which can be explained in terms of narrative theory. This process has been essentially completed in the case of "ethnographic realism" and has just begun on more "experimental" forms.

6. For a brief introduction to recent debates, see Caplan 1988; Clough 1992; Emerson 1983:253–311; Hammersley 1992; Harrison 1991; Reinharz 1992; Sjoberg 1967; Spradley and Rynkiewich 1976; Strathern 1987b; and M. Wolf 1992.

"Ethics" are also a stock topic of attention in field manuals for a number of related disciplines (Gorden 1975; Hammersley and Atkinson 1983; Ives 1980; B. Jackson 1987; McRobbie 1980). The literature on ethics in journalism is also relevant, though a special case in the United States, where journalists have extraordinary legal rights and duties. Humanistic social scientists might gain the most by reviewing the literature on ethics in nonfiction filmmaking. Ethical criticism of film aesthetics, poetics, objectivity, reflexivity, political economy, and representational practices more generally dates from the earliest days of the medium. A good place to start would be the collection edited by Alan Rosenthal (1988). See also Becker 1967; Becker and Freidson 1964; Cassell 1978; Cassell and Wax 1980; Duster, Matza, and Wellman 1979; Galliher 1973; Langness and Frank 1981:117–155; Orlans 1973; and Rainwater and Pittman 1967.

7. Most professional associations in the social and psychological sciences adopted formal codes of ethics in the 1960s (American Psychological Association in 1963, American Sociological Association in 1968, American Association on Mental Deficiency in 1969, Society for Research in Child Development in 1972). The American Anthropological Association adopted a rudimentary code as early as 1948 and full "Principles of Professional Responsibility" in 1971. The AAA amended the principles of November 1976, and thoroughly revised them in 1989–90. Among the differences in these versions, 1948–90, are bolder claims for the rights of subjects (vs. producers or consumers) of ethnographic texts. The newsletter's "Ethics Column" covers interpretations of more particular cases, and division reports include yet more specialized codes.

8. The U.S. Department of Health and Human Services established and continually updates "Policy for the Protection of Human Research Subjects." See, for example, U.S. Department of Health and Human Services 1981. For an introduction to some of the attending issues in jurisprudence, see Greenwald, Ryan, and Mulvihill 1982; or Hershey and Miller 1976.

9. Their range might be suggested by contrasting two narrators of my fieldwork: the side-stage nebish in Horwitz 1987 and the bar-graph–wielding absence in Horwitz 1989. More commonly I try to combine such variations and others to effect a kind of cubism. See Horwitz 1985.

10. Loosely speaking, a study qualifies as "minimal risk" if the procedures so resemble those of everyday life that, in agreeing to participate, a subject is not entering particularly unfamiliar or dangerous terrain. In practice most committees imagine the terrain of ordinary life to be something like the Cleavers' living room, a place with fewer surprises and less bloodshed than any place I've actually encountered. The payoff for qualifying as minimal risk is radically shortened red tape.

11. Of course, too, published criticism may also help. See Adams 1989; Lauritsen 1989; Rappoport 1989; and Shilts 1988.

Collaboration: Sally McBeth and Esther B. Horne. Photo by D. Wallwork (July 1992). Used by permission.

10

Myths of Objectivity and the Collaborative Process in Life History Research

Sally McBeth

Current ethnographic writing is seeking new ways adequately to represent the authority of "informants" and to explore methodologies that more accurately legitimize the expertise of the members of the culture being investigated. This effort to share out authority, or, in other words, to acknowledge who the authorities and sources of our data really are, is part of a broader questioning of the motives and the objectivity of the anthropological endeavor. This concern stems not only from the fact that the people we write about read what we write, but also from a renewed concern with the nature of the ethnographic encounter.

This chapter participates in the discussion and debate concerning the relationship among anthropological fieldwork, text, and audience. My focus is an ongoing life history of and with a Shoshone Indian woman, Esther Burnett Horne (Essie). While it is true that life histories are not typical ethnographic texts, they are nonetheless a legitimate pursuit in anthropology. They are self-examined lives, made public, that allow the native voice to be heard. Life histories provide a context from which to reconsider anthropological methods and to question the rationale of ethnographic enquiry; these concerns are germane to the formidable issues that currently dominate many discussions within the social sciences and humanities.

My description of a collaborative life history illustrates the strengths and weaknesses of the process itself. I begin with a brief introduction to the subject of the collaboration, Esther Horne, and then move into related issues. Specifically, three areas will be examined here. First is the life history approach itself.

The benefits and problems inherent to this approach will be investigated. Second, I will examine both Horne's self-representation and my cultural representation of her. Both are integral to the life history as the subject and researcher work together to create a story that is satisfactory to their concerns and goals. Questions of representation raised in the fieldwork include: How is the "subject" of the study represented in the final product?, How do individuals actually experience their culture?, and How do we (the fieldworker and audience) come to understand and interpret that experience? Third, I will discuss dialogue, discourse, and audience as they relate to the collaborative life history method. My discussion of these three areas is not intended to provide a comprehensive overview of the collaborative approach as used in life history collection, but rather to initiate debate on the process itself. In the partnership method described herein, both the positive values and the dilemmas encountered in collaborative fieldwork are discussed.

While these three concerns create the framework of my inquiry, the real foundation unifying the above is the value placed on the relationships formed as a result of the collaborative method. The crucial catalyst for this project, for me, is the intimacy that results from listening to and telling stories. The entire chapter, therefore, brings into question the goal of the anthropological venture in light of the impossibility of objectivity. I propose here an alternative to objectivity: informed intersubjectivity. This is achieved through familiarity, through collaboration, through listening, and through sharing. It is the knowledge of an individual that is informed by such subjective criteria as friendship, camaraderie, and shared experiences over time. It is the insight (limited as it may be) that results from mutual interests and mutual friends. It is the understanding that individuals from diverse cultures share because of our commonalities. The value of this personal theme may be questioned by those who wish for detachment and distance from the objects of their study, and by those who question the subjective nature of fieldwork in the social sciences. It is impossible to document the objective value of an interpersonal and intercultural friendship. But when meaningful relationships are established, native points of view can be presented more accurately, and a more balanced picture results.

THE COLLABORATIVE PROJECT

The postmodern turn in anthropology and feminist theory have directed my focus toward a methodology suited for the complexities of life history fieldwork. Both require reflection on the researchers' role and on their interference in the data. Postmodernism redefines cultural discourse by privileging heterogeneity and difference; it rejects large-scale interpretations purportedly of universal application. It also begins to grapple with deconstructing the myth of objectivity through self-reflection and an acknowledgement of the power-laden relationships of ethnographic (and other) writings. While some of the self-reflexive preoccupation of postmodernism seems narcissistic, the notion of reevaluating and questioning the fieldwork process has provided valuable insights for this collaborative project.

Feminism certainly shares many of the philosophies of postmodernism, although the connections between the two and derivations of one from the other are hotly debated by scholars who define themselves as feminists or postmodernists. Feminist efforts to challenge typical assumptions and views about everyday reality and to understand the different voices of social reality seem to be compatible with the theories of postmodernism. The methods that Horne and I use in our collaboration combine the relevant aspects of postmodernism and feminism with the more traditional anthropological approach. I believe that experimental or postmodern cultural anthropology must include not only a change in writing (as proposed, for example, by Clifford and Marcus 1986, and Marcus and Fischer 1986), but a change in field methods and techniques as well.

The subject of the collaborative life history is Esther Burnett Horne, an eighty-three-year-old mixed-blood Shoshone Indian woman. Horne has been willing to explore with me ways that we might create a text that would be collaborative, but at the same time allow her to maintain a maximum of control over certain sections of the final product. Not surprisingly, the areas of text Essie wants to control are those that concern her reminiscences about and interpretations of the meanings of her life.

Our endeavor has evolved into one that is truly collaborative. We do not stand in the traditional positions of informant and ethnographer, in which the former "speaks" and the latter "writes." Instead our relationship casts Essie as a native consultant rather than as an informant. Not only is the collaboration defined by us both, but the very direction of the project is a part of the mutual endeavor. An additional value of this collaborative method (given that Essie's life is the focus of the text) is that it respects Horne's life experiences as she chooses to present, explain, and interpret them.

The life history project that Essie and I are working on began (as do most) with a friendship. The source of our connection was a mutual interest in the effects that the boarding school experience had on American Indian youth in the twentieth century. My research interests in Bureau of Indian Affairs (BIA) boarding schools and Horne's firsthand experiences as pupil and teacher in this system led to our initial meeting in 1981. I had recently completed research for my dissertation on Oklahoma Indians' perceptions of their boarding school experiences in western Oklahoma (McBeth 1983a, 1983b, 1984). Shortly thereafter, I moved to North Dakota and became interested in comparing the experiences of Northern Plains tribal members who had attended BIA or church sponsored boarding schools with those of tribes from the Southern Plains with whom I had worked.

In the process of interviewing and collecting data, Mrs. Horne's name came up again and again. Her students at the Wahpeton Indian School in Wahpeton, North Dakota (a BIA school), lauded her teaching as a highlight of their schooling experience. She was one of a group of Indian teachers who had dedicated their lives to mitigating the negative effects of a boarding school education on Indian youth and accentuating the positive aspects of that experience.

Horne was also a well-known figure in North Dakota and Minnesota due to her status as a descendant of Sacajawea, the Shoshone woman who accompanied Lewis and Clark on their exploratory trip from St. Louis, Missouri, to the Pacific coast from 1804 to 1806. In addition to devoting her life to Indian children whose education took place in a boarding school environment, she also labored to keep the memory of her great-great-grandmother alive. The oral traditions that surrounded the life of the "girl guide" were recounted to her by her grandparents and tribal elders, and Essie was singularly influenced by the tribal memories of Sacajawea.

Many historians believe that Sacajawea died on December 20, 1812, at Fort Manuel Lisa in South Dakota. She would have been about twenty-four or twenty-five years old. The evidence for this date is contained in particular written records and accounts that have convinced some historians that Sacajawea died as a young woman. Horne and others have worked to encourage historians to consider Indian oral traditions and the writings of other scholars who believe that Sacajawea lived to be an old woman and died on the reservation, venerated by her Wind River Shoshone people. Those who hold this opinion believe that she was buried on April 9, 1884, at the cemetery on the Wind River Reservation in Wyoming. Sacajawea would have been in her nineties at this time. As a great-great-granddaughter of Sacajawea, Horne believes that she bears the legacy of this heritage. Her sense of personal and cultural worth is entwined with her ancestry, and many of her life experiences are understood as a part of this legacy.

It was not until I left North Dakota in 1984, however, that the idea of a collaborative life history project with Essie began to take shape. It was a result not only of our friendship, but also because I believed that Essie had lived her life convinced of its importance. It was apparent that Essie had contemplated the meaning of her past and that she looked forward into the future; she has a remarkable memory and is thoughtful and articulate. She has always believed that the traditions, values, and beliefs impressed on her by her parents and teachers need to be handed down to the next generation. We began the project in 1987, and I have made numerous trips to her home on the White Earth Chippewa Reservation in Naytahwaush, Minnesota, to continue work on the project. Needless to say, the project has become much more involved than either of us anticipated.

We began by taping Essie's life story chronologically, frequently including successive versions of specific events, so that we could more easily negotiate the life history. The notion of negotiation (Crapanzano 1977b) in the life history method refers to recording incidents and remembrances more than once. Collecting successive versions of life events is valuable because it aids in the process of editing the transcribed tape, and it also provides insights into how one goes about rendering a narrative that makes a life coherent and meaningful. We then began work (which is still ongoing) on the collaborative editing of the transcriptions, page by page. As we work slowly through each of the 400-plus pages, refining and condensing, we are daily made aware that our conversations are not easily translatable into a written form. As a former fourth grade teacher and a woman frequently called on by the community to address educational and cultural issues, Essie is a busy woman. She has many friends and visitors, and the physical distance between our homes means that our taping and editing sessions occur only once or twice a year. But Essie is concerned that her story be written in a way that she has a hand in creating and enjoying; she also insists that her health and still-busy schedule are not conducive to writing her own story. Our diversionary discussions on politics, mothering, growing old, and survival set the tone for the life history and also, at times, become a part of it. We evaluate each step as we proceed and move toward an appreciation of the complexities of our mutual endeavor.

THE LIFE HISTORY APPROACH

Life histories have long been regarded in anthropology as legitimate, if not perfect, approaches to understanding other cultures, for they emphasize the experiences of individuals and provide an insider's view of their life and culture. The virtues, then, of life histories are that they provide a platform for the native voice and a lens through which to see the native world. Life histories, however, are also problematical. Their limitations include subjectivity, accuracy of the informant's memory, as well as interference and/or romanticization by the researcher.

An early debate drawn from the works of two anthropologists whose writings were influential in the first half of the twentieth century exemplifies the strengths and weaknesses of the approach. Paul Radin, an early proponent of the life history method in anthropology, suggests that life histories or personal documents may be the only truly acceptable form of ethnology (1933:238, 252). While most anthropologists would disagree, it is nonetheless a valid contention that life histories ideally mirror the individual's perspectives, rather than the interpretations or speculations of the observer.

Franz Boas, however, disagreed with Radin, and was skeptical of the reliability of autobiographies and life histories. "They are not facts but memories and memories distorted by the wishes and thoughts of the moment. The interests of the present determine the selection of data and color the interpretation of the past" (1943:334). Anthropologists often deride life histories as little more than derived narratives and an embarrassment to academic anthropology.

Following this early contention concerning the shortcomings and efficacies of the life history, numerous scholars have discussed the pros and cons of this approach. The early works of Dollard (1935), Allport (1942), and Kluckhohn (1945) were instrumental in legitimizing the personal document as an important source of materials for the social scientist. The history of the biographical approach to anthropological fieldwork has also been well documented. Many publications over the past twenty-five years have reviewed the theoretical background and provide useful bibliographies (cf., e.g., Langness 1965; Olney 1972, 1980, 1988; Mandelbaum 1973; L. Watson 1976; Shaw 1980; Bertaux 1981; Langness and Frank 1981; L. Watson and Watson-Franke 1985, to name a few). The works of these and other scholars, who represent a number of disciplines, point out that the strengths of the approach are that it has the potential to demonstrate what individuals consider to be important in their own experiences, and how they think and feel about those experiences. Life history studies emphasize the experiences of people as members of the culture and how they cope with their society, rather than the general view of how the society shapes individuals. They also demonstrate that the major weaknesses of the approach are its subjective nature, including the accuracy of the informant's memory, and the intrusive role of the researcher. Given my goal of informed intersubjectivity, I believe that the components of this approach cannot so easily be divided into the disparate categories of effective versus ineffective research techniques, or strengths and weaknesses of the approach.

As Essie and I began working on the life history, I came to understand that the limiting factors of this approach are also what make it dynamic and innovative. The criticism that a life history is subjective is acknowledged. Life histories *are* subjective, and they are a difficult body of data to analyze by conventional standards. The very process of telling a life is retrospective and reflective. The tellers remember and reflect on their lives in the presence of others. They can and certainly do distort, avoid, or idealize in their life history reports—to themselves as well as to the listener. While questions of reliability and bias may be interpreted as a weakness of this approach, they may also be perceived as a unique strength, for self-interpretation is a part of the human expression, and a part of what life histories are. Memory is, in the words of Samuel Beckett (1931:7), an "instrument of discovery," not just one of reference. Many scholars of autobiography and life history (e.g., Gusdorf 1980 [1956]; S. Smith 1987; Personal Narratives Group 1989; T. Adams 1990) have focused on this relationship between history and memory, and between memory and one's personal and cultural significance. "Memory is the after-life of history" (Bauman 1982:1), and history continues to live and be passed down to the next generation as individuals seek to make sense of their lives, as communities try to find pattern in chaos, and as both discover solutions to the universal problems that each new generation encounters.

In relation to the above, researchers who work with the elderly have also documented this phenomenon of making sense of our lives by remembering and talking about specific events. They suggest that the construction of a coherent, unified sense of self is an ongoing process and that reminiscences or "life review" may be a universal feature of old age that is therapeutic (Butler 1968). The reconstruction of the past and interpretation of one's self chances as one grows older (Myerhoff and Tufte 1975), and the opportunity to tell one's story to an interested listener both validates one's life and helps one to discover its significance. The reader and writer must recognize that autobiographies and life histories are constructions and creations. They reflect the human need to examine a life and to know one's self and one's past through the insights gained. The truths that they reveal are metaphorically rather than historically accurate, which is to say that the truths of experience are not open to empirical verification.

Since human memory selects, emphasizes, rearranges, and even alters past episodes, an understanding of the selective process and strategic decisions involved can help us understand and discover this essential part of human behavior. Essie is aware that as she remembers her past, she interprets it in accordance with her present ideas of what is important and what is not. Like all of us, she begins her "story" by acknowledging the trick that memory plays on us. She combines memory and imagination in her initial remembrance:

I was born in 1909, on November ninth and the earliest thing I can remember is being on top of a very tall dapple gray horse. It seems to me I still had a diaper; I don't know whether this memory is something that I made up, or images remembered from what I've been told, or truth personified. Could I remember being that young?

Where memories come from, how we create them, and how "true" they are, are questions that require perceptive and thoughtful consideration, for memories illuminate what it means to be human and alive. Through them, we can understand the important happenings of the past from the perspective of an individual, or collectively from community members who may remember the past differently than historians have recorded it. Memories reveal truths of experience and situate a person's life in cultural, social, and historical contexts. (An example of this from Horne's life history that relates to the Shoshone oral traditions of Sacajawea will be discussed later.)

Memory, then, is central to the life history, since the events of a life are reinterpreted over and over and over. The fascination and frustration of this approach are revealed in this reinterpretation, for not only are events and remembrances of the past discovered, interpreted, and reinterpreted by the individual who has lived them, but they are also interpreted and reinterpreted by the individual who is recording them, and later by the reader of the documented life. A second criticism of the life history, the intrusive role of the researcher, needs to be considered. For, in addition to the idealized memories of the subject, one must also acknowledge the biases and interpretations of the recorder.

The collaborative encounter incorporates the consciousness and biases of the investigator as well as those of the subject. The life history is filtered through the perspectives of the recorder and interpreter—both must be aware of the consequences of the telling of the life in the presence of another. Cruikshank has recently noted that while autobiographical writing is a solitary exercise, the recording of a life history is a social activity (Cruikshank et al. 1990:x). This is a critical component of the life history approach and methodology, for it relates not only to the interference of the researcher, but also to the interpretations that will be made when the manuscript becomes public. Crapanzano reminds us that the anthropological endeavor "is a continuous movement of construction, deconstruction, and reconstruction in the field and in the academy" (1977b:3) and that "it is, as it were, doubly edited, during the encounter itself and during the literary re-encounter" (1977b:4).

So all of these concerns—her subjectivity, my interference, and the fact that the story would be made public—became integral to the development of the project. Horne and I chose to collaborate in the collection and editing of the text. Every step of the process is discussed at length. Our collaborative efforts, evolving decision making, and mutual problem solving have created a dynamic arena for learning about and understanding the complexities of life history research as well as the nature of the relationship between "researcher" and "subject." One day as I contemplated the complexities of the project, including the form that the final manuscript would take, I asked Essie why she had agreed to work on this project with me. Her response illuminates *her* sense of the difficulties and rewards of our collaboration:

To begin with, I was hesitant about doing this work with you until I got to know you real well, personally, and sized you up as to whether you'd be one of those people who was going to glorify or put in your own way what *you* had to say and not take into consideration *my* feelings or *my* right to privacy. I would not have agreed to do the project at all if I had thought that I was not going to be able to have a say about what was going to be on the written page. . . . I think there is value in sharing my philosophies and perspectives on the twentieth century, and I would not have agreed to have told you my whole life story unless I felt that it was going to be historically significant, at least as compared to what has taken place before and what might take place after.

As we discussed it further, we agreed that her life history would be a testimony of her life's personal meanings as well as a chronicle of her perspectives on the twentieth century.

REPRESENTATION, SELF-REPRESENTATION, AND INTERPRETATION

The recognition that cultural representation is inherently problematical is not new, and is not confined to anthropological study. For at least the last twenty years, scholars have debated how we can resolve the problem of how adequately to represent the subjects of our studies (cf., e.g., Rabinow 1977; Marcus and Cushman 1982; Clifford 1983; Fabian 1983; Bruner 1986; Marcus and Fischer 1986; Geertz 1988). They raise important questions, but rarely provide comprehensive answers. Questions that I ask of myself concerning how I represent Essie include: Do I allow Essie to act as the real authority? Do our words preserve a privileged authorial standpoint despite our best intentions? Are my interests in Essie self-serving? And to all, I answer a partial and hesitant yes. But since this is a collaborative project which Essie also controls, how she represents herself through her reminiscences is also a central component of the project.

In a collaborative life history, both the subject of the study and the researcher contribute to the "representation" as presented in the published manuscript. This complex endeavor for Horne and myself is further complicated by the evolving nature of this project. Even the definition of the project is nonstatic. Initially, when Essie talked to her family and friends about our work together, it was in vague terms. We discussed this and discovered that neither of us knew exactly how to talk about the project, because we weren't really sure what it would become. Our mutual friends would ask of me, "Are you writing a book about Essie?" My confused and vague answers or blank stares left them even more confused. Eventually I learned to reply, "*We* are. But we will have to see if we think it's publishable. If not, it's a record of Essie's life, for her, and for her family." But for most, this answer was still too vague. "Are you or aren't you?" was a frequent comeback directed at me, not Essie. After some thought, I realized that I was uncomfortable with this line of inquiry because of the very nature of anthropological representation, especially as it relates to the unequal relationship of the colonizer and the colonized.

Anthropology and the "work" that anthropologists do have often been equated with the colonial encounter and as a part of the colonial drive (Asad 1973; Todorov 1982; Rabasa 1987; Said 1989; Mason 1990, etc.). I knew that this view of anthropology has some currency, and that the very word "anthropologist" could elicit anything from laughter to disgust in Indian communities. Nonetheless, I wanted to work through these negative stereotypes and did not want the way that I represented Essie or even that *we* represented her to itself defuse her power or authority.

American Indian people no longer tolerate the intrusions of social scientists into their lives without some guarantee that they will not only see the final research product, but also have some control over it. They don't allow anthropologists to conduct research that is not of value to them, that resists their own perception of themselves, or that perpetrates stereotypes. Historically, the life history has moved from a method in which the aim was to salvage the last vestiges of a vanishing people, to one that records the lives of natives as adaptive players, resisters, actors, and collaborators in the preservation of their own pasts and presents (cf. Bruner 1986; Clifford 1983; McBeth 1989).

This change in the format and content of life histories appears to signal a preliminary paradigm shift in the social sciences. I believe this is especially evident among the life histories of Native Americans, who have by far been the most popular subject material for life histories (cf. Brumble 1981; Bataille and Sands 1984; Krupat 1985 for references to this phenomenon). Indian and Inuit autobiographies and life histories vary tremendously in their candor, their honesty, and their ability to draw the non-Indian into the world of tribal existence. They offer different answers to the question of what it means to be a Native

American and mark the beginning of an era of public interest in the popular accounts of Indian lives.

Many anthropologists working with native peoples in the early 1900s used personal accounts or life histories to reflect the growing interest in the individual within a cultural framework. Many of what today are considered "classic" examples of the American Indian life history were published in the first half of the twentieth century. These include *Crashing Thunder* (Radin 1926), *Plenty-Coups* and *Pretty Shield* (Linderman 1930, 1932), *Black Elk Speaks* (Neihardt 1932), *Papago Woman* (Underhill 1936), *Son of Old Man Hat* (Dyk 1938), *Smoke from Their Fires* (Ford 1941), *Sun Chief* (Simmons 1942), *Gregorio* (Leighton and Leighton 1949), and many others.

In these and other American Indian life histories, the most consistent and prevalent criticism focuses on the role of the researcher and how he or she has chosen to represent the subject. The reason for this is that life histories as understood in the work of anthropologists are usually translated, edited, interpreted, reorganized, and sometimes even rewritten by a collector. These intrusions violate the integrity of the storytellers' words and style, and hence diminish the intrinsic value of the document. In response to this concern there has been a shift in the collection methods of some life histories during the second half of this century. *Lame Deer: Seeker of Visions*, for example, which appeared in 1972, was the result of a literary collaboration between John Lame Deer and his good friend, the journalist Richard Erdoes. Other recent American Indian life histories that admit to being collaborative endeavors on one level or another include *Life Lived Like a Story* (Cruikshank et al. 1990) and *Lakota Woman* (Crow Dog with Erdoes 1990) to name a few. In addition, native authors themselves have begun authoring their own stories. Zitkala-Sa's *American Indian Stories* (1986 [1921]), Campbell's *Halfbreed* (1973), and Momaday's *The Names* (1976) are just a few. How an individual is represented in the final published account has become a central concern, since the subjects themselves and their communities read what is written by and about them.

Collaboration is gaining in popularity and respectability, and may offer a technique that will begin to resolve the methodological weaknesses of the life history approach. The partnership method allows the individual recounting a life to do so with less interference, and allows the subject of the document a role in presenting the text in its final form and receiving authorship credit. Collaboration is also the only means by which *some* life histories can be written at all. An example is that of Esther Horne. Due to her age, arthritis, and busy schedule, she is unlikely to write her own autobiography or organize and edit the tapes single-handedly, so we work together.

The nature of representational authority is a contested one. As Horne and I recorded her reminiscences of the life of a twentieth-century mixed-blood woman, it was not to record a "vanished" past but to celebrate persistence, change, and survival. Her life history does not need to be represented by me, the outsider, but as we interpret the recordings of the events of her life, we do so not out of nostalgia, but in an effort to translate her experiences into a text. We do so with an understanding of the complexity of moving from oral form to written form, and with the knowledge that we both become a part of the text. We do not pretend that the story is an aboriginal one, nor do we do mourn the passing of "traditional" Indian societies or glorify the colonial encounter. This life history will never be a national best-seller. We explore our relationship, the past, the present, and the future in the process of writing, translating, and transforming. We attempt to explore the multiple points of view that go into the construction of any life history, exploring individual experience and the relationship between the ethnographer and her subject. We have agreed that my interpretation of her roles as mediator, bricoleur, and master teacher should be confined to the sections on methodology and background. Her story (collaboratively edited) will stand alone.

We recognize that there are restrictions embedded in the very nature of writing, that is, that the story will be read. We are admittedly constrained by audience, and by family and community reactions to the text. Nonetheless, we began the project with the intent that Horne's memories of the oral traditions of Sacajawea, her experiences as pupil and teacher in the BIA boarding school system, and her reflections on changing gender roles and aging would be of interest to our readers. We still believe these things are of importance and interest.

One example of how Essie represents and interprets herself through our writing is in her relationship to Sacajawea and the controversy surrounding this legendary woman. The story that she (as well as others) tells of Sacajawea's later life is an empowering one for the Shoshone tribe and for all Indian people. Her discourse emerges as a challenge to the authoritative writings and voices of historians as she debates their interpretations of the past of her people. It is an opportunity for her to refute the established historical position that Sacajawea died in 1812. In recounting her early memories, she says:

For as long as I can remember, my mother and father taught us about our relationship to Sacajawea . . . about her travels and about the things that she had done. I can remember my mother showing us roots and berries that could be used for medicine, and then she would tell us that her great-grandmother had used these when she traveled westward with a group of white men who had gone out to the Pacific Ocean, and that these roots had saved their lives. . . .

Basil, Sacajawea's sister's son who she adopted, was very solicitous of his mother and her comfort throughout her life. Maggie Basil, my maternal grandmother, was Basil's daughter. We had connections to Sacajawea through both sides of our family. We were biologically related through our mother's side, but my father's side of the family had a long-standing relationship with her too.

My grandfather, Finn Burnett, the frontiersman, who later became the agricultural agent or boss farmer for the Shoshones, worked with Sacajawea and knew her personally. He said she was anxious to help teach the Shoshones agriculture because in her wanderings she remembered the Mormon wheat fields and she'd eaten bread and she liked it and she wanted her people to be able to make T'de Cup, that's how we say bread in Shoshone.

My great-great-grandmother and paternal grandfather were friends and co-workers and had a great deal of respect for each other. Sacajawea returned from her wanderings through Comanche country and Mormon country, until she finally got home to Fort Bridger, just before the Shoshones were put on the reservation. Her sons were already at Fort Bridger with the rest of the Shoshones. Sacajawea was more or less a liaison between the Shoshone people and the military. You see, Fort Washakie was established as a military post to keep the Shoshones where the government wanted them to be: confined on a reservation. We had been a tribe of nomadic people, and the government did not want us roaming around. . . . Some historians believe that Sacajawea died as a young woman, but how could all that we knew about her later life have been fabricated?

The above excerpt, from an early portion of the life history, refutes the position accepted by most historians that Sacajawea died at Fort Manuel Lisa in 1812. Tribal traditions and Essie's family records support that Sacajawea wandered westward from St. Louis, eventually moving through Indian Territory (Oklahoma) and north to what is now Wyoming and the homeland of her tribe, the Shoshones. She lived out her later years there and died in 1884. When Essie speaks about why she agreed to work on this project with me, one of the reasons that she gave was the opportunity to voice the native perspectives on the controversy one more time:

I think it's important to keep on insisting that the oral traditions are very important; that they are truth personified. I was careful to allow the historians their view, and I respected their historical perspectives, but I thoroughly believed what I said. I knew it was true. I knew people that had known Sacajawea whose integrity was just beyond reproach—I'm talking of my grandfather Finn Burnett and the Reverend John Roberts who officiated at her burial as well as the tribal elders. Anyone who visited with these people would not doubt for one moment the things they said. They had really known her and really had worked with her and really been friends of hers. I think it's hard for non-Indian to give credit to the Native American. They're so used to always stepping on our necks and grinding us down. And of course, there's the fact that what is written is considered more important than what is verbally passed down. I think there is an effort to discredit the Native position and those who side with our views.

The above example demonstrates that the life history is, by its very nature, an interpretive process. It is a given that experience (life as lived) structures expression (life as told) and that expression restructures the experience. As we narrate an event or even a life, we interpret it. We create our personal sense of continuity through time as we interpret and relive our experiences through our expressions of them. That is, we express who we are as individuals and members of groups, and we assign meanings to our experiences by talking about them. Neither Essie nor I stand beyond the interpretive context, and the concept of narrative self-expression or authoring oneself has become a predominant theme of our cooperative text. Following Foucault (1972), Rabinow (1977), Ricoeur (1979), Marcus and Cushman (1982), Clifford (1983), Geertz (1986), and others, part of the intent of the collaboration is to experiment with interpretive modes and representations.

Essie is self-reflective about her world and her life. Stories that she tells of herself as teacher, mother, and grandmother reflect her sense of who she is. She says:

I'm not ashamed of my life. . . . I think that I have fought for my rights as a woman and a mother—continuing full time teaching even after the birth of my first child. Throughout my life I've had the desire and the discipline and the dependability to get what I wanted; women didn't used to do that. We were supposed to be seen but not heard. I was not afraid to question men's authority.

Essie endows certain episodes of her life with a symbolic meaning that she and I discuss and interpret. As much as I might try to stand outside of the story, we both know that I do not. If one of the aims of the life history is understanding by insight and acquaintance rather than by explanation (Little 1980:217), then the interactions of the collaborative method are valuable for many reasons. They create a more balanced perspective from which the problems of representation can be addressed; the interpretations that result from the intersubjectivity are more reliable, and, most important, they create an arena for understanding, sharing, and friendship.

DIALOGUE, TEXT, AND AUDIENCE

The notion of the dialogic has become a fashionable metaphor for modern and postmodern concerns, recognizing as it does that dialogue and discourse are the very basis of cultural description. Dialogue with informants in the field is not only the most prevalent form of acquiring information, but it is part of the give and take that creates precise and insightful cultural descriptions and understanding. The realization that people get to know each other by telling each other stories about themselves is not privileged academic wisdom.

In this section I will address word play as a form of dialogue that creates connections for intersubjective understanding and interpretation, the translation of oral form to written form, and the audience to whom the writing is directed.

In this life history project, the recorded conversations of Essie and myself (our dialogues) are speech events of a peculiar type because they are spoken and *recorded* in the presence of the two of us. They are further complicated by the knowledge that they will be made public (in some form) in the future. The acknowledged purpose of taping our conversations was to transcribe them, edit them, and make them available to an audience. We also knew that they would be interpreted, critiqued, applauded, or criticized by our readers. The formidable aspects of this process certainly colored the nature of our dialogue, but did not alienate us from the work at hand. In fact, the regularity and frequent intensity of the sessions and what we came to call "the project" also taught us to poke fun at how seriously we were taking ourselves.

We often engaged in word play, the process of which is not detailed in the text, but which is nonetheless critical to the process of "creating" the text. The dialogue and laughter joined us together as coauthors. Certain verbal cues became the signal to move into a joking and teasing interplay where we created and constructed the text of the life history, and in the process deconstructed it, laughed at it, played with it, or imagined an exchange of words more playful than what we had already written down. A few examples will clarify the complexity and engaging nature of this collaborative process.

Transcription error was a source of much play. In the early phases of the project, I hired a high school student to begin transcribing the tapes. When she couldn't understand a spoken word (the tapes are all in English), she created a substitute. For example, after the death of her father, Horne's mother and five brothers and sisters moved back to Wyoming to the area around the Wind River Reservation, and her mother began working outside of the home. The transcription as recorded by this student reads, "My mother received a job as a chambermaid in the Union Pacific Deep Hole. Well it wasn't exactly a deep hole, it was more like a hotel where the firemen and railroad people stayed and had rooms when they were away from home." So, quips made by me, like, "Your mother works in a deep hole" (rather than depot) became a verbal cue for a break from the sometimes emotional remembering and listening in which we were involved.

Another example is taken from the period when Horne was a student at Haskell Institute in Lawrence, Kansas, an off-reservation boarding school for Indian youth. Ella Deloria and Ruth Muskrat Bronson, two influential Native American teachers at Haskell, produced and directed *A Midsummer Night's Dream* in 1923. Esther landed the role as Hermia, and on closing night was given a bouquet of roses by the cast, an event that held a special significance for her. Years later, Horne and Deloria happened to run into each other at a conference and were reliving some of their Haskell experiences. Deloria went out in the afternoon, and upon her return presented Esther with a single rose with a note which read, "This is for my Hermia." The transcriber had not read much Shakespeare, and so transcribed the note as "This is for my hernia." While this form of dialogue will not be evident in the final published product, it was and is an important part of maintaining the friendship and rapport that Essie and I have created.

We even experimented with recording the editing process, and when we listened to these tapes (which for us were the preservation of special times), we began to consider the idea of a never-ending narrative, and decided it was much like life itself. We make a tape, transcribe it, edit it, tape the editing process, transcribe it, edit it, ad infinitum. Essie once mentioned that life's events follow the pattern of the process, as we interpret, reinterpret, edit, forget, and re-remember. There were days when the process seemed slow and tedious, and there were days when we reveled in our insights and growing friendship. The process had become much more important than the product, the dialogue more significant than the text. But our goal was and is to complete the project. I cautioned Essie (and myself) that I knew of many life history projects begun by colleagues that lay in embryonic states because the ''author'' (and ''informant'') did not know where or how to begin with the hundreds of pages of transcribed tapes that are the result of most projects like ours. What to do with all of the transcribed tapes became our next methodological problem.

A life historian must from the outset concern herself with the fact that moving from interview to published account involves countless decisions. Even though each of these decisions affects the tone and often the very meaning of the final account, few life historians discuss this concern in the context of their work. Collaboration on some level with our informants thus becomes essential to insure that the presentation of the life respects the individual's experiences and interpretations. The text replaces oral communication, but may not represent it adequately.

Chafe (1982) and Cicourel (1985) note that the more integrated quality of writing contrasts with the fragmented nature of speaking, in which we often string together various ideas without connectives. Transcripts of conversational data frequently appear to be chaotic and unordered relative to written texts (Stubbs 1983:19; Alverson and Rosenberg 1990). This is not to say that the dialogue is without coherence, but rather that both have their own validity (Chafe and Tannen 1987). The ethnography of communication (Hymes 1962, 1967; Saville-Troike 1982), the study of discourse analysis (De Beaugrande 1980; Brown and Yule 1983; Stubbs 1983) and conversational analysis (Goodwin and Heritage 1990) contribute to the understanding of spoken as opposed to written language. These areas of study have informed my understanding of the complex interrelations between oral and written forms. The decisions made by us both as we transcribe from the oral to the written, however, require compatibility, trust, and time.

Essie and I are learning to translate and transform our oral communication into a more comprehensible written form without losing all of its spontaneity and informality in the process—a task both challenging and exceedingly difficult. Spoken language contains many incomplete sentences or sequences of phrases; it is more repetitive, less chronological, and more explanatory, and uses more general vocabulary and fillers (if you know what I mean) than written language. The coherence of conversation depends on understanding the above in the context of the dialogue, in addition to observing gestures, questions, intonation, tempo, rhythm, and voice quality. The discussions that Essie and I have about the process reveal the difficulties we encounter and are central to Essie's commitment to completing the project.

In the process of moving from the transcribed tapes to the edited manuscript, one form must be translated into another, and it is imperative that the process be collaborative, since the actual dialogue was shared and recorded together. But it is the audience that creates this need. Ricoeur (1979:80) explains: ''The

narrowness of the dialogical relation explodes. Instead of being addressed just
to you, the second person, what is written is addressed to the audience that it
creates itself.''

When we began the taping, we had not yet discussed the move from spoken
dialogue to written discourse or text. Since we were both novices, it never really
occurred to us to ask, What next? The social nature of our taping sessions was
fun and relatively easy. But when we began the editing process, all of the
theoretical and methodological problems inherent in the process began to confront
us. Initially we thought we might footnote my questions and requests for elaboration, so that the reader would know how much of what was said was a result
of my probings and promptings. But Essie finally said that she thought that
technique would be very cumbersome.

We both interrupt each other; we both backtrack, stop in the middle of sentences; we
slap a mosquito or watch your son fish off the dock, and digress into conversations about
mothering, mutual friends, and all. No one will want to check every footnote to discover
why we both said what we said. And we have the tapes and transcriptions anyway.

There was another (embarrassing) problem associated with my ''footnoting''
proposal. Sometimes my incomprehensible (in transcribed form) questions were
answered elegantly and at length by Essie. Often they were followed by three
to four pages of beautiful prose. My questions or requests for clarification were
interruptions to Essie's narrative. Our process was less an interview than a
recorded story of a life. So I agreed with Essie, but wanted the life history to
respect Essie's style and expressions. This is a difficult aspect to retain, since
Essie frequently is inclined to edit it out. While I attempt to be the somewhat
transparent medium for Essie's voice and for the native point of view, it is also
true that I hear some of what I have been taught to expect by my own training,
reading, and cultural background (Appadurai 1988:16). I do not lead or control
the dialogue, but merge with it as we join in the interpretive movement.

After much discussion of the nature of our dialogue, we finally concluded
that our questions, comments, digressions, and moods, while important in some
respects, would detract from the manuscript; and that we would therefore limit
the number of footnotes. Why? Because we were aware of our audience and
how they would react to our method, mode, and organization. The question of
audience surfaces again and again in the life history fieldwork approach. Who
will our audience be? Who is this document for? What are its purposes? These
are questions that we both raise and put aside regularly. We anticipate that the
audience for the completed text will combine academic and nonacademic readers.
Individuals interested in the boarding school experience, in oral traditions, and
in collaborative methodologies may have a particular interest in portions of the
completed book. A small historical press is likely to be our choice for a publisher
since we envision an audience with special interests in twentieth-century American Indian life in the Northern Plains area or in women's issues.

The book will also be read by Horne's extended family, her friends and acquaintances (in many areas of the western United States), and by former students and colleagues. In answer to my questions of what she thought community reactions will be to the document, Essie said:

It will depend on who reads it—I don't think there will be many negative reactions, but there will certainly be those who will find fault with me for baring myself on the written page and revealing my life to the public. When we live so close to people, they don't see us the way that others do. My family doesn't see me as an educator or historian or lecturer, but as mom or grandma.

We are aware that this text will be read by people who know or knew Esther Horne. While this anticipated audience does not directly control our writing process, we admit to a concern for their reactions and criticisms. As more of what is written by and about native people is read by the public, we must use techniques in the collection process as well as the writing process that begin to deal with "our" hegemonic position.

CONCLUSIONS

The move to the sharing out of authority in anthropology reflects contemporary efforts to strengthen alliances between anthropologists and native communities. It is an important component in understanding the complex relationships among text, audience, and ethnographic field techniques, for it requires that the ethnographer consider the issues of representation, interpretation, and dialogue.

Unlike some ethnographies described in this volume, where the members of a community claim a right to lead unexamined lives, a life history *is* a self-examined life. It reveals how an individual feels about himself or herself. Critics may respond that the collaborative method is feasible only when a single individual or a small group is the subject of the ethnographic research. While this may be true, the experimental nature of collaboration, dispersed authority, and acknowledging our "informants' " understanding of their own culture may provide insights for the broader anthropological undertaking.

The current anthropological interest in the life history approach focuses as much on the process of production as on the finished product. While the words of our project are Essie's, my presence and style (as unobtrusive as I may try to be) definitely affect the stories, the prose, and the final text. Since an underlying theme of this chapter is that detached objectivity is not only impossible, but undesirable, it is well to acknowledge and celebrate the relationship between researcher and subject. I would never have undertaken this life history project if I had not known Essie and if we had not been friends. Indeed, it was our friendship that made me believe the collaboration might be possible. Objectivity is impossible, and I do not pretend to be a neutral, uninvolved recorder. We both question the project along the way, but the questioning does not become so self-conscious that the purpose and utility of the inquiry are forgotten (cf. Mintz 1989:794).

The daunting reality of the situation is that the theoretical paradoxes of the anthropological endeavor will only be understood as we question our methods and motives. Essie and I acknowledge that our method is an imperfect one, and we do not expect the process that we experiment with to revitalize the way ethnography is done in the future. But it will add one more piece to the puzzle of how we represent and interpret the ''other.'' The method is also one that we learn from as we proceed in understanding how people go about creating a narrative that makes sense of a life, both for themselves and for their audience.

Essie and I believe our project to be important in that it is experimental, and we acknowledge that any experiment with dispersed authority is open to varying levels of success. It is exciting for me to work through some of the most pressing anthropological issues of the late twentieth century with an Indian educator, lecturer, and elder, and to have fun and become enlivened and touched in the process. Does this statement suggest that I am in control? That I am the authority? That I am the learner? Fortunately, my reflections on these questions are not done in a vacuum. Essie is not the object of my study, but the subject of our collaboration, and she is also my friend. The intersubjective understanding that results enables us to translate her words and sense of self into terms comprehensible to others.

It is my belief that life histories can provide powerful and valuable tools to understand other cultures when the observations and narratives on which they are based have been carefully weighed and refined over time and when the ''informant'' is an equal partner in the process. I believe that Essie agreed to work on her life history with me because of her need to orient herself to a world that has influenced her and that she has influenced in turn. Horne combines remembered experience with sage advice as she constructs a narrative that reveals who she is by assigning meanings to her experiences. Those experiences, coupled with her sense of identity, her narrative, and her interpretive strategies, lead us to value her experiences and visions (cf. S. Smith 1987). She has chosen not to remain silent, but to share her history with me and the reader.

NOTE

This collaborative life history project has been funded in part by grants from the Claire Garber Goodman Fund of Dartmouth College (1987, 1988), the University of Northern Colorado Research and Publications Board (1991), and the Minnesota Historical Society (1991).

11

THE CASE OF MISTAKEN IDENTITY: PROBLEMS IN REPRESENTING WOMEN ON THE RIGHT

Faye Ginsburg

> Dialogue represents not just a literary technique, or a way of connecting the isolated person to the outside world, but a reinterpretation of the nature of the self . . . the self cannot be understood or expressed except in relation to an audience whose real or imagined responses continually shape the way in which we define ourselves.
>
> (Kelly 1992:44)

The question of how anthropologists achieve some sense of participation and empathy with *some* "other" despite difference has been central to the ethnographic enterprise in its conventional cross-cultural form. However divided the field of sociocultural anthropology has become, Malinowski's axiom—that the ethnographer's task is to represent the native's point of view—is still widely accepted. The assumption is that the ethnographer should take a sympathetic position vis-à-vis his/her subjects. While this stance of identification informs much of the discussion on field methods and ethnographic writing, it is rare that audiences read into even the most seamless of ethnographic accounts a confusion between the identities of the anthropologist and the native. Malinowski's talent for grasping the native's point of view, for example, has not been mistaken for his becoming a Trobriand Islander (whatever other questions have been raised about his work). What happens, however, when the anthropological gaze is turned toward those with whom the investigator—and most of his or her anthropological colleagues—disagrees in some significant way?

In his pioneering study, *Tuhami* (1980), Vincent Crapanzano discusses the recognition of other ways of constituting reality in anthropological research as a sort of "epistemological vertigo." The threat of such an encounter and its possible transformative effects is striking when the subject is at some cultural or historical remove. When the "other" represents some very close opposition within one's own society, taking on the "native's point of view" is problematic in different ways, not only in the research but in the response of professional colleagues, especially when the work is focused on a social and political conflict that engages the hearts and minds of other anthropologists. This chapter explores a particular instance of this general case through discussion of work with American right-to-life activists.[1] In particular, I want to focus on the dilemmas of developing effective ethnographic representation for potentially hostile audiences; discuss textual strategies for encompassing the tensions between compassion and disagreement; and suggest how such ethnographic mediation can illuminate important social issues in our own society.

Most of the anthropological writing on methodological problems addresses the research processes. Much ink has been spilled over questions of rapport, objectivity, reflexivity, selection of informants, and the ethics and politics of the field situation. For those working in their own societies, the question of gaining distance and *de*familiarizing oneself takes on prominence. Recently, there has been a surge of interest in ethnographic writing itself and how the relationships made in ethnographic fieldwork are reconstituted textually (Geertz 1988). Such work raises questions about the representation of the anthropologist's voice in relation to that of the (often less powerful) natives (Clifford 1988). A number of writers have suggested less authoritative and more experimental rhetorical strategies, the better to represent the experience of cultural anthropology in a postmodern world (Marcus and Fischer 1986; Clifford and Marcus 1986).

With all this self-reflection, relatively little attention has been paid to problems of *reception* of ethnographic texts. The tropes and strategies used to familiarize so-called exotic cultures assumed a fairly predictable response to such material on the part of most readers. Whether or not that assumption was correct, it cannot be applied so easily to audiences for ethnographies written about people from the same society as the reader's. Texts must be written with an awareness that they will be read by those studied; *other* natives—even anthropologists—inevitably find it difficult to suspend judgment, particularly when they disagree politically with those represented. In my own anthropological research with right-to-life grassroots activists in the United States, I found that when I began to present my work and explain the way the world looked from the point of view of these "natives," I was frequently asked if I had, indeed, become one of "them." For the sake of discussion, I will call this problem "the case of mistaken identity." The challenge for the ethnographer is to find methods that anticipate and effectively counter such reader reactions.

This chapter addresses this challenge through a discussion of the strategies I chose to enable audiences momentarily to set aside preconceptions. Unlike the

Nuer, Australian Aborigines, or a variety of American subcultures, the people I studied are considered by most of my colleagues to be their enemies. When I offered representations that rendered the right-to-life position sensible or even as powerful as it is to those who adhere to it (as any good ethnographer must), often my "objectivity" or results were called into question, framed by queries as to whether I had "gone native." In this case, my colleagues (most of whom are in favor of abortion rights, i.e., pro-choice, as am I) meant that I had come to understand the right-to-life position, implying as well that this would undercut my credibility to make a valid ethnographic analysis.

In response, I shifted from a strategy of mediation, which sets up the anthropologist as defender and spokesperson for "the native." Instead, I used devices that (1) helped me to recreate for readers the counter-intuitive encounter that I experienced, (2) drew attention to the interpretations offered by informants, and (3) resituated the ethnographic case in the context of historical material, thus drawing attention away from the immediacy of politics and toward broader cultural patterns that are often "too close" to see in one's own society. The more general concern is how the interpretation of research is shaped when home audiences are often directly engaged in the issues being studied. This is the central point to which I will return, but first I want to provide some background and case material.

BACKGROUND

The example used here is a study of grassroots activists on both sides of the abortion conflict in the United States. I worked with pro-life and pro-choice women engaged in a struggle over the opening of the first abortion clinic in Fargo, North Dakota, which I followed closely from 1981 to 1984 (including two periods of fieldwork totaling twelve months). Though I was concerned with activists on *both* sides of the abortion issue, the work focused on the pro-life position because of the prominent role this movement has played recently in American politics and culture.

I began to explore the idea for this research on female grassroots abortion activists in 1980, the year Ronald Reagan was elected President of the United States, an event that has come to be associated with what is called the rise of the New Right.[2] My interest was in investigating the role played by women in this rightward swing in the United States from the point of view of those engaged in conservative social movements at the local level.

The activism of women on the right was, by 1981, a topic of concern among feminist scholars in particular, although few had had direct contact with any of these right-wing women working at the grassroots. These grassroots activists offered an important challenge to the burgeoning work in feminist scholarship in the United States that began in the 1970s and has proliferated since then.[3] The first premise of such research was an acknowledgment of women as active agents rather than passive victims, as well as a respect for how women cross-culturally shaped their identities and interests from their experiences as *female* social actors. What were feminist scholars to do with this right-wing social movement claimed by and for women? The right-to-life movement put forward an agenda that seemed contrary to American feminist desires, and yet had thousands of "average" white, middle-class American women (the same sociological profile of most feminists) across the country as its supporters. On more political grounds, I wanted to understand why feminism was losing its persuasive grip, and was interested to see if indeed there was any broader common ground between women opposed on single issues such as abortion.

The development of the right-to-life movement was part of the emergence of the American New Right in the 1970s, the rather peculiar coalition of economically and socially conservative politicians, fundamentalist Christians, and people engaged in single-issue social movements intended to reverse liberal gains of the 1960s such as abortion, affirmative action, and gun control (Himmelstein 1990). While most of these groups did not share ideologies with each other, their different interests in having a conservative president brought them together to gain a minority for the election of Ronald Reagan in 1980 and 1984 and then George Bush in 1988. With some exceptions (Fitzgerald 1986; Harding 1987; Klatch 1987; Luker 1984; Paige 1984), most authors who were writing on the New Right in the 1980s focused on the political organization and leadership of a few well-known groups and leaders who were central to these organizations. Few had gone out and talked to the different people these movement leaders claimed as their supporters, to find out who they are, how they live, and what motivates them. In particular, I wanted to understand what motivated women to become so active in political causes that, in my view as a feminist, were against their own interests.

THE RIGHT-TO-LIFE WORLDVIEW

In the 1980s, pro-life activity was most engaged and effective at the local level, and for that reason offered a setting particularly appropriate for anthropological research. In general, right-to-life groups draw their strength from local social life. Their activity, unlike the direct mass-mail organizing of many of the New Right groups, is embedded in the kind of ongoing face-to-face interaction that is the stock-in-trade of the anthropological enterprise.

Contrary to stereotype, the pro-life movement, like many other single-issue groups, encompasses a broad range of ideological positions, from radical pacifism—Pro-Lifers for Survival, an antinuclear group, for example—to progressive Catholics and Protestants, to fundamentalist Christians. While right-to-lifers are frequently considered to be unswervingly hostile to feminism, much of their rhetoric seeks to claim the same territory charted by the women's movement. In the book *A Private Choice* by John Noonan, one of the key philosophers of the movement, abortion is cast as antiwoman, the agenda of upper-class men. Noonan writes:

When strong and comprehensive anti-abortion statutes were enacted in 19th century America, the militant feminists had been outspoken in their condemnation of abortion. . . . Who wanted abortion in 1970? Only a minority of any section of the population favored it, but the stablest and strongest supporters of the liberty were white upper-class males. (1979:48–49)

Noonan goes on to quote from Eugene O'Neill's play *Abortion*, written in 1914. In it, the protagonist Jack Townsend, a rich young college student, impregnates a local girl for whom he arranges an abortion, which proves fatal to her and the fetus. Noonan musters this, along with statistics and legal arguments, as evidence for his case that abortion casts women as the victims of male lust and the uncaring penetration of upper-class privilege into the ranks of the less fortunate.

Noonan provides an example of how right-to-life activists' concerns go beyond the goal of recriminalizing abortion; they see abortion as symptomatic of other social problems. In particular they are concerned that materialism and narcissism are displacing nurturant ties of kin and community. Much of their agenda could be interpreted as a desire to reform the more dehumanizing aspects of contemporary capitalist culture. In this respect, although their solutions differ, many right-to-life concerns more closely resemble those of some of their pro-choice opponents than those of their supposed allies on the New Right who favor a more libertarian conservative social philosophy (Klatch 1987).

This complexity of position is not confined to leadership but was apparent among grassroots activists as well. ''Roberta'' provides a case in point. I first met her at a pro-life banquet and fundraiser. Born in 1953, Roberta is now married to an auto mechanic. Before giving birth to her first child, she worked as a college teacher and a graphic designer. In 1984 she was a full-time homemaker, raising two children, expecting a third, and active in the pro-life movement as well as Democratic politics.

They paint the job world as so glamorous, as if women are all in executive positions. But really, what is the average woman doing? Mostly office work, secretarial stuff. Even teaching gets routine after awhile. When you watch TV, there aren't women pictured working at grocery store checkouts. I just don't see homemaking as any worse than eight to five. I really like homemaking. It's something I've chosen. I bake, I garden, I sew, I see it as an art. I don't say everyone should do it that way. And my husband likes to do it too. People should be able to do what they like to do. That's the part of the women's movement I've really been in favor of.

In Roberta's construction, this is not simply a defense of homemaking as a choice of vocation. Her description of her own life is embedded in a critique of what she considers to be the dominant culture. What she *does* defend is the social and economic consequences of having made a decision that she senses is unpopular.

There are a lot of pro-life people who choose to stay at home with their children like me. A secondary income is not that important to us. My income would be pretty darn good if I took off for the work force again. My husband alone can support us but we have to pinch and budget and so we don't go to the fundraisers. And now that my husband and I have become evangelicals, we don't really believe in drinking for the sake of drinking. So we're severely criticized for that. Anyway, to completely exclude us for that one reason, being pro-life, just blows my mind.

In choosing to leave the work force, Roberta knew she would be greatly reducing the disposable income of her household. The economic consequences of her ideological choice, then, have restricted the activities in which she and her husband can participate. (Interestingly, pro-choice women only ten years senior to Roberta felt that their decision to do the opposite, leave homemaking for the work force, was similarly controversial. This indicates how rapidly the definition of "normal female behavior" has changed.) Roberta sees in the lack of recognition for domestic work an extension of a more pervasive condition: the increasing commercialization of human relations, especially those involving dependents.

You know, the picture painted these days is how much kids cost. These are the reasons given for most abortions. How much work kids are, how much they can change your lifestyle, how they interpret the timing of your goals. What is ten years out of a seventy-year life span? You know, I've done a lot of volunteer work in nursing homes and it's just a lonely world to see women who don't have families. If you don't have your family, if you don't have your values, then what's money, you know?

In her narrative, abortion is threatening because it suggests the public acceptance of sexuality disengaged from family formation and the values associated with the latter. Metaphorically, Roberta represents this as the triumph of material interests over the care of human beings, a loss of a locus of unconditional nurturance in the social order.

In general, pro-life activists stress the negative consequences for women of the dismantling of a system that links male sexuality to childbearing and marriage. Sally, a friend and pro-life colleague of Roberta, for example, uses her experiences as a social worker as evidence that abortion undercuts women's ability to gain the support of a man.

In my work, I saw a lot of people who were part of the middle class and then because of a divorce or having a child out of wedlock, they became part of the welfare system. I saw how really necessary, how many reasons there were to really maintain that relationship. There's a very real world out there. I feel sorry for men that they can't have the same feelings I do about pregnancy. But in the situation of a woman, where all of a sudden after twenty years of a marriage, she has nothing, and he at least has a business or a job or whatever. . . . Women just have a different kind of investment in the marriage situation.

Ironically, the same sorts of cases are used by pro-choice activists who attribute the viewpoints of their opponents to ignorance of the difficulties many women face. Almost all of the Fargo pro-life activists were aware of these stereotypes and addressed them in a dialectical fashion, using them to confirm their own position. Roberta, for example, expressed it in the following way:

If you take the pro-life stand, you're labelled as being against anything else that women stand for. And ironically, it's mostly women in our movement. The pro-choice people say about us, "Well, they must have feelings but they're so put down they can't make up their own minds, you know." And they think we're just saying what we do because that's what men have taught us. Well, if the men have taught us, why aren't the men helping us?

To write off the views of a Sally or a Roberta as naive is as much a misreading as are their claims that pro-choice women are unconcerned with raising families. They, along with other right-to-life activists, are well aware of the fragility of traditional marriage arrangements and recognize the lack of other social forms that might ensure the emotional and material support of women with children or other dependents. As Roberta made clear,

The women I have been talking to are strong and independent, hardly weak women, homemakers by choice because they value that. They support equal pay for equal work. I know about that because I sued the company I worked for and won. . . . No, we aren't quiet. You know, we couldn't have a movement if we were all the way we're stereotyped.

For the most recent wave of right-to-life activists in particular, the pro-life movement speaks to their concerns. Through it, their own dilemmas are framed as part of a larger struggle to reform the culture in the interests of women. For Roberta, the right-to-life cause legitimates choices she has made—as a woman, mother, and political activist. As she explained to me while I cleared my tape recorder from her kitchen table to make room for freshly baked bread:

The image that's presented of us as having a lot of kids hanging around and that's all you do at home and you don't get anything else done, that's really untrue. In fact, when we do mailings here, my little one stands between my legs and I use her tongue as a sponge. She loves it and that's the heart of grassroots involvement. That's the bottom. That's the stuff and the substance that makes it all worth it. Kids are what it boils down to. My husband and I really prize them; they are our future and that is what we feel is the root of the whole pro-life thing.

The collective portrait that emerges from such stories is much more complex than stereotypes that portray pro-life women as reactionary housewives and mothers passed by in the sweep of social change. They are astute, alert to social and political developments, and on many issues are not antifeminist. They approve of and endorse women seeking political power and economic equity. Roberta, for example, brought a comparable worth suit against a former employer. Most held or had held jobs, and some had careers. In the marriage relationships I observed, husbands helped regularly with domestic duties and were pragmatically and emotionally supportive of their wives' political work.

What is striking in the pro-life narratives is how most of these women had assimilated some version of feminist thought and woven it into their life choices. The plot of almost every story hinges on how the narrator either repudiated or reorganized these ideas into a right-to-life framework. Sally's narrative of how her ideas have changed since she joined the pro-life movement is illustrative.

You're looking at somebody who used to think the opposite. I used to think that sex outside of marriage was fine. Now I see I don't believe that anymore. I believe when you practice sex outside of marriage you are taking all kinds of chances, including walking out on each other and not having to accept the responsibility of children or whatever. And to me, once you engage in the act of sex, it's a big emotional commitment. If my boyfriend walked out on me I would be devastated. I think the world preaches you can have it all . . . doing lots of things without getting caught and I guess over the last few years, I've really changed my mind about a lot of things. And when I see the abortion clinic, there's proof positive to me that my values are right and an innocent human being is paying the price for all this.

This sort of negotiation of feminism into their life story distinguishes younger right-to-life women in particular, although it is present in more muted form with older activists. Rather than simply defining themselves in opposition to what they understand feminist ideology and practice to be, many, like Sally, claim to have held that position and to have transcended it. Sally, for example, describes her former "liberated" ideas about sexuality and heterosexual relationships as a repression of her true self.

I think there was part of me that never fully agreed. It wasn't a complete turnaround. It was kind of like inside you know it's not right but you make yourself think it's okay. When I was in college, I loved to read *Cosmopolitan* magazine, all kinds of magazines and I thought, "This is the kind of life I was meant to lead. . . . " You know, I think part of it is rebellion.

The same kind of appropriation of feminism is incorporated into political rhetoric; for example, a pro-life lecture popular in 1984 Fargo was entitled "I Was a Pro-choice Feminist, but Now I'm Pro-life." While such a claim provokes discussion of how the ideas of feminism are distorted, my concern here is to analyze what such assertions mean for those who make them. The lecture title is only one of many examples of right-to-life narratives in which activists assert a prior alliance to feminism, usually framed as a period of separation from the narrator's mother. The "conversion" to the pro-life position often follows a first birth or pregnancy. Thus, they narratively subsume their opponent's ideology into their own and thus claim authority over it.

In much the same way that pro-choice women embrace feminism, pro-life women find in *their* movement a particular symbolic frame that integrates their experience of work, reproduction, and marriage with shifting ideas of gender and politics that they encounter around them. It is not that they discovered an ideology that "fit" what they had always been. Their sense of identification evolves in the very process of voicing their views against abortion. In the regular performance of their activism, they are transforming themselves and their community, while projecting their vision of the culture into the future, both pragmatically and symbolically.

What underlies these narratives is a partially shared world of reference, the sociohistorical context of American women's lives and the social and cultural understandings of procreation and sexuality in particular. One can hear in the different emphases of activists' stories the dramatic shape of contradictions experienced by American women over the female life cycle in particular, the opposition between motherhood and wage work.

Proposed solutions to this dilemma are being argued in the abortion debate, a social arena marked as a contested domain. To succeed, each side must see and present its understanding of the cultural and personal meaning of reproduction as "natural" and correct. In order to legitimate their own position, proponents must make a persuasive case so that the formulations of the opposition appear unnatural, immoral, or false. On an individual and organizational level, then, each side constitutes itself in dialogue with the "enemy," real and imagined. The opposition is both incorporated and repudiated, understood and denied. This process is what gives the abortion debate its dialectical qualities. The "other" becomes a critical counterpoint on which one's own stance depends. While activists' actions are cast against each other, both sides provide ways for managing the structural opposition in America between wage work and parenthood that still shapes the lives of most women in this culture, and differentiates them from those of men.

Such data suggest to me that the we/they dichotomy marking the public side of the debate masks the points on which activists converge: issues such as comparable worth, women embracing political power, women reshaping the economy to meet their needs and responsibilities, and opposition to "male culture" insofar as it is identified with materialism and achievement and detrimental to women's needs as mothers. In addition, these activists' lives are embedded in social worlds with significant empirical and ideological overlap. Neighborhood and state politics, school boards, churches, PTA, pot lucks, canoe trips, backyard picnics are the arena of "local knowledge" occupied by activists on both sides.

The pro-life and pro-choice stances, like all genuine dialectical oppositions, have a number of elements in common, and both draw on an overarching understanding of gender prevalent in American society. Both sides voice a critique of a culture that increasingly stresses materialism and self-enhancement while denying the cultural value of dependents and those who care for them; in each case, they tie this perspective to women, claiming that it is women who represent nurturance, whether in the family or in the society at large. While their solutions differ, each group desires, in its own way, to ameliorate the unequal conditions faced by women in American culture.

THE RETURN OF THE NATIVE

Despite their obvious differences, the shared concerns of women activists on both sides, such as those that I have presented above, continued to come up, and so I wove the thread of their common discourse into my writing. After I returned from the field and began to present these ideas in public, the reactions of colleagues raised new problems for me. It is one thing, I learned quickly, for an anthropologist to offer her analysis of the native's point of view when the subjects are hidden in the highlands of New Guinea and have little impact on the lives of the assembled audience. Relativism has its limits, I discovered, especially when the subject is a controversial group from one's own society.

At first, I used a conventional anthropological strategy of attempting to mediate social distance by stressing what I saw as shared concerns in terms that the "natives" (pro-life activists in this case) would not use but which would be familiar and evocative to mostly liberal anthropological audiences. For example, I would speak of the critique of materialism and conspicuous consumption in American life that fuels much right-to-life sentiment as "critical of capitalism's dehumanizing effects," a phrase I think appropriate but one most pro-life people would be unlikely to use, because it suggests ties to secular, left-wing ideologies which they eschew, but which most anthropologists hold dear.

Initially, I was more successful at engaging my audiences when I began framing my material in this way; this rhetorical strategy succeeded in disarming those armed with preconceptions. However, in the end the overall effect was to create further hostility and doubt on the part of certain audiences who took offense at any possible identification between themselves (many of whom also were critical of materialism in capitalist life) and these "others" to whom they were politically opposed, I found myself fielding hostile responses from colleagues; one skeptic actually suggested that my data—transcripts of life story interviews—simply were not true!

As a way out of the dilemma, I decided to put less effort into mediation and to create a more direct sense of confrontation between the right-to-life activists and the audiences I was addressing. Because my work took place in the context of a social drama—a contest around an abortion clinic—the multiple points of view of activists and their dialectical intertwining could be presented and compared. My hope was that the response could no longer be deflected onto me as if I had become an advocate rather than an analyst of these people.

While the social drama of clinic protests allowed the complexities of perspectives to be presented, it became apparent to me that abortion activism also needed to be contextualized as an ongoing social form rather than an isolated phenomenon. The metaphors and issues of gender articulated in the abortion debate are not new in American history, as many scholars have pointed out. I began to read extensively the feminist research on women's social history in America (Cott and Pleck 1979; Degler 1981; L. Gordon 1977).[4] This perspective gave me a powerful historical framework for examining the cultural and historical roots of contemporary debates over gender as they are played out in the abortion debate. Such a framing drew attention to the structural determinants that have shaped American women's lives for over two centuries, allowing me to resituate both the specific ethnographic case and the broader abortion controversy as part of a legacy of women's activism in the United States. This drew attention away from the immediacy of politics and toward broader cultural patterns regarding gender that are often too close to see in one's own society. The danger of such a long view, however, is that one loses a sense of the social actors themselves, the complexity of their motivations, and the cultural possibilities of their actions.

DISTINGUISHING IDENTITIES/POLYPHONIC STRATEGIES

In trying to understand the meaningful location of abortion in the lives of contemporary women, I elicited "life stories" (Bertaux and Kohli 1984) from women from both sides, as part of an interest in activists' subjectivity. My initial intention in using this method was to grasp the significance that activism assumed in people's lives, to clarify the connections they saw between their sense of personal identity and abortion activism, and to see how engagement in these social movements was itself transformative. Life stories allowed me to present to readers long sections of narratives in which subjects interpreted their own actions, deflecting attention away from me as ethnographer and forcing a vicarious encounter between the reader and the subjects.

My method was simple. How, I asked activists, did they see their own lives in relation to their current work on the abortion issue? During my fieldwork, I carried out thirty-five such interviews, twenty-one from pro-life activists, and fourteen from pro-choice activists. The result was a set of narratively shaped fragments of more comprehensive life histories in which women used their activism to frame and interpret their historical and biographical experiences, in ways that distinguish the memberships of each group. I call them "procreation stories" because in them, activists on either side constituted provisional, narrative resolutions of their dissonant experience of what they regard as a coherent cultural model for the place of reproduction, motherhood, and work in the female life course in contemporary America.[5]

When I began to carry out these interviews, I discovered that most of the activists shared my interest in these questions. We were, in a sense, interested in figuring out the same problems. People seemed to enjoy the process, and when I would see them after the interviews, they would often recall things they had forgotten to tell me. This desire to continue telling me a life story indicated to me that the interview was part of an active reconstruction of experience, providing continuity between the past and current action and belief. These women also are engaged in convincing others of the rightness of their position; in a sense, I had positioned myself as a potential convert. Certainly the life stories were shaped in part by what these women imagined would persuade me to agree with them. This response was not entirely unexpected; what had not occurred to me was that the material generated by this method would help me to mediate their worldview to incredulous audiences to whom right-to-life activists otherwise had no access; finally, it became apparent to me that my informants saw me as a vehicle for doing so.

To capture the tension that framed the life story interviews, I realized I needed to generate a more direct sense of confrontation between the right-to-life activists and the audiences I was addressing to avoid the trap of mistaken identity, as if I had become an advocate rather than an analyst of these people. I turned to the emerging feminist scholarship on women's personal narratives which has developed more dialogical approaches to the re-presentation of textual material—drawing on the use of extensive direct quotes, presented as a counterpoint to the author's words.

I used personal narratives as a central element in the text, which helped me to recreate for readers what I experienced and drew attention to the contrast between my interpretations and those offered by the women themselves. To clarify and elaborate this distinction is part of a larger trend in work with women's personal narratives, as noted by the editors of a recently published collection on that topic:

In positing the centrality of the interpretive act, we recognize the possibility that the truths the narrator claims may be at odds with the most cherished notions of the interpreter. Personal narratives cannot be simply expropriated in the service of some good cause, but must be respected in their integrity. . . .

The interpretation of women's personal narratives often entails a cautious juxtaposition of alternative truths and feeds into the feminist project of revising not merely the content of our knowledge of human society, but the very criteria that guide our search for truths. (Personal Narratives Group 1989:264)

By juxtaposing sections of life stories with my analyses of them and of other women activists in American history, I hoped to create a richer sense of the positions held by activists and how their identities emerge from lived experience as well as the historical construction of gender in the United States.

CONCLUSION

Working in as contested a situation as the one I had chosen, I could not rely on prior styles of ethnographic representation in which the cultural object is presented as homogeneous and stable, nor could I let my voice stand for my subjects. I also had to consider a complex readership, which included other anthropologists and feminist scholars, as well as my informants and other activists on both sides of the abortion debate. This was not simply a problem of popu-larizing, which was not my goal, but of developing a representational strategy that would challenge preconceptions on received political wisdom.

My struggle for an approach that more accurately reflected my experience coincided with the emergence of a greater "experimentalism" in the writing of ethnography that challenged its underlying political and poetic conventions (Mar-cus and Fischer 1986). Texts in which the voices of the anthropologists and subjects are made distinct and placed in dialogue with each other and with historical material can help to render sensible challenging cases such as that of women right-to-lifers, and ensure that they are not mistakenly identified with the anthropologist. Such polyphonically structured strategies reflect recent fem-inist anthropological work, which has insisted on a complex interrogation of the ways in which a text emerges out of relationships between the ethnographer and the subject, and which has drawn attention to the often forgotten historical dimensions that illuminate the lives and often contested social action of contem-porary women.

A number of people interested in innovation in ethnographic writing have been influenced by the work of the late Russian social and literary theorist Mikhail Bakhtin. In particular, they took up Bakhtin's idea of "polyphony" as a rhetorical strategy in which "no single voice is the bearer of definitive truth," especially characteristic of complex heterogeneous societies such as the United States (Kelly 1992:44). For example, in his introduction to the book *Writing Culture*, historian of anthropology James Clifford invokes Bakhtin's ideas of dialogue and poly-phony in both language and literature as guides to ethnographic textual produc-tion:

[Dialogism] locates cultural interpretations in many sorts of reciprocal contexts, and it obliges writers to find diverse ways of rendering negotiated realities as multisubjective, power-laden, and incongruent. In this view, "culture" is always relational, an inscription of communicative processes that exist, historically, *between* subjects in relations of power. (1986:15)

In creating a text that convincingly represented opposing political positions to anthropologists and activists alike, I would invoke Bakhtin even more radically than Clifford does. While Clifford argues in favor of the decentered, complex text, Bakhtin himself refused to draw the line between text and context. In his ideas of historical poetics, no cultural production exists outside of language; the context is already textualized by what he calls "prior speakings" and the "already said" (Stam 1990). When an anthropologist's informants are close but contro-versial neighbors, one is made acutely aware of the power of prior speakings in one's own community of academia, as these become particularly loud and dif-ficult to subvert.

By shifting from a strategy of analytic mediation, which inevitably sets up the anthropologist as spokesperson for "the native," to one of a dialogue in which the voice of the "other" is audible, the author is able to recreate for her audience the counterintuitive encounter that she herself experienced across a boundary of difference in her own society. In this way, the audiences for such work must encounter this other set of voices more directly. Such polyphonically structured encounters are, of course, still mediated by the author. However, when the voices of the anthropologist and the informants are presented, distinguished, and placed in dialogue with each other, our efforts to render sensible the lives of controversial subjects in our own society are less likely be misapprehended as cases of mistaken identity.

NOTES

I would like to thank Caroline Brettell, Fred Myers, and Susan Carol Rogers for their insights in editing this chapter. Research was funded by the Charlotte Newcombe Fellowship in Ethics and Values, an American Association of University Women Fellowship, a Sigma Xi Research Award, and a David Spitz Award in the Social Sciences, CUNY Graduate Center.

1. "Right-to-life" (or "pro-life") is the name used by American social activists who are against abortion and euthanasia. Following standard anthropological practice, I will call members of the group by the name they prefer.

2. More recently, conservative analyst and New Right architect Kevin Phillips has argued that the Reagan administration was the economically destructive finale of a coalition built by Goldwater, Nixon, and Wallace in the 1960s rather than the debut of a new conservativism (Dionne 1987).

3. For example, see M. Rosaldo and Lamphere 1974; Reiter 1975; and MacCormack and Strathern 1980.

4. A more obvious context that I also addressed was the long history of changes not only in the interpretation of abortion, but in its practice as well (Luker 1984; Mohr 1978).

5. For a full discussion of my analysis, see Ginsburg 1987.

BIBLIOGRAPHY

Abu-Lughod, Lila. 1991. "Writing Against Culture." In Richard G. Fox, ed., *Recapturing Anthropology: Working in the Present*. Santa Fe, N.M.: School of American Research, pp. 137–162.

Adams, Jad. 1989. *AIDS: The HIV Myth*. New York: St. Martin's Press.

Adams, Timothy Dow. 1990. *Telling Lies in Modern American Autobiography*. Chapel Hill: University of North Carolina Press.

Agar, Michael. 1980. *The Professional Stranger: An Informal Introduction to Ethnography*. New York: Academic Press.

———. 1986. *Speaking of Ethnography*. Beverly Hills, Calif.: Sage Publications.

Allport, Gordon. 1942. *The Use of Personal Documents in Psychological Science*. Social Science Research Council, Bulletin 49. New York: Social Science Research Council.

Alverson, H., and S. Rosenberg. 1990. "Discourse Analysis of Schizophrenic Speech: A Critique and Proposal." *Applied Psycholinguistics* 11:167–184.

American Anthropological Association. 1989. "Report of the Administrative Advisory Committee," *Anthropology Newsletter* 30 (8):22–23.

———. 1990. "Revised Principles of Professional Responsibility." Ballot to Members, March 15, 1990. Washington, D.C.

Appadurai, Arjun. 1981. "The Past as a Scarce Resource." *Man* 16:201–219.

———. 1988. "Introduction: Place and Voice in Anthropological Theory." *Cultural Anthropology* 3 (1):16–20.

Arensberg, Conrad M., and Solon T. Kimball. 1940. *Family and Community in Ireland*. Cambridge, Mass.: Harvard University Press.

Asad, Talal, ed. 1973. *Anthropology and the Colonial Encounter*. New York: Humanities Press.

Badone, Ellen. 1992. Review of *Nationalism and the Politics of Culture in Quebec*, by Richard Handler. *American Ethnologist* 19 (4):in press.

Bahloul, Joelle. 1991. "France-USA: ethnographie d'une migration intellectuelle." *Ethnologie Française* 21 (1):49–55.

Barbichon, Guy. 1991. "Le Huron chez Narcisse: un regard renouvelé de l'anthropologie americaine sur la France." *Ethnologie Française* 21 (1):56–66.

Barley, Nigel. 1986. *The Innocent Anthropologist*. London: Penguin Books.

Bataille, Gretchen M., and Kathleen M. Sands. 1984. *American Indian Women: Telling Their Lives*. Lincoln: University of Nebraska Press.

Bauman, Zygmunt. 1982. *Memories of Class*. London: Routledge and Kegan Paul.

Becker, Howard S. 1964. "Problems in the Publication of Field Studies." In Arthur J. Vidich, Joseph Bensman, and Maurice R. Stein, eds., *Reflections on Community Studies*. New York: John Wiley and Sons, pp. 267–284.

———. 1967. "Whose Side Are We On?" *Social Problems* 14:239–248.

Becker, Howard S., and Eliot Freidson. 1964. "Against the Code of Ethics." *American Sociological Review* 29:409–410.

Beckett, Samuel. 1991. *Proust*. New York: Grove Press.

Behar, Ruth. 1986. *Santa Maria del Monte: The Presence of the Past in a Spanish Village*. Princeton, N.J.: Princeton University Press.

Bell, Earl. 1959. "Freedom and Responsibility in Research: Comments." *Human Organization* 18:49.

Bennoune, Mafhoud. 1985. "What Does It Mean to Be a Third World Anthropologist?" *Dialectical Anthropology* 9:357–364.

Berger, Bennett M. 1985. *The Survival of a Counterculture*. Berkeley: University of California Press.

Bertaux, Daniel, ed. 1981. *Biography and Society: The Life History Approach in the Social Sciences*. Beverly Hills: Sage Publications.

Bertaux, Daniel, and Martin Kohli. 1984. "The Life Story Approach: A Continental View." *Annual Review of Sociology* 10:215–237.

Birth, Kevin K. 1990. "Reading and Righting of Writing Ethnography." *American Ethnologist* 17 (3):549–557.

Blacking, John, May McCann, Graham McFarlane, Eileen Kane, and Lee Komito. 1983. "Social Anthropology in Ireland." *RAIN* 54 (February):2–3.

Blackman, Margaret. 1992. *During My Time: Florence Edenshaw Davidson, a Haida Woman*. Rev. ed. Seattle: University of Washington Press.

Bloch, Maurice. 1977. "The Past and the Present in the Present." *Man* 12:278–292.

Boas, Franz. 1943. "Recent Anthropology 11." *Science* 98 (2546):334–337.

Borofsky, R. 1987. *Making History: Pakapukan and Anthropological Constructions of Knowledge*. New York: Cambridge University Press.

Bourguignon, Erika. 1988. "Who Are We? Where Do We Come From? Where Are We Going? Malinowski, Mead, and the Present State of Anthropology." *Central Issues* 8:71–92.

Brady, Ivan, ed. 1991. *Anthropological Poetics*. Lanham, Md.: Rowman and Littlefield.

Breen, T. H. 1989. *Imagining the Past: East Hampton Histories*. Reading, Mass.: Addison-Wesley.

Brettell, Caroline B. 1985. "From Catholics to Presbyterians: French-Canadian Immigrants in Central Illinois." *American Presbyterians, Journal of Presbyterian History* 63:285–298.

————. 1990. "The Miracles of Frenchtown: Religious Pilgrimage in a Midwestern French-Canadian Immigrant Community." Unpublished paper.

Briggs, Charles L. 1986. *Learning How to Ask*. Cambridge, Eng.: Cambridge University Press.

Briggs, Jean. 1970. *Never in Anger*. Cambridge, Mass.: Harvard University Press.

Brown, Gillian, and George Yule. 1983. *Discourse Analysis*. Cambridge, Eng.: Cambridge University Press.

Brumble, H. David. 1981. *An Annotated Bibliography of American Indian and Eskimo Bibliographies*. Lincoln: University of Nebraska Press.

Bruner, Edward. 1986. "Ethnography as Narrative." In Victor M. Turner and Edward M. Bruner, eds., *The Anthropology of Experience*. Urbana: University of Illinois Press, pp. 139–155.

Butler, Robert N. 1968. "The Life Review: An Interpretation of Reminiscences in the Aged." In B. L. Neugarten, ed., *Middle Age and Aging*. Chicago: University of Chicago Press, pp. 486–496.

Campbell, Maria. 1973. *Halfbreed*. Lincoln: University of Nebraska Press.

Caplan, Pat. 1988. "Engendering Knowledge: The Politics of Ethnography." *Anthropology Today* 4 (5):8–12; 4 (6):14–17.

Cassell, Joan. 1978. "Risk and Benefit to Subjects of Fieldwork." *American Sociologist* 13:134–143.

Cassell, Joan, and Sue-Ellen Jacobs, eds. 1987. *Handbook on Ethical Issues in Anthropology*. Special Publication of the American Anthropological Association, No. 23. Washington, D.C.

Cassell, Joan, and Murray Wax. 1980. "Editorial Introduction: Toward a Moral Science of Human Beings." *Social Problems* 27:259–264.

Chafe, Wallace. 1982. "Integration and Involvement in Speaking, Writing, and Oral Literature." In D. Tannen, *Spoken and Written Language: Exploring Orality and Literacy*. Norwood, N.J.: Ablex, pp. 171–184.

Chafe, Wallace, and Deborah Tannen. 1987. "The Relation Between Written and Spoken Language." *Annual Review of Anthropology* 16:383–407.

Chapman, Malcolm, Maryon McDonald, and Elizabeth Tonkin. 1989. "Introduction—History and Social Anthropology." In Tonkin, McDonald, and Chapman, eds., *History and Ethnicity*. London: Routledge, pp. 1–21.

Chilungu, Simeon W. 1976. "Issues in the Ethics of Research Method: An Interpretation of the Anglo-American Perspective." *Current Anthropology* 17 (3):457–481.

Cicourel, Aaron V. 1985. "Text and Discourse." *Annual Review of Anthropology* 14:159–185.

Clifford, James. 1983. "On Ethnographic Authority." *Representations* 1 (2):118–146.

————. 1986. "Introduction: Partial Truths." In James Clifford and George Marcus, eds., *Writing Culture: The Poetics and Politics of Ethnography*. Berkeley: University of California Press, pp. 1–26.

————. 1988. *The Predicament of Culture: Twentieth-Century Ethnography, Literature and Art*. Cambridge, Mass.: Harvard University Press.

Clifford, James, and George Marcus, eds. 1986. *Writing Culture: The Poetics and Politics of Ethnography*. Berkeley: University of California Press.

Clough, Patricia Ticineto. 1992. *The End(s) of Ethnography: From Realism to Social Criticism*. Newbury Park, Calif.: Sage Publications.

Cohen, Stanley. 1972. *Folk Devils and Moral Panics*. London: McGibbon and Key.

Collard, Anna. 1989. "Investigating 'Social Memory' in a Greek Context." In Elizabeth Tonkin, Maryon McDonald, and Malcolm Chapman, eds., *History and Ethnicity*. London: Routledge, pp. 89–103.

Cook, Ramsey. 1989. Review of *Nationalism and the Politics of Culture in Quebec*, by Richard Handler. *Queen's Quarterly* 96 (2):540.

Cott, Nancy, and Elizabeth Pleck. 1979. Introduction to Nancy Cott and Elizabeth Pleck, eds., *A Heritage of Her Own*. New York: Simon and Schuster, pp. 9–24.

Crane, Julia G. 1991. "Experimentation and Change in Contemporary Strategies for Ethnography." *Reviews in Anthropology* 19:11–40.

Crapanzano, Vincent. 1977a. "On the Writing of Ethnography." *Dialectical Anthropology* 2 (1):69–73.

———. 1977b. "The Life History in Anthropological Field Work." *Anthropology and Humanism Quarterly* 2 (2–3):3–7.

———. 1980. *Tuhami: Portrait of a Moroccan*. Chicago: University of Chicago Press.

———. 1986. "Hermes' Dilemma." In James Clifford and George Marcus, eds., *Writing Culture: The Poetics and Politics of Ethnography*. Berkeley: University of California Press, pp. 51–76.

———. 1992. *Hermes' Dilemma and Hamlet's Desire: On the Epistemology of Interpretation*. Cambridge, Mass.: Harvard University Press.

Crocombe, Ron. 1976. "Anthropology, Anthropologists, and Pacific Islanders." *Oceania* 47 (1):66–73.

Crow Dog, Mary (with Richard Erdoes). 1990. *Lakota Woman*. New York: Harper.

Cruikshank, Julie, ed., in collaboration with Angela Sidney, Kitty Smith, and Annie Ned. 1990. *Life Lived Like a Story*. Lincoln: University of Nebraska Press.

Davis, Dona. 1983a. *Blood and Nerves: An Ethnographic Focus on Menopause*. St. John's: Memorial University of Newfoundland Institute of Social and Economic Research.

———. 1983b. "Woman the Worrier: Confronting Archetypes of Stress." *Women's Studies* 10 (2):135–146.

———. 1986a. "Changing Self-Image: Studying Menopausal Women in a Newfoundland Fishing Village." In T. Whitehead and M. E. Connaway, eds., *Self, Sex and Gender in Cross-Cultural Fieldwork*. Urbana: University of Illinois Press.

———. 1986b. "The Meaning of Menopause in a Newfoundland Fishing Village." *Culture, Medicine and Psychiatry* 10 (1):73–94.

———. 1987. "Celebrating Women in a Newfoundland Fishing Village." *Plainswoman* 11 (4):4–14.

———. 1989. "The Newfoundland Change of Life." *Journal of Cross-Cultural Gerontology* 3 (4):1–24.

———. 1990a. "Reservations about Newfoundland: Community and Crisis in a North Atlantic Fishery." Unpublished manuscript.

———. 1990b. "Dependable to Dangerous: Changing Gender Ideologies in Rural Newfoundland." Paper presented to the Canadian Anthropology Society, Calgary, May 2.

———. In press. "Gender, Generation and Culture Change: Community Crisis in Newfoundland." Memorial University of Newfoundland, Institute of Social and Economic Research.

De Beaugrande, Robert. 1980. *Text, Discourse, and Process*. Norwood, N.J.: Ablex.

DeBuys, William Eno, and Alex Harris. 1990. *River of Traps: A Village Life.* Albuquerque: University of New Mexico Press.

DeFleur, Melvin L., and Everette E. Dennis. 1981. *Understanding Mass Communication.* Boston: Houghton Mifflin.

Degler, Carl. 1981. *At Odds: Women and the Family in America from the Revolution to the Present.* New York: Oxford University Press.

DeVita, Philip R. 1992. *The Naked Anthropologist: Tales from Around the World.* Belmont, Calif.: Wadsworth Publishing.

Dionne, E. J., Jr. 1987. "High Tide for Conservatives, but Some Fear What Follows." *New York Times*, October 13.

Dollard, John. 1935. *Criteria for the Life History.* New Haven, Conn.: Yale University Press.

Dumont, Jean-Paul. 1978. *The Headman and I: Ambiguity and Ambivalence in the Fieldwork Experience.* Austin: University of Texas Press.

Duster, Troy, David Matza, and David Wellman. 1979. "Field Work and the Protection of Human Subjects." *American Sociologist* 14:136–142.

Dwyer, Kevin. 1977. "Dialogue of Fieldwork." *Dialectical Anthropology* 2:143–151.

———. 1982. *Moroccan Dialogues.* Baltimore: Johns Hopkins University Press.

Dyk, Walter. 1938. *Son of the Old Man Hat: A Navajo Autobiography.* New York: Harcourt, Brace.

Eisenstadt, S. N. 1973. "Post-Traditional Societies and the Continuity and Reconstruction of Tradition." *Daedalus* (Winter):1–28.

Emerson, Robert M., ed. 1983. *Contemporary Field Research: A Collection of Readings.* Prospect Heights, Ill.: Waveland Press.

Evans-Pritchard, E. E. 1962. *Social Anthropology and Other Essays.* New York: Free Press.

———. 1968 (1940). *The Nuer.* Oxford: Clarendon Press.

Fabian, Johannes. 1983. *Time and the Other: How Anthropology Makes Its Object.* New York: Columbia University Press.

Fahim, Hussein. 1977. "Foreign and Indigenous Anthropology: The Perspectives of an Egyptian Anthropologist." *Human Organization* 36 (1):80–86.

Farrel, Franklyn. 1982. "The Doctrines and Rituals of the Spiritual Baptists." Unpublished thesis, University of the West Indies, Trinidad.

Fienup-Riordan, Ann. 1988. "Robert Redford, Apanuugpak, and the Invention of Tradition." *American Ethnologist* 15:442–455.

Fischer, Michael M. J. 1977. "Interpretive Anthropology." *Reviews in Anthropology* 4 (4):391–404.

Fish, Stanley. 1980. *Is There a Text in This Class? The Authority of Interpretive Communities.* Cambridge, Mass.: Harvard University Press.

Fitzgerald, Frances. 1986. *Cities on a Hill.* New York: Simon and Schuster.

Fluehr-Lobban, Carolyn, ed. 1991. *Ethics and the Profession of Anthropology: Dialogue for a New Era.* Philadelphia: University of Pennsylvania Press.

Foley, Douglas E. (with Clarice Mota, Donald Post, and Ignacio Lozano). 1988. *From Peones to Politicos: Ethnic Relations in a South Texas Town, 1900–1977.* Austin: University of Texas Press.

Ford, Clellan S. 1941. *Smoke from Their Fires: The Life of a Kwakiutl Chief.* New Haven, Conn.: Yale University Press.

Forrest, H. J. 1991. *Publish or Perish?* Dublin: Glendale Publishing.

Foster, George F., Thayer Scudder, Elizabeth Colson, and Robert V. Kemper. 1979. *Long-Term Field Research in Social Anthropology*. New York: Academic Press.

Foucault, Michel. 1972. "The Discourse on Language." Appendix to *The Archaeology of Knowledge*. New York: Pantheon, pp. 215–237.

Fox, Richard G., ed. 1991. *Recapturing Anthropology*. Santa Fe, N.M.: School of American Research Press.

Gagnon, Nicole. 1989. Review of *Nationalism and the Politics of Culture in Quebec*, by Richard Handler. *Recherches Sociographiques* 30 (1):125–127.

Galliher, John F. 1973. "The Protection of Human Subjects: A Reexamination of the Professional Code of Ethics." *American Sociologist* 8:93–100.

Geertz, Clifford. 1973. *The Interpretation of Cultures: Selected Essays*. New York: Basic Books.

———. 1983. *Local Knowledge: Further Essays in Interpretive Anthropology*. New York: Basic Books.

———. 1986. "Making Experiences, Authoring Selves." In Victor Turner and Edward Bruner, eds., *The Anthropology of Experience*. Urbana: University of Illinois Press, pp. 373–380.

———. 1988. *Works and Lives: The Anthropologist as Author*. Stanford: Stanford University Press.

Gibbs-de-Peza, Hazel Ann. 1989. "Correcting Misconceptions: A Review of Caribbean Studies Theses on the Topic—The Spiritual Baptist Church." Caribbean Studies thesis, University of the West Indies.

Gill, Bartholomew. 1989. *The Death of a Joyce Scholar*. New York: William Morrow.

Gilligan, Carol. 1982. *In a Different Voice: Psychological Theory and Women's Development*. Cambridge, Mass.: Harvard University Press.

Ginsburg, Faye. 1987. "Procreation Stories: Nurturance, Reproduction, and Procreation in Abortion Activists' Life Stories." *American Ethnologist* 14 (4):623–636.

Glassie, Henry. 1982. *Passing the Time in Balleymenone: Culture and History of an Ulster Community*. Philadelphia: University of Pennsylvania Press.

Glazier, Stephen D. 1991. *Marchin' the Pilgrims Home: A Study of the Spiritual Baptists of Trinidad*. Salem, Wis.: Sheffield Publishing.

Gmelch, Sharon. 1986. *Nan: The Life of an Irish Travelling Woman*. New York: W. W. Norton.

———. 1992. "From Beginning to End: An Irish Life History." *Journal of Narrative and Life History* 2 (1):29–38.

Gold, Gerald. 1988. Review of *Nationalism and the Politics of Culture in Quebec*, by Richard Handler. *Culture* 8 (2):108–109.

Golde, Peggy, ed. 1986. *Women in the Field: Anthropological Experiences*. 2nd ed. Chicago: Aldine.

Goldner, Fred H. 1967. "Role Emergence and the Ethics of Ambiguity." In Gideon Sjoberg, ed., *Ethics, Politics and Social Research*. Cambridge, Mass.: Schenkman Publishing, pp. 245–266.

Gonzalez, Denyse. 1987. "The Hand that Rocks the Cradle: A Bibliographical Case Study of a Woman in Religion." Unpublished thesis, University of the West Indies, Trinidad.

Goodwin, Charles, and John Heritage. 1990. "Conversation Analysis." *Annual Review of Anthropology* 19:283–307.

Gorden, Raymond L. 1975. *Interviewing: Strategy, Techniques, and Tactics*. Homewood, Ill.: Dorsey Press.

Gordon, Deborah. 1988. "Writing Culture, Writing Feminism: The Poetics and Politics of Experimental Ethnography." *Inscriptions* 3/4:7–24.

———. 1990. "The Politics of Ethnographic Authority: Race and Writing in the Ethnography of Margaret Mead and Zora Neale Hurston." In Marc Manganaro, ed., *Modernist Anthropology: From Fieldwork to Text*. Princeton, N.J.: Princeton University Press, pp. 146–162.

Gordon, Linda. 1977. *Woman's Body, Woman's Right: A Social History of Birth Control in America*. New York: Penguin Press.

Greenwald, Robert, Mary K. Ryan, and James E. Mulvihill. 1982. *Human Subjects Research: A Handbook for Institutional Review Boards*. New York: Plenum Press.

Gusdorf, Georges. 1980. "Conditions and Limits of Autobiography." In James Olney, ed., *Autobiography: Essays Theoretical and Critical*. Princeton, N.J.: Princeton University Press, pp. 28–48 [originally published 1956].

Hall, John R. 1989. *Gone from the Promised Land: Jonestown in American Cultural History*. New Brunswick, N.J.: Transaction.

Hammersley, Martyn. 1992. *What's Wrong with Ethnography? Methodological Explorations*. New York: Routledge.

Hammersley, Martyn, and Paul Atkinson. 1983. *Ethnography: Principles in Practice*. London: Tavistock Publications.

Handler, Richard. 1988. *Nationalism and the Politics of Culture in Quebec*. Madison: University of Wisconsin Press.

———. 1991. "Who Owns the Past? History, Cultural Property, and the Logic of Possessive Individualism." In Brett Williams, ed., *The Politics of Culture*. Washington, D.C.: Smithsonian Institution Press, pp. 63–74.

Handler, Richard, and Jocelyn Linnekin. 1984. "Tradition, Genuine or Spurious." *Journal of American Folklore* 97:273–290.

Hanson, Allan. 1989. "The Making of the Maori: Culture Invention and Its Logic." *American Anthropologist* 91:890–902.

———. 1991. "Reply to Langdon, Levine and Linnekin." *American Anthropologist* 93:449–450.

Haraway, Donna. 1988. "Situated Knowledges: The Science Question in Feminism and the Privilege of Partial Perspective." *Feminist Study* 14:575–599.

Harding, Susan. 1987. "Convicted by the Holy Spirit: The Rhetoric of Fundamental Baptist Conversion." *American Ethnologist* 14 (1):167–181.

Haring, Douglas. 1956. *Personal Character and Cultural Milieu*. Syracuse: Syracuse University Press.

Harrison, Faye V., ed. 1991. *Decolonizing Anthropology: Moving Further Toward an Anthropology of Liberation*. Washington, D.C.: Association for Black Anthropologists, American Anthropological Association.

Hatch, Elvin. 1987. "Comment on Marilyn Strathern, Out of Context: The Persuasive Fiction of Anthropology." *Current Anthropology* 28 (3):271–272.

Hau'ofa, Epeli. 1975. "Anthropology and Pacific Islanders." *Oceania* 45 (4):283–289.

Herndl, Carl G. 1991. "Writing Ethnography: Representation, Rhetoric, and Institutional Practices." *College English* 53 (3):320–332.

Hershey, Nathan, and Robert D. Miller. 1976. *Human Experimentation and the Law*. Germantown, Md.: Aspen Systems.

Herzfeld, Michael. 1980. "Honour and Shame: Problems in the Comparative Analysis of Moral Systems." *Man* 15:339–351.

———. 1983. "Looking Both Ways: The Ethnographer in the Text." *Semiotica* 46 (2/4):151–166.

———. 1984. "The Horns of the Mediterraneanist Dilemma." *American Ethnologist* 11 (3):429–454.

Himmelstein, Jerome. 1990. *To the Right: The Transformation of American Conservatism.* Berkeley: University of California Press.

Hobsbawn, Eric, and Terence Ranger. 1983. *The Invention of Tradition.* Cambridge, Eng.: Cambridge University Press.

Holub, Robert C. 1984. *Reception Theory: A Critical Introduction.* New York: Methuen.

Holy, Ladislav. 1987. *Comparative Anthropology.* Oxford: Basil Blackwell.

hooks, bell. 1989. *Talking Back, Thinking Feminist, Thinking Black.* Boston: South End Press.

Horwitz, Richard. 1985. *The Strip: An American Place.* Lincoln: University of Nebraska Press.

———. 1987. "An Artist Makes History: Peter Feldstein and Oxford '84." *North Dakota Quarterly* 55 (1):78–92.

———. 1989. " 'Foreign Expertise': American Studies in Taiwan." *American Studies International* 27 (1):38–62.

Howes, David. 1990. "Controlling Textuality: A Call for a Return to the Senses." *Anthropologica* 32:55–73.

Hymes, Dell. 1962. "The Ethnography of Speaking." In T. Gladwin and W. C. Sturtevant, eds., *Anthropology and Human Behavior.* Washington, D.C.: Anthropological Society of Washington, pp. 13–53.

———. 1967. "The Anthropology of Communication." In F. Dance, ed., *Human Communication Theory: Original Essays.* New York: Holt, Rinehart and Winston, pp. 1–39.

———., ed. 1969. *Reinventing Anthropology.* New York: Pantheon.

Iamo, Warilea. 1988. "The Stigma of New Guinea—Reflections of Anthropology and Anthropologists." *Central Issues* 8:56–69.

Ives, Edward D. 1980. *The Tape-Recorded Interview: A Manual for Fieldworkers in Folklore and Oral History.* Knoxville: University of Tennessee Press.

Jackson, Anthony, ed. 1987. *Anthropology at Home.* London: Tavistock Publications.

Jackson, Bruce. 1987. *Fieldwork.* Urbana: University of Illinois Press.

Jackson, Jean. 1989. "Is There a Way to Talk about Making Culture Without Making Enemies?" *Dialectical Anthropology* 14:127–143.

Jackson, Michael. 1989. *Paths Toward a Clearing: Radical Empiricism and Ethnographic Inquiry.* Bloomington: Indiana University Press.

Jacobson, David. 1991. *Reading Ethnography.* Albany: State University of New York Press.

Jaffe, Alexandra. 1989. "L'Angoisse de l'être et l'enjeu du Corse." *Publications Universitaires Linguistiques et Anthropologiques Université de Corté* No. 1:17–29.

Jones, Delmos. 1970. "Towards a Native Anthropology." *Human Organization* 29:251–259.

Kane, Eileen. 1979. "Is Ireland Blighted?" *Irish Press* (Dublin), November 13.

———. 1982. "Cui Bono? Do Aon Duine (To Whose Advantage? Nobody's)." *RAIN* 50 (June):2–3.

Kaplan, Bernice. 1988. "To the Memory of Eleanor (Happy) Leacock." *Central Issues* 8:1.

Karp, Ivan, and Martha B. Kendall. 1982. "Reflexivity in Fieldwork." In Paul F. Secord, ed., *Explaining Human Behavior: Consciousness, Human Action and Social Structure*. Beverly Hills, Calif.: Sage Publications, pp. 249–273.

Keesing, Roger. 1989. "Exotic Readings of Cultural Texts." *Current Anthropology* 30 (4):459–479.

Kelly, Aileen. 1992. "Revealing Bakhtin." *New York Review of Books* 39 (15):44–48.

Kennedy, Theodore. 1980. *You Gotta Deal with It: Family Relations in a Southern Community*. New York: Oxford University Press.

Kim, Choong Soon. 1990. "The Role of the Non-Western Anthropologist Reconsidered: Illusion Versus Reality." *Current Anthropology* 31 (2):196–200.

Kirk, Jerome, and Marc L. Miller. 1986. *Reliability and Validity in Qualitative Research*. Beverly Hills, Calif.: Sage Publications.

Klatch, Rebecca. 1987. *Women and the New Right*. Philadelphia: Temple University Press.

Kluckhohn, Clyde. 1945. "The Personal Document in Anthropological Science." In L. Gottschalk, C. Kluckhohn, and R. Angell, eds., *The Use of Personal Documents in History, Anthropology, and Sociology*. New York: Social Science Research Council, Bulletin 55, pp. 78–173.

Korovkin, Michael. 1989. Review of *Nationalism and the Politics of Culture in Quebec*, by Richard Handler. *Annali Accademici Canadesi* 5:168–179.

Krupat, Arnold. 1985. *For Those Who Came After: A Study of Native American Autobiography*. Berkeley: University of California Press.

Laforest, Guy. 1988. Review of *Nationalism and the Politics of Culture in Quebec*, by Richard Handler. *Canadian Journal of Political Science* 21 (4):843–844.

Lame Deer, John [Fire], and Richard Erdoes. 1972. *Lame Deer: Seeker of Visions*. New York: Simon and Schuster.

Langdon, Robert. 1991. "Caucasian Maoris: Sixteenth Century Spaniards in New Zealand." *American Anthropologist* 93 (2):440–444.

Langness, Lewis L. 1965. *The Life History in Anthropological Science*. New York: Holt, Rinehart and Winston.

Langness, Lewis L., and Gelya Frank. 1981. *Lives: An Anthropological Approach to Biography*. Novato, Calif.: Chandler and Sharp.

Larcom, Joan. 1982. "The Invention of Convention." *Mankind* 13:330–337.

Lauritsen, John. 1989. *Poison by Prescription: The AZT Story*. New York: Pagan Press.

Lawless, Elaine J. 1992. " 'I was afraid someone like you . . . an outsider . . . would misunderstand.' Negotiating Interpretive Differences Between Ethnographers and Subjects." *Journal of American Folklore* 105 (417):302–314.

Lederman, Rena. 1990. "Unpacking Fieldnotes: Pretexts for Ethnography." In Roger Sanjek, ed., *Fieldnotes: The Makings of Anthropology*. Ithaca: Cornell University Press, pp. 71–91.

Leighton, Alexander, and Dorothea Leighton. 1949. "Gregorio, the Hand Trembler: A Psychobiological Personality Study of a Navajo Indian." *Papers of the Peabody Museum of American Archaeology and Ethnology*, Vol. 40.

Leone, Mark. 1990. Review of *Nationalism and the Politics of Culture in Quebec*, by Richard Handler. *Anthropological Quarterly* 63 (1):61–62.

Levine, H. B. 1991. "Comment on Hanson's 'The Making of the Maori.' " *American Anthropologist* 93 (2):444–446.

Levi-Strauss, Claude. 1955. *Tristes Tropiques.* New York: Athenaeum.

Levitt, Joseph. 1989. Review of *Nationalism and the Politics of Culture in Quebec*, by Richard Handler. *Canadian Review of Studies in Nationalism* 16 (1–2):377–379.

Linderman, Frank B. 1930. *Plenty-Coups.* Lincoln: University of Nebraska Press.

———. 1932. *Pretty Shield.* Lincoln: University of Nebraska Press.

Linnekin, Jocelyn S. 1983. "Defining Tradition: Variations on the Hawaiian Identity." *American Ethnologist* 10:241–252.

———. 1991. "Cultural Invention and the Dilemma of Authenticity." *American Anthropologist* 93:446–448.

Lippmann, Walter. 1965 (1922). *Public Opinion.* New York: Free Press.

Little, Kenneth. 1980. "Explanation and Individual Lives: A Reconsideration of Life Writing in Anthropology." *Dialectical Anthropology* 5:215–226.

Lofland, John. 1987. "Reflections on a Thrice-Named Journal." *Journal of Contemporary Ethnography* 16:25–40.

Lowenthal, David. 1989. "The Timeless Past: Some Anglo-American Historical Preconceptions." *Journal of American History* 75:1263–1280.

Luker, Kristin. 1984. *Abortion and the Politics of Motherhood.* Berkeley: University of California Press.

McBeth, Sally. 1983a. *Ethnic Identity and the Boarding School Experience of West-Central Oklahoma American Indians.* Washington, D.C.: University Press of America.

———. 1983b. "Indian Boarding Schools and Ethnic Identity: An Example from the Southern Plains Tribes of Oklahoma." *Plains Anthropologist* 28 (100):119–128.

———. 1984. "The Primer and the Hoe." *Natural History* 93 (8):4–12.

———. 1989. "Collaboration." In B. Benson et al., eds., *Day in, Day out: Women's Lives in North Dakota.* Grand Forks: University of North Dakota Press, pp. 64–67.

MacCormack, Carol, and Marilyn Strathern, eds. 1980. *Nature, Culture and Gender.* New York: Cambridge University Press.

McDonald, Maryon. 1986. "Celtic Ethnic Kinship and the Problem of Being English." *Current Anthropology* 27 (4):333–346.

———. 1987. "The Politics of Fieldwork in Brittany." In Anthony Jackson, ed., *Anthropologists at Home.* London: Tavistock Publications, pp. 120–138.

———. 1989. *We Are Not French.* New York: Routledge.

McRobbie, Angela. 1980. "Settling Accounts with Subcultures: A Feminist Critique." *Screen Education* 34:37–49.

Mandelbaum, David G. 1973. "The Study of Life History: Gandhi." *Current Anthropology* 14 (3):177–196.

Manganaro, Marc, ed. 1990. *Modernist Anthropology: From Fieldwork to Text.* Princeton, N.J.: Princeton University Press.

Marcus, George E., and Dick Cushman. 1982. "Ethnographies as Texts." *Annual Review of Anthropology* 11:25–69.

Marcus, George E., and Michael M. J. Fischer. 1986. *Anthropology as Cultural Critique: An Experimental Moment in the Human Sciences.* Chicago: University of Chicago Press.

Mascia-Lees, Frances, Patricia Sharpe, and Colleen Ballerino Cohen. 1989. "The Postmodernist Turn in Anthropology: Cautions from a Feminist Perspective.'' *Signs* 15 (1):7–34.

Mason, Peter. 1990. *Deconstructing America: Representations of the Other*. London: Routledge.

Mead, Margaret. 1932. *The Changing Culture of an American Indian Tribe*. New York: Columbia University Press.

———. 1963. *Sex and Temperament in Three Primitive Societies*. New York: William Morrow.

Messenger, John. 1969 (1983). *Inis Beag: Island of Ireland*. Prospect Heights, Ill.: Waveland Press.

———. 1984. ''Problems of Irish Ethnography.'' *Royal Anthropological Institute Newsletter* 3:2–13.

———. 1988. ''Islanders Who Read.'' *Anthropology Today* 4 (2):17–19.

———. 1989. *Inis Beag Revisited: The Anthropologist as Observant Participator*. Salem, Wis.: Sheffield Publishing.

Mies, Maria. 1983. ''Towards a Methodology for Feminist Research.'' In G. Bowles and R. Klein, eds., *Theories of Women's Studies*. London: Routledge and Kegan Paul, pp. 15–26.

Minh-ha, Trinh T. 1989. *Woman, Native, Other: Writing Postcoloniality and Feminism*. Bloomington: Indiana University Press.

Mintz, Sidney W. 1989. ''The Sensation of Moving While Standing Still.'' *American Ethnologist* 16 (4):786–796.

Modleski, Tania. 1986. ''Feminism and the Power of Interpretation.'' In T. de Lauretis, ed., *Feminist Studies/Critical Studies*. Bloomington: University of Indiana Press.

Mohr, James. 1978. *Abortion in America: The Origins and Evolution of National Policy*. New York: Oxford University Press.

Molohon, Kathryn. 1989. Review of *Nationalism and the Politics of Culture in Quebec*, by Richard Handler. *American Anthropologist* 91:795–796.

Momaday, N. Scott. 1976. *The Names: A Memoir*. Tucson: University of Arizona Press.

Moore, Joan W. 1967. ''Problems in Large-Scale Study of a Minority Population.'' In Gideon Sjoberg, ed., *Ethics, Politics and Social Research*. Cambridge, Mass.: Schenkman Publishing, pp. 225–244.

Mowat, Claire. 1983. *The Outport People*. Toronto: Seal Books.

Myerhoff, Barbara. 1978. *Number Our Days*. New York: E. P. Dutton.

Myerhoff, Barbara G., and Virginia Tufte. 1975. ''Life History as Integration: An Essay on an Experimental Model.'' *Gerontologist* (December):541–544.

Myers, Fred R. 1986. ''The Politics of Representation: Anthropological Discourse and Australian Aborigines.'' *American Ethnologist* 13 (1):138–153.

Narayan, Kirin. 1989. *Storytellers, Saints, and Scoundrels: Folk Narrative in Hindu Religious Teaching*. Philadelphia: University of Pennsylvania Press.

Nash, Dennison, and Ronald M. Wintrob. 1972. ''The Emergence of Self-Consciousness in Ethnography.'' *Current Anthropology* 13:527–542.

Neihardt, John G. 1932. *Black Elk Speaks*. New York: William Morrow.

Noelle-Neumann, Elisabeth. 1974. ''The Spiral of Silence: A Theory of Public Opinion.'' *Journal of Communication* 24 (1):43–51.

Noonan, John. 1979. *A Private Choice: Abortion in America in the Seventies*. New York: Free Press.

Olney, James, ed. 1972. *Metaphors of the Self: The Meaning of Autobiography*. Princeton, N.J.: Princeton University Press.

——., ed. 1980. *Autobiography: Essays Theoretical and Critical*. Princeton, N.J.: Princeton University Press.

——., ed. 1988. *Studies in Autobiography*. New York: Oxford University Press.

Orlans, Harold. 1973. *Contracting for Knowledge*. San Francisco: Jossey-Bass.

Ortner, Sherry. 1978. *Sherpas Through Their Rituals*. Cambridge, Eng.: Cambridge University Press.

——. 1984. "Theory in Anthropology since the Sixties." *Comparative Studies in Society and History* 26:126–166.

Paddock, John. 1965a. "Oscar Lewis' Mexico." *Mesoamerican Notes of the Department of Anthropology, University of the Americas* 6:3–34.

——. 1965b. "Private Lives and Anthropological Publications." *Mesoamerican Notes of the Department of Anthropology, University of the Americas* 6:59–66.

Paige, Connie. 1984. *The Right-to-Lifers*. New York: Summit Books.

Paredes, Americo. 1978. "On Ethnographic Work among Minority Groups: A Folklorist's Perspective." In Raymond Romo and Raymond Paredes, eds., *New Directions in Chicano Scholarship*. La Jolla: University of California at San Diego, Chicano Studies Program, pp. 1–32.

Personal Narratives Group. 1989. *Interpreting Women's Lives*. Bloomington: Indiana University Press.

Pina-Cabral, João de. 1989. "The Mediterranean as a Category of Regional Comparison: A Critical View." *Current Anthropology* 30 (3):399–406.

Pitman, Mary Anne, and Joseph A. Maxwell. 1992. "Qualitative Approaches to Evaluation: Models and Methods." In Margaret D. LeCompte, Wendy Millroy, and Judith Preissle, eds., *Handbook of Qualitative Research in Education*. San Diego: Academic Press, pp. 729–770.

Polier, Nicole, and William Roseberry. 1989. "Triste Tropes: Post-modern Anthropologists Encounter the Other and Discover Themselves." *Economy and Society* 18 (2):245–264.

Powers, William K. 1990. "Comment on the Politics of Orthography." *American Anthropologist* 92 (2):496–497.

Pratt, Mary Louise. 1986. "Fieldwork in Common Places." In James Clifford and George Marcus, eds., *Writing Culture: The Poetics and Politics of Ethnography*. Berkeley: University of California Press, pp. 27–50.

Punch, Maurice. 1986. *The Politics and Ethics of Fieldwork*. Beverly Hills: Sage Publications.

Rabasa, Jose. 1987. "Dialogue as Conquest: Mapping Spaces for Counter-Discourse." *Cultural Critique* 6:131–159.

Rabinow, Paul. 1977. *Reflections on Fieldwork in Morocco*. Berkeley: University of California Press.

——. 1985. "Discourse and Power: On the Limits of Ethnographic Texts." *Dialectical Anthropology* 10 (1):1–13.

——. 1986. "Representations Are Social Facts: Modernity and Post-modernity in Anthropology." In James Clifford and George Marcus, eds., *Writing Culture: The Poetics and Politics of Ethnography*. Berkeley: University of California Press, pp. 234–261.

Radin, Paul. 1926. *Crashing Thunder: The Autobiography of an American Indian*. New York: Appleton.

———. 1933. *The Method and Theory of Ethnology*. New York: Basic Books [1965].

Rainwater, Lee, and David J. Pittman. 1967. "Ethical Problems in Studying a Politically Sensitive and Deviant Community." *Social Problems* 14:357–366.

Rappoport, Jon. 1989. *AIDS Inc*. San Bruno, Calif.: Human Energy Press.

Read, Kenneth. 1965. *The High Valley*. New York: Charles Scribner's Sons.

Reinharz, Shulamit. 1992. *Feminist Methods in Social Research*. New York: Oxford University Press.

Reiter, Rayna Rapp, ed. 1975. *Toward an Anthropology of Women*. New York: Monthly Review Press.

Ricoeur, Paul. 1979. "The Model of the Text: Meaningful Action Considered as a Text." In Paul Rabinow and W. M. Sullivan, eds., *Interpretive Social Science: A Reader*. Berkeley: University of California Press, pp. 73–101.

Rivière, Peter. 1989. "New Trends in British Social Anthropology." *Cadernos do Noroeste* 11:7–24.

Rogers, Susan Carol. 1991. "L'Ethnologie nord-américaine de la France: entreprise ethnologique 'près de chez soi.'" *Ethnologie Française* 21 (1):5–12.

Rosaldo, Michelle Z. 1980a. *Knowledge and Passion: Ilongot Notions of Self and Social Life*. New York: Cambridge University Press.

———. 1980b. "The Use and Abuse of Anthropology: Reflections on Feminism and Cross-Cultural Understanding." *Signs* 5(3):389–417.

Rosaldo, Michelle, and Louise Lamphere, eds. 1974. *Woman, Culture and Society*. Stanford: Stanford University Press.

Rosaldo, Renato. 1986. *When Natives Talk Back: Chicano Anthropology since the Late Sixties*. Tucson: University of Arizona, Mexican American Studies and Research Center, Renato Rosaldo Lecture Series Monograph, Vol. 2.

———. 1989. *Culture and Truth: The Remaking of Social Analysis*. Boston: Beacon Press.

Rose, Dan. 1987. *Black American Street Life: South Philadelphia 1969–1971*. Philadelphia: University of Pennsylvania Press.

———. 1990. *Living the Ethnographic Life*. Newbury Park, Calif.: Sage Publications.

Roseberry, William. 1989. *Anthropologies and Histories: Essays in Culture, History and Political Economy*. New Brunswick, N.J.: Rutgers University Press.

Rosenthal, Alan, ed. 1988. *New Challenges for Documentary*. Berkeley: University of California Press.

Roth, Paul A. 1989. "Ethnography Without Tears." *Current Anthropology* 30 (5):555–569.

Ruby, Jay, ed. 1982. *A Crack in the Mirror: Reflexive Perspectives in Anthropology*. Philadelphia: University of Pennsylvania Press.

Sahlins, Marshall. 1985. *Islands of History*. Chicago: University of Chicago Press.

Said, Edward. 1978. *Orientalism*. New York: Pantheon.

———. 1989. "Representing the Colonized: Anthropology's Interlocutors." *Critical Inquiry* 15 (Winter):205–225.

Sangren, P. Steven. 1988. "Rhetoric and the Authority of Ethnography: 'Postmodernism' and the Social Reproduction of Texts." *Current Anthropology* 29 (3):405–435.

Sanjek, Roger, ed. 1990. *Fieldnotes: The Making of Anthropology*. Ithaca, N.Y.: Cornell University Press.

Saville-Troike, Muriel. 1982. *The Ethnography of Communication*. Oxford: Basil Black-
    well.
Scheper-Hughes, Nancy. 1979 (1982a). *Saints, Scholars and Schizophrenics: Mental
    Illness in Rural Ireland*. Berkeley: University of California Press.
———. 1981. "Reply to Ballybran." *Irish Times*, February 21, p. 9–10.
———. 1987. "The Best of Two Worlds, The Worst of Two Worlds: Reflections on
    Culture and Fieldwork among the Rural Irish and Pueblo Indians." *Comparative
    Studies in Society and History* 29 (1):56–75.
———. 1982b. "Ballybran." *RAIN* 51 (August):12–13.
Schneider, Jane. 1971. "Of Vigilance and Virgins: Honor, Shame and Access to Re-
    sources in Mediterranean Society." *Ethnology* 10:1–24.
Schoen, Donald. 1983. *The Reflexive Practitioner*. New York: Basic Books.
Shankman, Paul. 1984. "The Thick and the Thin: On the Interpretive Theoretical Program
    of Clifford Geertz." *Current Anthropology* 25(3):261–280.
Shaw, Bruce. 1980. "Life History Writings in Anthropology: A Methodological Re-
    view." *Mankind* 12 (3):226–233.
Sheehan, Elizabeth A. 1990. "The Academics and the Powers: Colonialism, National
    Development and the Irish University." Ph.D. dissertation, City University of
    New York.
———. 1991. "Political and Cultural Resistance to European Community Europe: Ireland
    and the Single European Act." *Socialism and Democracy* 13 (May):101–118.
———. 1992. "Architecture as Destiny? Trinity College and University College Dub-
    lin." *Eire-Ireland* 26:7–24.
———. Forthcoming. "The Academic as Informant: Methodological and Theoretical
    Issues in the Ethnography of Intellectuals." *Human Organization*.
Shilts, Randy. 1988. *And the Band Played On: Politics, People, and the AIDS Epidemic*.
    New York: Penguin Books.
Shokeid, Moshe. 1988. "Anthropologists and Their Informants: Marginality Reconsi-
    dered." *Archives Européennes de Sociology* 29:31–47.
Simmons, Leo. 1942. *Sun Chief: The Autobiography of a Hopi Indian*. New Haven,
    Conn.: Yale University Press.
Sjoberg, Gideon, ed. 1967. *Ethics, Politics, and Social Research*. Cambridge, Mass.:
    Schenkman Publishing.
Slater, Mariam. 1976. *African Odyssey: Anthropological Adventure*. Garden City, N.J.:
    Anchor Books.
Smith, Carolyn D., and William Kornblum. 1989. *In the Field: Reading on the Field
    Research Experience*. New York: Praeger.
Smith, Sidonie. 1987. *A Poetics of Women's Autobiography*. Bloomington: Indiana Uni-
    versity Press.
Spencer, Jonathan. 1989. "Anthropology as a Kind of Writing." *Man* 24:145–164.
Spradley, James P., and Michael Rynkiewich, eds. 1976. *Ethics and Anthropology:
    Dilemmas in Fieldwork*. New York: John Wiley and Sons.
Stacey, Judith. 1988. "Can There Be a Feminist Ethnography?" *Women's Studies In-
    ternational Forum* 11 (1):21–27.
Stam, Robert. 1990. "Mikhail Bakhtin and Left Cultural Critique." In A. Kaplan, ed.,
    Postmodernism and Its Discontents. Bristol, U.K.: Verso, pp. 116–145.
Stoller, Paul. 1989a. "A Conversation in the Future." *Anthropology Newsletter* 30 (7):17.

————. 1989b. *Fusion of the Worlds: An Ethnography of Possession among the Songhay of Niger*. Chicago: University of Chicago Press.

————. 1989c. *The Taste of Ethnographic Things: The Senses in Anthropology*. Philadelphia: University of Pennsylvania Press.

Strathern, Marilyn. 1987a. "The Limits of Auto-Anthropology." In Anthony Jackson, ed., *Anthropology at Home*. London: Tavistock Publications, pp. 16–37.

————. 1987b. "An Awkward Relationship: The Case of Feminism and Anthropology." *Signs* 12 (2):276–292.

Stubbs, Michael. 1983. *Discourse Analysis*. Chicago: University of Chicago Press.

Szklut, Jay, and Robert Roy Reed. 1991. "Community Anonymity in Anthropological Research: A Reassessment." In Carolyn Fluehr-Lobban, ed., *Ethics and the Profession of Anthropology*. Philadelphia: University of Pennsylvania Press, pp. 97–114.

Tedlock, Barbara. 1991. "From Participant to Observation to the Observation of Participation: The Emergence of Narrative Ethnology." *Journal of Anthropological Research* 47 (1):69–94.

Thelen, David. 1989. "Memory and American History." *Journal of American History* 75:1117–1129.

Thiers, Jacques. 1986. "Elaboration linguistique et individuation sociolinguistique." In J. B. Marcellesi and G. Thiers, eds., *L'Individuation sociolinguistique corse*. Mont Saint-Aignan: GRESCO-IRED, pp. 19–25.

Thomas, Eudora. 1987. *A History of the Shouter Baptists in Trinidad and Tobago*. Ithaca, N.Y.: Calaloux.

Todorov, Tzvetan. 1982. *The Conquest of America: The Question of the Other*. New York: Harper and Row.

Tompkins, Jane P., ed. 1980. *Reader-Response Criticism*. Baltimore: Johns Hopkins University Press.

Trouillot, Michel-Rolph. 1991. "Anthropology and the Savage Slot: The Poetics of Otherness." In Richard G. Fox, ed., *Recapturing Anthropology*. Sante Fe: School of American Research, pp. 17–44.

Tyler, Stephen A. 1984. "The Poetic Turn in Post-modern Anthropology: The Poetry of Paul Friedrich." *American Anthropologist* 86 (2):328–336.

————. 1986. "Post-modern Ethnography: From Document of the Occult to Occult Document." In James Clifford and George Marcus, eds., *Writing Culture: The Poetics and Politics of Ethnography*. Berkeley: University of California Press, pp. 122–140.

————. 1987. "Still Rayting." *Critique of Anthropology* 7:49–51.

Underhill, Ruth. 1936. *Papago Woman*. New York: Holt, Rinehart and Winston.

U.S. Department of Health and Human Services. 1981. "Policy for the Protection of Human Research Subjects." *Federal Register* 46 (116):8306–8392.

Valencia, Anselmo, Heather Valencia, and Rosamond B. Spicer. 1990. "A Yaqui Point of View: On Yaqui Ceremonies and Anthropologists." In Richard Schechner and Willa Appel, eds., *By Means of Performance: Intercultural Studies of Theatre and Ritual*. Cambridge, Eng.: Cambridge University Press, pp. 96–108.

Van Maanen, John. 1988. *Tales of the Field: On Writing Ethnography*. Chicago: University of Chicago.

Verrey, Robert, and Laura Henley. 1991. "Creation Myths and Zoning Boards: Local

Uses of Historic Preservation." In Brett Williams, ed., *The Politics of Culture*. Washington, D.C.: Smithsonian Institution Press, pp. 75–108.

Vidich, Arthur J. 1960. "Freedom and Responsibility in Research: A Rejoinder." *Human Organization* 19 (1):3–4.

Vidich, Arthur J., and Joseph Bensman. 1958a. *Small Town in Mass Society*. Princeton, N.J.: Princeton University Press.

———. 1958b. "Freedom and Responsibility in Research: Comments." *Human Organization* 17 (4):1–7.

———. 1964. "The Springdale Case: Academic Bureaucrats and Sensitive Townspeople." In Arthur J. Vidich, Joseph Bensman, and Maurice R. Stein, eds., *Reflections on Community Studies*. New York: John Wiley and Sons, pp. 313–349.

Wade, Mason. 1950. "The French Parish and Survivance in Nineteenth-Century New England." *Catholic Historical Review* 36 (2):156–190.

Waite, P. B. 1988. Review of *Nationalism and the Politics of Culture in Quebec*, by Richard Handler. *Choice* 25 (July-August):1726.

Watson, Graham. 1987. "Make Me Reflexive—But Not Yet: Strategies for Managing Essential Reflexivity in Ethnographic Discourse." *Journal of Anthropological Research* 43:29–41.

Watson, Lawrence. 1976. "Understanding a Life History as a Subjective Document." *Ethos* 4:95–131.

Watson, Lawrence, and Maria-Barbara Watson-Franke. 1985. *Interpreting Life Histories: An Anthropological Inquiry*. New Brunswick, N.J.: Rutgers University Press.

Wengle, John L. 1988. *Ethnographers in the Field: The Psychology of Research*. Tuscaloosa: University of Alabama Press.

Werner, Dennis. 1984. *Amazon Journey: An Anthropologist's Year among Brazil's Mekranoti Indians*. New York: Simon and Schuster.

Whyte, William F. 1958. Editorial. *Human Organization* 17 (2):1–2.

Wilson, Thomas M. 1984. "From Clare to the Common Market: Perspectives on Irish Ethnography." *Anthropological Quarterly* 57:1–15.

Wolf, Eric R. 1990. "Distinguished Lecture: Facing Power—Old Insights, New Questions." *American Anthropologist* 92:586–596.

Wolf, Margery. 1992. *A Thrice-Told Tale: Feminism, Postmodernism, and Ethnographic Responsibility*. Stanford: Stanford University Press.

Woolgar, Steve, ed. 1988. *Knowledge and Reflexivity: New Frontiers in the Sociology of Knowledge*. London: Sage Publications.

Wrobel, Paul. 1979. *Our Way: Family, Parish and Neighborhood in a Polish-American Community*. Notre Dame: University of Notre Dame Press.

Zitkala-Sa [Gertrude Bonnin]. 1986. *American Indian Stories*. Lincoln: University of Nebraska Press [originally published 1921].

INDEX

About the Editor and Contributors

CAROLINE B. BRETTELL (Department of Anthropology, Southern Methodist University) is the author of *Men Who Migrate, Women Who Wait: Population and History in a Portuguese Parish* (1986) and *We Have Already Cried Many Tears* (1983). She has coauthored *Painters and Peasants in the Nineteenth Century* (1982) and coedited *International Migration: The Female Experience* (1986) and *Gender in Cross-Cultural Perspective* (1992).

DONA L. DAVIS (Department of Social Behavior, University of South Dakota) is the author of *Blood and Nerves: An Ethnographic Focus on Menopause* (1983) and *The "Ruination of Us All": Community and Crisis in Newfoundland* (in press). She is coeditor (with Jane Nadel-Klein) of *To Work and to Weep: Women in Fishing Economies* (1988).

FAYE GINSBURG (Department of Anthropology, New York University) is the author of *Contested Lives: The Abortion Debate in an American Community* (1989) and coeditor of *Uncertain Terms: Negotiating Gender in American Culture* (1990). She writes in the areas of symbolic anthropology, visual anthropology, and gender.

STEPHEN D. GLAZIER (Department of Anthropology, University of Nebraska, Kearney) has been conducting fieldwork on the island of Trinidad since 1976, and in 1983 he published *Marchin' the Pilgrims Home: Leadership and Decision Making in an Afro-Caribbean Faith* (Greenwood). A 1991 paperback version of this book has been widely distributed in the Caribbean.

OFRA GREENBERG (Western Galilee College/Open University, Israel) is the author of *Women in an Israeli Prison* (1982, in Hebrew) and *A Development Town Visited* (1989, in Hebrew), and coauthor of *A Voluntary Women's Association in a Society in the Making* (1980). Currently, her research interests are in the field of medical anthropology.

RICHARD HANDLER (Department of Anthropology, University of Virginia) is the author of *Nationalism and the Politics of Culture in Quebec* (1988) in addition to a number of important articles focusing on the politics of culture and the invention of tradition. With Daniel Segal he has coauthored *Jane Austen and the Fiction of Culture* (1990).

MARYCAROL HOPKINS (Department of Sociology, Anthropology, and Philosophy, Northern Kentucky University) has academic interests in African arts and culture, women, the anthropology of education, and ethnic minorities in the United States.

RICHARD P. HORWITZ (American Studies Program, University of Iowa) has conducted fieldwork in East and South Asia as well as in Western Europe and North America. Among his publications are *The Strip: An American Place* (1985), *Anthropology Toward History* (1978), and *Exporting America* (1993). He is currently studying family farmers and anecdotes of everyday life in the United States.

ALEXANDRA JAFFE (Department of Anthropology, SUNY-Cortland) is currently working on a book based on her research on the island of Corsica. She is interested in the relationship between language and culture and the politics of identity, and is organizing an international working group on European regional languages.

SALLY MCBETH (Department of Anthropology, Black, and Women's Studies, University of Northern Colorado) is the author of *Ethnic Identity and the Boarding School Experience* (1983). Her research interests and publications are in the areas of folklore, gender, education, and contemporary Native American and multicultural issues. She is currently working on a collaborative life history of and with a Shoshone Indian woman.

ELIZABETH A. SHEEHAN (Department of Anthropology, Johns Hopkins University) has research interests in intellectuals, national identity, and public history in Western Europe. She is currently writing a book based on her research on intellectuals and politics in Ireland.